The Outside Story

Robert Scammell

Illustrations by Jack Cowin

 A Reidmore Book

 Fleet Books, Toronto

A Reidmore Book
9115 39 Avenue
Edmonton, Alberta, Canada T6E 5Y2

Published by Fleet Publishers
A Division of International Thomson Limited
1410 Birchmount Road
Scarborough, Ontario, Canada M1P 2E7

Canadian Cataloguing in Publication Data

Scammell, Robert
 The outside story

  ISBN 0-919091-15-6

  1. Hunting. 2. Fishing. 3. Outdoor life.
I. Cowin, Jack L., 1947- II. Title.
SK33.S28 799 C82-091256-5

ACKNOWLEDGEMENTS

My thanks to: The Red Deer Advocate, *in which all of the columns in this book were first published and to* The Calgary Herald *and* The Lethbridge Herald *in which some appeared; Jack Cowin, artist, and words do not suffice; Herself who did the typing in the good old days and Ann Watson who does it now; and to the characters in the columns, named and anonymous, there and then, here and now, what we enjoyed together are the good old days.*

DEDICATION

To the memory of a couple of good old boys:
Harry C. Scammell, the Guv,
who left me his love of the outdoors,
and to one who needled me to write about it,
Allen H. Bill, Alberta's pioneer outdoor writer.

6. Flora, Fauna, and Fungi

7. Tips, Hints, and Help

8. Grousing in Paradise

9. Pheasants and Other Phoul

PREFACE

In May of 1966, prodded by the late Allen H. Bill, who, many readers will recall, was for many years the outdoors columnist of *The Calgary Herald*, I submitted my first outdoors column to *The Red Deer Advocate*.

My experience as a journalist and columnist in other areas led me to prepare a list of 50 topics, a year's supply, for columns concerned with matters I had to get off my chest. So urgent was my desire to write about the outdoors pursuits I love that I offered to do the column for nothing. Pat O'Callaghan, then publisher of *The Advocate*, insisted I had to be paid something; now I recognize that it is difficult to fire a volunteer.

More quickly than I can believe, 17 years have flown by, during which the column has appeared each week. My original list of things to get off my chest still exists with not half the original entries struck off and thus flushed from my mind. My experience parallels that of many long-time columnists in that sometimes the readers take over, sometimes events dictate the column, and at other times the column seems to have a life and a reason for living all its own.

There have been changes over the years. The first column was titled "Sportsman's Luck", words that mean much to me and to many of my readers but which did not appeal much to publishers. As I write this, the column now appears weekly in Alberta in one weekly newspaper and four dailies, generally under the heading "Alberta Outdoors" or the name of the paper plus "Outdoors", as in *"Herald* Outdoors".

After the death of Allen Bill, *The Calgary Herald* took the column, a source of no little pleasure to me, since I had also toiled for *The Herald* previously as newsboy and journalist. Next came *The Lethbridge Herald*, and then I got together with Pat O'Callaghan again in *The Edmonton Journal*. My most recent publisher has been my only weekly, my home town *Brooks Bulletin.*

The columns in this collection are selected from the 500 or so written in the first 10 years. They are favorites of mine and, some of them, of readers. In reading through the full 500 to select these few, I was struck that since each column was written, there have been changes in me, my life, and my

Alberta. In the time I have been writing the columns, "the Guv", mentioned in so many columns, has died, as has my mother. The Guv, of course, was my father, who so frequently took runny-nosed brat, then lout, then young adult with him and shared the only expertise I know he had and the only one I will profess: a deep love of the outdoors. In that time, too, my own son and daughter have been born. Soon the process comes full circle and leads me to hope I can do with the Guv's grandchildren as well as he did with me.

Reading the columns convinces me I have changed, too, and I think for the better. When I started I was exclusively a warm-water fisherman, a painfully enthusiastic new trout fly fisherman, a bird hunter, and a dedicated conservationist. The column and its readers have broadened me: big game hunting is now a passion and I shoot a little skeet, tie flies, take pictures, load ammunition, pick mushrooms, cross-country ski, train dogs, and do too many other enjoyable things to mention, all connected with the outdoors in some way.

It is painful and difficult for me to reflect on how different a place Alberta is now in 1982 from what it was when the column began only 17 years ago. The column has frequently dealt, in plain words, with those changes that have made Alberta a worse place to live for people like me and people who like to read outdoors columns. Few of those heavy, issue-oriented conservation columns will be found in this collection; unfortunately, nothing is as stale as yesterday's controversy. It is enough here to say that the locales of many of these columns, the quiet, unspoiled places where fish and game were to be found, exist no longer, having been destroyed to create a Heritage Trust Fund, the billions of which, as I write, are being used to finance the destruction of still more quiet, unspoiled places.

The inspiration for this collection has come from readers who seem to delight in contacting me as much as I delight in hearing from them. On a simplistic level, the book is an answer to the question I hear so often: "Is there a book of your early columns?" But there must be other reasons, and for me the motivation to read, cull, correct, and collect for this book is tied to that word "heritage" and the way things change. Those who so easily destroy the quiet places forget that living off the land—hunting, fishing, berrying, collecting—is part of the heritage of every one of us born in western Canada. Allen Bill recorded some of it, and I read him avidly as a young lout and young adult. I wish the Guv had done a column somehow, but at least I can pass on his stories of the good old days sometimes, even though to the day of his death the Guv believed, as I do, that in hunting and fishing the good old days are here and now. Simply, for those thousands of westerners who still have hunting and fishing in their blood, I wish to add to the record of how it was, in a form slightly more permanent than newsprint, just in case things continue to change at the pace I have observed since I started the column.

Among the many reasons people hunt and fish is simply that they enjoy it. They also enjoy reading about it. The literatures of angling and hunting remain the richest among all the recreational pursuits of man. My final justification and hope is that those who read this collection will enjoy reading just some of the columns as much as I enjoyed writing all of them.

1. Opening Daze

When to Start

Just as I was planning that first fishing trip for 1967, the March lion gave its belated miaow. Until the blow came I was all jitters and anticipation; afterwards, like a hundred other anglers with plans, I was all depression.

It seems to me that things were easier on the nerves back a few years when the fishing season started on a particular date. In my youth it was May 16th or thereabouts. Plans were made and a party formed, every member of which would writhe the night away until 4 or 5 a.m. of sundry May 16ths. Then up and away, pedalling like maniacs to Johnson's Lake a couple of miles north of Brooks. Every year a few half-frozen pike would be yarded out, and every year some kid would lose all his hooks on the submerged barbed wire where we insisted on fishing. Invariably, this unfortunate would strip off all his clothes and go diving for his hooks among the biggest ice cubes in the world. All further trips would be postponed until the diver ended his courageous battle with pneumonia.

Come what would, irate mother or act of God, you went fishing on May 16th because the government decreed that was when the season started. Now, as is the case with certain religions, things are a matter of personal conscience. For a number of years now it has been up to each individual angler to decide when his personal season is to start. No doubt the policy of no closed season can be justified on fish management principles, but the responsibility of deciding when to take that first trip is making ulcer-ravaged basket cases of formerly carefree anglers.

One must pick just the right time so as not to be early and disappointed by ice-bound creeks or fish metabolisms chilled below the biting point. It is even worse to be late. The despair of any angler hearing of a good catch made before he has made his first trip of the year is so excruciating that I mention it only in hushed tones.

In the interest of lending some science to the mental gyrations involved in picking the date of the first fishing trip, I offer the following first-trip observations from the fishing diary I have kept since I started fishing in the west country.

March 18, 1963, was my first trip ever to the west country. I found where what had to be Alford Creek crossed the road. The Creek seemed high and discolored. Water temperature: 38° F. Too cold. I just get back up on the road and a hoary-handed son of the soil stops his truck and gives me hell just for thinking about fishing in Alford Creek. Snow starts. On the way home, my trusty compass locates Caroline Bar. Friendly people. Beer temperature: just right. I buy two rounds, participate in seven. Net catch three beer.

On March 30, 1964, I stood up to the nexus of my waders in a snowdrift beside Stauffer Creek and caught five brown trout of from 12 to 15 inches on seven casts of a Mepps spinner without moving my feet from their tracks. It was cold that year. Feet were probably frozen.

March 6, 1965. Bright day, a cruel wind blowing down Alford Creek. I hooked only one fish all day and lost him in the confusion resulting when the bank I was standing on suddenly turned out to be a snowdrift hanging over the water. I was pleased to see that my waders had wintered well: no water escaping from them.

March 26, 1966. Beautiful sunny day on a tributary of the Clearwater. I got a 14-inch bull trout on the first cast of the year. Only fresh air and sunshine the rest of the day. Stayed dry inside and out.

Like most anglers I appear to start the season a trifle early. I may just swear off going fishing before the end of March unless, like my old friend Bert Mitten, I can take an early trip to Vancouver Island

and conquer 19-pound steelhead.

There are certain sly old veterans of many a west country piscatorial encounter who claim they never venture out fishing until, as one of them with a poetic turn puts it, "the trees are furred with green." They do not fool me, for I have seen their nostrils flare and withers quiver at the mere rumour of a March-caught mess of trout.

This being March 17, a fellow tells me that the headwaters of the Raven have been open for some time and some nice fish have been coming out. He says all you need is a pair of snowshoes.

Year of the Skunk

For about the first three months of each of the past 10 years I have had this chronic nightmare. I head out, heart on sleeve, all palpitating expectation, for the first fishing trip of the year, and the second, and the third—but nothing happens. There are no fish there. Either that or the last fish to chomp vittles containing a hook has met his demise, and natural, or unnatural, selection has left nothing but trout who unfailingly scorn anything containing a hook. Either way, angling, as a sport, is dead. I wake up screaming.

This year that nightmare is old news. The new nightmare is whether or not my old nightmare would come true. Oh, I did the expected and started going out much too early this year. Those first few trips, just being out there is joy enough. You don't really expect to catch fish. I mean a man is so dozy out there in all that fresh air and sunshine that a fish would scare the hell out of him.

Then you have to allow a couple of extra fruitless trips for the fact that I start the season with flies, being so stubborn that I would rather catch no fish casting flies. That, of course, is exactly what happens.

Throw in a couple of fruitless fiascos, too, for the fact that I am in the big-fish phase of my dementia: I scorn places that are sure early-season producers of average-size trout in favour of places that produce the odd very large trout, but much later in the season.

Five or six fishless trips I can take, but no matter how high-minded you get about it, the name of the game is catching fish. Up to about trip five this year it was truly the year of the skunk, and not only for me. Everywhere I run into anglers, they are complaining about the poor fishing this season. The odd one would tell of a trip or two where it seemed to him he just happened to be in the right place at the right time.

All this does have one advantage. Eventually your best fishing buddy will get so desperate to catch a fish that if he is helplessly along with you, he will direct you to take him to a spot he has selfishly been keeping from you for lo these umpteen years.

I thought I knew Mike Burrington, and about trip five he up and directed me to take us to a spot I never knew existed, although I presume I could have deduced it had I seriously thought that known stream A-Z must, somehow, pass intervening points B-C. Beautiful water, too, so beautiful that as I flailed away at it with flies and got nothing I got madder and madder at Mike for keeping it a secret, or maybe I just wanted to see if there really were fish out there.

Whatever the reason, I made sure Mike was nowhere around, snuck back to the car, rigged a spinning rod, and went back to the starting point to prospect the water again with a Mepps #0 gold. That was almost to no avail also, but I finally caught a 13-inch brown. I nearly had a nervous breakdown when some sneaky kid, the kind every man should take fishing and then throw in, came quietly up behind me and asked, "How you doing?" while I was obviously doing just fine unhooking the fish.

Mike caught me with the spinning rod anyway, and if he'll forgive me that, I'll forgive him for not showing me the place sooner. Besides, Mike has not caught a fish yet. He announced in a broken voice last Saturday that he guessed he would have to break out the golf clubs again. Now *that*, sports fans, is desperation. After all, Mike is my fishing buddy, and he and I have often toasted the golfers in diet Kool Aid and other potables because golfing keeps so many of them off the streams. But if he wishes to forego the streams for the links, so be it. I shall propose my lonely toasts to one more golfer.

Actually, the scientific theories I have heard discussed among fishermen about why the fishing is so lousy this spring makes an international conclave of nuclear physicists sound like a convention of land surveyors at happy hour. One gent even quoted Theodore Gordon's theory that fish would not bite when snow water was in the stream, and observed there is still a lot of unmelted snow in the woods owing to the cool spring.

My own observation is that aquatic insects simply do not hatch in the wind, and the wind has been howling on the only two spring-like days we have had since April first. Last Saturday I remembered Stauffer Creek where there are big fish and where the fishing is usually easy in the spring. The water was an unaccountable 58° F, whether from the brushburning at the top end or not, I do not know.

I do know that for the first hour the wind howled and the fishing was as lousy as everywhere else in the country. Then it let up and gay little fleets of "Quill Gordon" duns started cruising downstream, the odd one being tumbled tail over antenna back upstream by the odd wayward zephyr.

Through the smoke haze the bright sun put a pewter glare on the water, and I could so poorly see the gray Quill Gordon fly that I reefed it a couple of times from the gaping mouths of considerable brown trout. So I tied on a Light Cahill, that strawberry blond confection that is so visible. The result was two brookies and two browns of about 10 inches each: not great, but not bad, considering the hell I had been through to catch my first trout of the year on flies.

Despite knowing that her that lives with me has gone through hell for her first spring trout on a plate, I shook each of the four off. After all, that nightmare has been so real this year. What if these four were the last in the west country that would take a fly?

For the Birds

BROOKS—It couldn't have been more than 8:30 a.m. on the opening morning of pheasant season when I knew that if I had any sense at all I would go home and back to bed.

This is my home town, and the Guv, now known as Granddad, had arranged an itinerary for my first whack in many years at the opening of pheasant season down here where men are maniacs and pheasants are Philistines.

The first stop was to be an isolated island of willow in a barley stubble field. In the past week the barley stubble had been plowed under, but the dose of heaves I got walking the half mile over that loose ground bothered me not at all. Then old Quince, my Brittany, went on a point that was so vibrant I thought he would shatter like fine crystal. As I got to him he lunged, then deposited into my hand a chickadee that had obviously expired of old age during the night. I just chuckled.

But I knew it was going to be one of those days when I knocked down a cock pheasant that flushed silently ahead and to my left and flew back behind me and I couldn't find a feather of that fowl despite about an hour of my time and Quince's.

The next sight to greet these tired old eyes was a ground swell of

13

pheasants surging down the ditch we had not blocked, emphasizing that while it may be early season for us, the birds were in mid-season form. Then I went back to look for that downed rooster, and Quince bumped a lone Hungarian partridge which I missed with both barrels as it went straight away.

The gun I was using was a new Model 280 Ithaca side-by-side double 12-gauge, the same fowling piece around which I had managed to entwine myself sufficiently a couple of weeks ago to break a lousy 15 of 25 at trap. With pheasants there was not time for the contortions, and by 2 p.m. when the Guv wore out, I had completely missed the only other two cock pheasants I had seen.

About that time I heard the Guv making very heavy weather of it indeed trying to take my car up to the end of the long island of willows we were hunting in an ocean of prairie. It turned out that the emergency brake was on and had been for some time. The clutch was smelling the medium-rare side of well-done when I arrived to the rescue.

As I nursed the expiring clutch through the extravaganza of sport that pheasant season opening is supposed to be, I had plenty of time to muse upon the comment I heard so often from many of the hundreds of hunters out there: that the government ended its ill-conceived experiment in hen-pheasant seasons just short of wiping out 40 years of work in establishing the critter here in the first place. Particularly noticeable is the remarkable lack of hens, to the point that I saw more cocks than hens the first day, and three times as many cocks as hens the second.

The first hunting day ended with me missing the fourth cock of the day, which promptly flew over my ailing auto, in which the Guv was ensconced, sound asleep. But the day was not over. After the evening post-sprinkling tour, Quince, on a leash, caught the Guv with his head down and on his wrong foot and bounced him on his *gluteus maximus* down the front steps. No broken hip, but a little finger sufficiently torn from its moorings that three stiches were required.

The next day I was out alone with the dog after arranging for a new clutch to be shipped down here. I was loaded for bear with my $65 double, cylinder-choke riot gun, a cure-all for my shooting problems, and hunting not for pheasant but for places the other hunters had missed. I remembered one from my high school days and found it was still there, the same as ever. Two roosters were home. The first came to bag and the second just kept going.

The rest of the day was nothing but too many hunters and pheasants that were running for the prairie before the car stopped. On the way home, on a hunch, I went to that secret little corner that had produced in the morning. About three minutes into it, Quince pointed and a rooster went up over the canal bank and the road and dropped at the first shot. Someone had opened the gate since morning and the "empty" canal I piled into after the bird was half full of water. Quince and I arrived soaked and in a dead heat at the bird.

Back in front of the family home, feeling at once like a million dollars and an old wrung-out dishrag, I am hailed from a passing pick-up by an old school buddy, jowly and successful and with a nasty memory for faces: "Hey, Scammell, you're too old and fat to be running around like that!"

Faith, Hope, and Insanity

An early spring trip seldom fails to confirm the faith, the hope, and the insanity that is trout fishing. A point such as this is driven home even more firmly if the angler chooses his home water for that first trip, water that day in and day out, season after season, he fishes more than any other.

Thus did I, on three days of an Easter weekend, set out to slay them on the south Alberta stream I have fished about 15 days each of the last nine seasons to the tune of about 500 trout each season. What mattor that I had never caught a fish in this water before May 15th? The ice—well, most of it—was out, was it not? Was the water not clear, almost to noon each day? The clincher was that the snow had been long gone down here and a man does not have to wade before he gets to the water.

All weekend the wind blew from the northwest at a velocity known down here as "Whar's the barn?" and the tunes it played on my sinuses sounded like hillbillies in a jug band. The resulting sinusitis attack merely caused me to set a new family record in trumping partners' aces in the après fish bridge tournament.

Much preparatory work had been done on my equipment, and of course, one boot leaked right at the instep. It wouldn't be a season if a man couldn't spend most of it just trying to find that one elusive pinhole in the waders.

The first cast demonstrated that if my memory were as good as the memory of nylon monofilament that has been left on the reel all winter, I would change my lines every spring and hang the expense.

Each cast looks like a sprung spring, and 33°F water and 35°F air do little to remove the temper from the spring. A pair of elk-hide gloves, however, does add to the sport of untangling the snarls.

But these things are as nothing to a man who really knows the stream and all the tricks. I went to all the places, the deep holes under overhanging banks, the pools where springs enter from the bottom, and I fished that bottom where all the fish are supposed to be in spring, to the tune of $10.83 worth of hooks, etc. And—may the Federation of Flyfishermen forgive me—I even backslid to worms after three years of total abstinence.

Crazed by the hope that springs eternal, I went to other waters that I find closed until May 15th, for the first time in umpteen years. The only people who should be more embarrassed than I and the dozen fishless anglers who actually wet a line there, are the game officers who neither post the water nor appear on the scene to make a nifty haul of miscreants.

Back I go to that home water where I startle a starving merganser into flight. Instead of cursing the fish-eating beast as I generally do, I wish him luck as he wobbles wearily on his way and sneak up to try my luck in the pool where he was sitting, on the theory that he may know this water even better than I do. But he doesn't.

Finally the hard fact gets itself accepted: in many small streams on the east slope of the Rockies there just are no fish at all in early spring. Not only is this a convenient excuse for skunked anglers; it is fact. On this stream, for example, I have long known that fish appear in droves with the first big spring rain. Where they come from and where they go to about the middle of October is a mystery to me and to science. But each spring hope, faith, and insanity drive me again to learn that they are not in my favorite stream until early summer.

So I decide to go and fly a kite for nephew and niece. Just as I finish building it, father-in-law cackles gleefully and tells me she'll never get off the ground as the wind blows downhill in these parts. I sneer and head out. Up she struggles for 40 feet, then the wind smashes her to the ground and into wood chips and confetti. Just as Franklin learned something from flying a kite, I now know why each summer I stick at least six flies in my ears when fly casting down here, even with the wind.

Nothing for it but to drag my burgeoning sinuses into the house and read the paper until happy hour and the qualifying rounds of the bridge tournament. In his outdoors column for *The Lethbridge Herald*, complete with pictures, Joe Balla reports on another great fishing discovery: the proliferation of dead trout and empty liquor and beer bottles on the shores of Henderson Lake this spring proves the fish are getting polluted on alcohol and running themselves aground.

Shattered faith, faint hope or not, spring fishing can't be all that insane when you learn such things as these.

Avoiding Agriculture

Certainly I'd caught a trout or two in the past couple of months on hardware and during blizzards, but for me spring has not arrived until I have taken just one trout on a fly. Thus went my lament to myself last Saturday, as I suspected that spring had arrived out west. Something in the air suggested trout with fins aquiver over bugs, and there I was engaged in agriculture.

We bought a place in darkest suburbia last fall, one with about two townships of grass, one section of which I broke for a vegetable garden. About 1:30 p.m. Saturday I had just finished mulching the begonias or something under the direction of my beloved and was foundered on the back stoop considering whether I would get a government subsidy if I kept that new broken section out of production, when here comes Mike Burrington, slinking in from the lane.

Now Mike engages in agriculture in the same neighborhood, had somehow given his beloved the slip, and was suggesting we check for the arrival of spring about 50 miles to the west. I resent the suggestion that it was haste to get away rather than confidence that spring had arrived that caused me to take only a fly rod. After all, was it not a never-tried Para/metric fly rod, and do I not always have to catch fish the first time I use a new rod?

Streams such as the South Raven and the Clearwater were unseasonably cloudy, the result of a recent heavy snowstorm, but the first sight of the spring creek we intended to fish revealed its customary clarity. A bluebird beckoned me on by flying from fencepost to fencepost ahead of me down the road to the creek. The sight of no other bird cheers me more. I have seen so many this spring that I believe Kerry Wood is right, as he always is in matters of this sort, when he writes that bluebirds are making a comeback.

As I eased myself into the water, the sun came out full blast and the wind died obligingly. My thermometer showed the temperature of the water to be 49°F, which is springtime for the fish in most of the waters in this country. All the systems were go, as they say, but though I belted and flayed the water my best lick for the first 200 yards, indications were that prophets of doom such as I were absolutely right: the oil companies had killed all the fish.

But around the next bend came the sudden sight which never fails to astonish me no matter how often I see it. In a deep still pool about 60 feet long, eight fish were industriously earning their livings: the first rises I have seen in this young season. The rise was the characteristic humping of the water without breaking the surface, which in this country generally indicates the trout are snatching just below the surface the beetle-like water boatman abundant in central Alberta streams.

So I fumbled a Despickable onto the leader, a fly I tie to imitate the boatman and in which every fly fisherman in central Alberta but me has supreme confidence. I even remembered to slosh it around in water and mud to make it sink properly. Out it went 10 feet above the lowest rise and dead-drifted back toward the waiting fish. As usual, I did not believe the hesitation in the line, struck too late, and felt the hook merely graze a tooth.

The next fish snatched the Despickable like a kid swiping cherries, humped the water, and I got him. So did the next, and the next, all purple and orange brook trout of about 11 inches with ivory-edged fins and bright red flesh. These, I self-righteously decided, would be enough for eating; the rest would be for fun. But the remaining fish had made their own decision and, although they continued to feed, would have no truck with the Despickable.

Then the fish stopped rising, a result, I decided, of two anglers clomping down the bank and through the creek just upstream of the pond. I waited around, and one playful trout started slashing at the odd caddis fly that would skitter over the surface in its egg-laying run. I tried two or three dry-flies, caddis imitations, with absolutely no result.

At the appointed hour Mike appeared on the bridge, and as we walked up the road he admitted to seeing only one rise and to having taken two brown trout. On a black beetle? Not at all. Mike took them both on a Joe's hopper, a July and August fly, fished high and dry!

Spring has arrived, and much is still right in the west country. Once again it is doubtless that God could have made a more engaging creature than the trout, but doubtless He didn't.

2. Trout:
Dark Brown and Otherwise

Cutthroat, Our Native Trout

On a rainy weekend earlier this summer I found myself a rare treat. In a tiny, crystal-clear creek flowing through a valley between a roily Castle River and a raging Carbondale River, I caught biting, battling little native cutthroat trout up to 12 inches, all decked out in their rose and gold nuptial colors.

Creeks containing only native cutthroat in Alberta are rare and becoming rarer today because of the tendency of cutthroat to cross with rainbow trout which were stocked in many cutthroat waters in Alberta between 1930 and 1950. In the mixing process, the cutthroat characteristics give way to the dominant rainbow characteristics.

A set of statistics I have gathered over the last five years from a favorite stream near the one I have already spoken of illustrates the hybridization process in action: about one fish caught in 20 is pure cutthroat, four in 20 are hybrids, and about 15 in 20 appear to be pure rainbow. This crossing process we now see going on in Alberta has already almost eradicated the cutthroat as a pure strain in the U.S., except for high mountain lakes and portions of rivers, like the Yellowstone, made inaccessible by falls.

Many Alberta anglers feel sorry at the passing of the pure cutthroat, as it is the only trout native to Alberta from the international boundary north to and including the Bow River system. (Contrary to popular belief, in Alberta the rainbow is native only to the Athabasca River system, and the brown trout is not native even to this continent.)

The cutthroat may not disappear from Alberta as a pure strain. Central Alberta anglers can sample many rare treats owing to one of the more successful experiments conducted by our Alberta Fish and Wildlife Division. Following studies carried out by biologists, the late Dr. R. R. Miller and Martin Paetz, Chief Provincial Fisheries Biologist, in 1955 cutthroat were stocked in the Ram River system about 120 miles west of Red Deer in a conscious effort to preserve cutthroat fishing in Alberta.

Because of accidents of nature and the many falls in the Ram system that are impassable to fish, Miller and Paetz could find no fish whatever in the main Ram above the first falls. In Fall Creek and in the Ram near Fall Creek, they found some Dolly Varden; in the North Ram they found only longnose suckers. The water appeared to them to be too cold for browns or rainbows, but it did look to them like typical cutthroat water, and they felt that the cutthroat would be superior to the brook trout both in size and longevity. The clincher of all reasons was that the same impassable falls that had kept the Ram system barren of fish over the centuries would prevent rainbow trout from invading and committing their acts of love and miscegenation with the planted cutthroats.

In 1955 eyed cutthroat eggs were stocked in the North Ram, Smallpox, Cripple, and Hummingbird Creeks and in the main Ram. The streams were closed for about five years with no further plantings. In about 1960 there was evidence that the cutthroat were reproducing naturally and that the introduced population was self-sustaining, so open seasons have been allowed ever since. Many anglers, especially earlier this season (1966), have reported excellent catches. Although I have heard of larger cutthroat being taken from the Ram, my young friend Brian Caddy did successful battle with a 16-incher about three weeks ago.

Many anglers claim that owing to the coldness of the waters they inhabit and the lateness of their spawning season, the cutthroat of the Ram do not really come into their own until August. On my trip last weekend, the water was 51°F, extremely cold for so late in the summer.

An August trip to the Ram will reward any angler who likes fishing clear, rushing waters in unspoiled mountain scenery. The diet of the Ram cutthroat is probably composed mainly of caddis flies, mayflies, and stonefly larvae. I know of these fish having been taken on male Black Gnat flies, grasshoppers, Mepps spinners and, of course, worms. A couple of interesting-looking fly patterns on sale in local stores purport to be tied especially to the specifications of the Ram cutthroats.

The irony in all the wonders the Ram experiment has produced for the Alberta angler is that when he catches one of these fish he will not be catching a true native fish of Alberta. Because the eggs of native Alberta east slope cutthroat were not available when the stocking was done in 1955, eggs from the Cranbrook hatchery in British Columbia were used. Somehow I think satisfied Alberta anglers will not allow this fact to spoil their sport.

The Dolly Varden, a Native Char

Sometimes I think I'm the only person in the world who gives a damn about the bull trout. About a month ago, I had the opportunity of admiring two fine strings of fish taken from the mouth of one of the many little creeks that flow into the Clearwater River. On each string, among the many whitefish and the few small browns and brookies were a couple of whopping great bull trout. When I got enthusiastic over the big fish, as is only polite, their owners gave rapid voice to the usual attitude: "Yeah, but they're just bulls".

I acquired a great affection for the bulls way back when their great numbers in the North Fork of the Belly River provided a prairie lad with his first real trout fishing. Even that appears gone now, as too many people have found where the wild North Fork rushes by all that beautiful mountain scenery.

At any rate, I decided I should tell everyone a few things about bull trout. I decided not to tell anyone that the proper name is Dolly Varden and that the name is after a character in Charles Dickens' novel *Barnaby Rudge* who wore a dress very like the delicate coloring of the fish. Nor, I decided, would I offer that old chestnut that the Dolly Varden is not really a trout at all but a char and spawns in the fall, like the brook and lake trout, our other chars.

Most people know these things, so I decided to say that the Dolly is native to Alberta, that he has been here for many thousands of years, and that he will become the first native Alberta fish to become extinct unless the attitudes of a few people are changed and changed soon. Somehow the bull trout got the reputation of a cannibal, an eater of fish and fish roe, to the extent that in Alaska for many years pressure of the commercial fishing industry kept a bounty on his tail and millions of the great game fish were slaughtered. Tails were strung 40 to a wire and brought one dollar in bounty or barter. The bounty is gone now because it was discovered that the charge was false, that the Dolly Varden is no more a cannibal than many other sport fish, but the evil reputation given to the fish by the bounty persists today.

The bull trout is found in clear, cold wilderness streams, and as streams of this type disappear, so does the native char. Complicating the disappearing habitat is the curious attitude of our fisheries biologists toward the Dolly. The biologists explain the complete absence of any Dolly Varden stocking program by giving in to the old Alaska myth and saying, "the fishermen don't like them". This is plain, unrefined applesauce. My experience has been that anglers, particularly occasional anglers, like bull trout just fine when they get to know them. The Dolly is easy to catch, puts up an unspectacular but stubborn battle when hooked, often grows to great size in strange little streams, and is nectar of the mountains in the skillet. In Alberta we leave the Dolly to fend for himself as we destroy his habitat, and instead import a foreign char, the brook trout, that has already proved unable to survive the advances of civilization against the little streams of its native eastern Canada and United States. Somehow the brook trout does not thrive in Alberta streams. He is every bit as gullible and probably as much cannibal as any fish, but he remains stunted and puny in many streams where the Dolly Varden would be muscular and magnificent, if we would only plant some there. It is a tragedy to let a native species sink to extinction while promoting a foreign species that has proved to be inferior in its new surroundings.

The bull trout is a valuable native fish who has proved his ability to live and reproduce in our streams. But because of the Dolly's tendency to co-operate with anglers, a stream can have its population reduced very quickly.

A restocking program should be set up to assist him before it is too late. A reduction of the catch limit would probably also help because it is so much easier to catch a limit of char than it is of trout. There

22

could also be some attractive trophy fishing available if steps would be taken to allow the bull trout the time he needs to attain the great weights of which he is capable. The finest bull trout fishing in the world is to be found just to the south of us in Montana's Flathead River and in its North, Middle, and South Forks. The Dollies there are big: Montana regulations provide that no Dolly Varden may be taken from the Flathead under 18 inches in length. It would be interesting to see what would happen if we gave the bull trout in the Clearwater River the same kind of break.

Bull Trout, for Kids

No matter how old the boy, bull trout are child's play. Two years ago, my then five-year-old friend, Iain Johnston, was along in his capacity as chief in charge of netting the fish. While his father and I were stringing the rods, Iain, taking a couple of practice swipes down at the creek, lost his grip and the net floated gaily away in complete defiance of anyone knee-high to the head of water in a half-filled bathtub.

Last Sunday the much older boy next door was bowing deeply to land a sprightly little bull trout when what he erroneously thought was the only bottle of beer west of the 5th meridian slipped its moorings in his pocket and sank: an excellent example of protective coloration, the amber bottle blending nicely with the amber water. Iain's net was retrieved, but the bottle, as they say in some trade or other, disappeared without a trace. I will not breach the confidence of either of my friends by revealing which of them howled the louder. On each occasion, however, the slight misfortune was insignificant compared with the magnificent time had by all present with the fierce little bull trout in the creek.

I have a vague hope for a huge bull trout some day, but little 10- to 15-inchers inhabit these tiny, winding meadow creeks. I guess you could say bull trout are not my bag any more, but there was a time when the combination of a little bull trout and my father taught me a lot of what there is to know about fish, creeks, and fishing.

The thing about bull trout is that they are often found in abundance in cold, pure water in fantastically interesting little creeks winding their way through settings worth glancing at from time to time. They are also fish of simple tastes, meat-and-potatoes fish: a boy equipped with gobs of worms, lots of split shot, and #8 snelled hooks to go on the terminal end of line, rod, and reel, is outfitted in style for his expedition.

With this equipment, on this type of creek, fishing is reduced to its bare essentials. The type of creek I have in mind is fairly abundant in our west country, winding and unwinding upon itself through flat glacial meadows. On such a creek a boy learns about the holes in the bends, the beauties of undercut banks, and the subtleties of creeping up just so to get the worm right to the bottom in such a place where, with bull trout, it does the most good. The kid may even be a sophisticate who loves to wind up a spoon or spinner like a bolo wizard, with or without the meat garnish. The lack of high vegetation along such creeks allows for all youthful casting styles, and there is no disaster should the creek be missed completely.

Gradually the character of the Dolly Varden will reveal itself as the bull trout, the bulldog of the fish world. Sometimes he will clamp down so hard on the bait itself that the hook cannot be pulled home. In such cases he invariably opens his mouth, lets the bait go, and goes free just as he was about to be derricked over the bank. Then doesn't youth grapple with a vocabulary inadequate to the occasion! But the lesson to be learned is that in angling the fascination is most often found in the ones that get away. Besides, being a bull trout, his memory is dwarfed by his appetite, and he will glom on again the next time the meat goes by.

The only real difficulty with bull trout is that they occasionally have dour periods during which they high-hat everything. They are not hungry or angry, just full, and cannot be moved by the right approach as browns and rainbows can. During such periods the young fellow learns that, contrary to popular myth, a really good stream fisherman has no patience at all. With bull trout, lack of patience is always rewarded, as they soon get hungry again.

The great worry of some of our biologists is that the bull trout is eating himself out of existence, that he is becoming scarce because he is so easy to catch. The problem is compounded by the fact that we do not stock bull trout in Alberta, despite the fact that he is our native char, and society, particularly fledgling anglers, has a need for a handsome little trout that is always easy to catch.

Perhaps if we are going to do nothing else, we should reserve the bull trout in some of his creeks for the training of future anglers. The regulation: no person over 12 can fish certain bull trout havens unless accompanied by at least one person under 12. The bull trout would be grateful and so would a considerable number of today's tads in about 30 years or so.

The Brown Trout, an Immigrant

The message came from a mystified non-fishing partner that Fred Lowe had a fish he was willing to show me. A fish indeed! Fred slid from the fridge a 4½-pound brown trout he had seduced with a Five of Diamonds spoon during the long weekend in the often-praised but hard to locate "Out West Creek".

The description of the event was brief but graphic. Fred fought it for a few minutes, got it on the bank somehow, and then subdued it with a full body slam. The fish was a female and contained well-developed roes. This fact started my romantic musing that brown trout everywhere are preparing for the annual fall population explosion.

Despite the fact that a brown over six pounds which he caught a few years ago hangs on the wall, the glint in Fred Lowe's eye started me thinking about how the brown trout's introduction and subsequent multiplying has brought so much pleasure to so many sportsmen.

The brown trout, *Salmo trutta*, is the native trout of Europe and was first introduced into the United States in 1883 by men of vision in an attempt to provide angling in the face of native brook trout populations that were even then beginning to decline as the land was stripped of its cover and the water warmed up. Early American angling literature is filled with derogatory remarks about the new immigrant. We hear derogatory remarks today, but they come mostly from anglers who have been frustrated in their efforts to catch tho wily browns.

American angling literature today is filled with the praises of the brown as the adversary most worthy of an angler's skill. Browns are not wise, as their fans will claim, but they are a cautious fish. A frightened brown seldom scurries in disorder as a rainbow will. When a brown moves, he is going somewhere, generally to his lair under a bank or a brush tangle; sometimes he will just fade to the bottom and fix the careless angler with a steely stare. The caution of the brown, his ability to tolerate environmental change, to live and multiply in waters no longer suitable for native species of trout, keep his numbers up without stocking and produce specimens the size of Fred Lowe's fish.

In Alberta, because the gradual disappearance of the cold, clear waters they love and their own gullibility was resulting in a decline of Dolly Varden and cutthroat populations, our own men of vision imported brown trout eggs from Montana in 1927. Records are sparse, but the imported eggs were hatched at the Banff hatchery and the fingerlings were planted in Grant, Castle, and Schrader Creeks, all tributaries to the Red Deer River. Between 1927 and the early 1930's, browns were planted in most of the Alberta streams that now contain them: the Raven, Dogpound, Fallen Timber, Grease, Swan, and other west-central Alberta creeks.

Chief Alberta Fisheries Biologist Martin Paetz says that in streams where the first stockings of browns were successful, natural reproduction has maintained their populations since. If the environment is suitable, browns require little or no stocking assistance to keep their populations at a good level. Most central Alberta anglers would be hard-pressed, for example, to recall the last time the North and South Ravens were stocked with browns, yet these streams teem with them.

Our biologists, looking to the future when there will be few waters suitable for the native Dolly Varden and cutthroat, and when there will be many more fishermen, are working to extend the range of *Salmo trutta* to most major watersheds in Alberta. Recently browns have been successfully introduced to: Cottonwood Creek, tributary to the Waterton River; Open Creek, tributary to the Medicine River; Elk Creek, tributary to the Clearwater River; and Obed Creek, tributary to the Athabasca River.

The attempt to extend the range of the brown trout can be nothing but good news to Alberta's burgeoning army of anglers, for, since 1883, the brown has proved himself to be the species most likely to maintain quality trout fishing for large fish in heavily-fished waters.

Logjam Trophy

Night after night the drab giant stonefly nymphs kept moving, later and later into the day, toward the rocks at the shore. Once on the rock, the nymphal case would split and a giant orange and grey stonefly would emerge, abandon its former skeleton, and flutter clumsily off into the riverside vegetation.

Gradually, through the nights, the big brown trout broke his nocturnal feeding habit and hunted later and later away from the safety of his deep hole under the logjam to gorge on the succulent nymphs.

Now the giant flies had abandoned the bushes and were flying high, but dipping always closer and closer to the surface of the water, pulled back to the stream that gave them life by the weight of the mature eggs they carried. The sight of one of these fluttering forms stopped the big fish by the entrance to his hole. As more appeared, instinct and a vague memory of past pleasures drew him further up the run and higher in the water until he lay in feeding position just under the broken surface of the water near the middle of the run.

There was a fluttering on the water just upstream that moved toward him. He drifted back, tilted slowly, and a smacking sound was the only evidence to the unhearing world of the demise of a giant stonefly. One after another they came, and the fish fell into so satisfying a rhythm of meeting all comers that he forgot the dangers of revealing his position in daylight. Nor did he turn from the form that did not flutter. It struggled more violently than the others and pulled away, as did another just seconds later. Somewhat later the still form came again. He clamped down hard, was annoyed by a strange pressure pulling him back, tried to expel the thing, could not, and angrily swam upstream and stopped at the very head of the run.

Gradually, the push of the water and the pull from behind forced the big fish down to the tail of the run. Even then he remained calm, confident of his powers. Only when he saw the two strange upright forms was he frightened, and only then did he twist violently. The thing came free and the big fish was washed over the tail of the run, then fled to rest under a cutbank far below. The big fish feasted no more on the fluttering stoneflies that day and used the cover of darkness only to return to his home under the logjam.

When we arrived at the stream, a few stoneflies could be seen flying high over the treetops. Now, after noon, females could be seen from time to time swooping to the surface, dipping their tails in the water to lay the eggs while beating their way upstream in a losing battle against the current. Few got further than 10 feet before there would be an explosive eruption from below and the fly would be gone.

It was a sparse hatch, and the small fish were tempted first, but eventually my companion proved there were big ones there by taking a two-pound brown. I worked up a narrow run flowing along a logjam. As I false-cast, I felt a "tick" on the back cast, thought nothing of it, and shot the fly above the broken water at the head of the run. A huge golden form rose under the fly and took it. There was the slightest resistance to my strike and the fly came back.

Excitement made me break two rules: I did not inspect the fly, and I cast immediately over the big fish. Incredibly for a brown, he came again, and again we felt each other, but the fly came back. This time I cast to another part of the run without looking at the fly, and was annoyed to be fast to a 14-incher which I horsed to the tail of the run to avoid disturbing the big fish. The small fish shook once and was free.

A hopeless third time? Ridiculous. Why check anything? Again the big fish took it, but was stuck this time. The reel buzzed momentarily in response to the short but powerful surge of the fish to the head of the run. There he stopped and stayed against all the bend of the rod I dared for as long as I cared to bend it, and I cared as long as I could stand, because I did not want a fish this big in the shallow riffle below or under the logjam beside me.

Back he came, grudgingly, tail first. At the tail of the run, not four feet from me and my net-bearing witness, he saw us, lost his dignity, and struggled violently for the first time. Again the fly came back, this time to be examined. It was without point and without barb and, since I tied it myself, probably had been since I knocked both off on that "tick" on the back cast I now remember only too well.

A few days later I was back at the run to collect my trophy, checking knots and fly at every cast. At the critical spot there was a slashing rise, and when I dropped back into my waders I found I was fast to a 10-incher whose huge run-mate has probably taught to eat in a rush or be eaten. As I put him back I heard what I know was only the water chuckling under that logjam.

3. Fish and Tell

Truth in Fishing

Somewhere there is a quip about the angler who returneth late at night smelling of strong drink, and the truth is not in him. Like most anglers, I think so little of that slander that I probably do not even quote it right.

An erstwhile fishing companion turned up at my door wearing a grin that would slice sod and bearing in one hand a hat that no longer fit him and in the other a 22½-inch, 4¾-pound brown trout he said he had taken on a dry fly that evening.

I must admit my first impulse was to give him the classic response: "the man who caught that fish is a liar!" But I know him well, and there was neither the odor of strong drink nor of mendacity about him, who can sometimes be held down for a cold beer to be poured in after 10 hours on a blistering day fishing water unfit to drink.

So I congratulated him, made the enthusiastic inquiries about which pool, which fly, how long to land, and so on. The next day at noon I embarked for the Mountain Aire Lodge west of Sundre, filled with awe by the accomplishments of my fellow anglers and the selfless way they, particularly the fly fishermen, will give help and information to their fellows.

Trouble with the Mountain Aire Lodge for a man bent on my type of research is that this is the year every stream on the Forestry Road north from the lodge to Moose Creek is closed to angling. The two capable and charming cooks we brought along chuckled bitterly about going 98 miles and coming back 60 to get into fishing country. It even upset me a little to pass up the beautiful but closed runs and riffles of the James River that, somehow, I have never fished, probably because nobody has ever told me how awful the fishing is in the James.

But I was determined to examine Fallen Timber Creek. After all, where we wanted to fish was a mere 56 miles back towards civilization, and every fisherman I have ever encountered who knew something about Fallen Timber seemed most helpful and generous with his information on the creek. If this latter bit seems paradoxical, let me give some of the data from which I formulated Scammell's Umpteenth Law of Contrariness.

Anglers with uncrossed fingers have assured me Fallen Timber is muddy and unfishable until August. On June 2nd we found it, to avoid the gin cliche, vodka-clear. I have been told by gentlemen who crossed their hearts and spat to die that the holes are too few and far between to make for good fishing. Never have I seen such an abundance of superb brown trout cover as I saw on the stretch of Fallen Timber i fished.

Brethren in anglerhood have sadly shaken their heads and sobbed at how logging has silted in the spawning beds and warmed the waters until only suckers, whether they be fish or anglers, frequent the Fallen Timber. On June 2nd I saw clean gravel spawning beds on the upper end of Fallen Timber, the like of which I have not often seen. On that blistering day the water temperature at the upper end was a crisp 40° F and three hours later the temperature at the lower end was an ideal 60° F.

"Don't seem to be no insect hatches on Fallen Timber," grizzled old veterans have assured me as they examined the far horizons. While I was at the creek, only a couple of hours, there was activity from two species of mayfly and one each of stone and caddis flies. Such abundance of feed was lost on the fish, as I saw no rises. So I tied on a #8 Bird's stonefly nymph and promptly caught a beautiful 14-inch brown and lost two just as big, no further than a cry for "nanny" from a public campground.

If you suspect that my kindly friends were so anxious to spare me the pain of a fruitless trip that they would out and out lie to me, then you are catching on. You also begin to understand why I was so anxious to get to Fallen Timber. My expectations were borne out. Fallen Timber has many attributes of an outstanding brown trout stream, and I intend to visit frequently. I could, of course, have believed Dr. Richard B. Miller who surveyed Fallen Timber in 1952 and reported in "Preliminary Biological Surveys of Alberta Watersheds 1950-52":

> This beautiful, large stream . . . is an ideal trout stream. The broad shallows, quiet pools and undercut banks make it a dry-fly fisherman's delight.

But I was not taken in for a moment by the fact Dr. Miller was a scientist. He was, first of all, an angler who had to use a fly rod to sample streams because he had no stream-shocking equipment. He even claims to have caught a 17-inch brown while testing Fallen Timber, and no angler, after all would have revealed *that* if it were true.

You see, Scammell's Umpteenth Law of Contrariness is: Never believe what a fisherman tells you, only what he does not tell you. Which makes me wonder whether my buddy really did catch that 22½-inch brown where he says he did, or whether I would believe myself if I were reading this column.

The Home Stream

Many incurable anglers have a special place in their hearts for the one river they consider their home river. The home river may be the stream upon which the angler, as a mere fingerling, learned most of what he knows about the ways of trout, or it may be the river beside which an angler lives, or the one he fishes more than any other.

Unfortunately, I do not live beside my home river, but fortunately this circumstance does not oblige me, by implication, to reveal its name. My home river is a scurrying little foothills stream and, because I fish it so often, it has taught me most of the little I know about trout.

I am just back from 10 days on my home river, humbled that I should ever have thought it had no more hard lessons to teach me.

Never before had I fished this river in the middle of July, and never at any other time on the stream have I seen conditions as strange as they were during my recent trip. Heavy late snowstorms had kept the water raging and black six weeks later than usual this particular spring. When I arrived this July, three weeks of drought had left the water as clear as late August, but it was still higher than it usually is in June. Every day while I was there, a scorching sun beat down on the tumbling water.

Despite the fact that this has been somewhat less than a vintage year for grasshoppers, I went out the first day to search the water with a hopper fly, a Joe's hopper, and by suppertime had seduced, subdued, beached, and returned to the stream at least five rainbows of no less than six inches long. Not a good fish had I seen and, had I been in a humming mood, it would have been "Where have all the big fish gone?" When the guilty sun finally slunk behind the mountains, in quick succession I took two 12- and one 14½-inch rainbows from two pools on that same Joe's hopper. This is so small a river that a 14½-inch fish is generally herd bull, so the big fish were there.

In the days that followed, I found the big fish that were there to be in an evil and ugly mood, driven by heat to strange madnesses and prodigious feats of craftiness and strength. The sun continued to heat the water as much as 20 degrees in a day, so that a stream in the low 50's in the morning was steeping in the low 70's by late afternoon.

Fish were seldom in their usual sunny pools, but could be caught in the mornings in the strangest new places, so long as they were shady places: under bushes and under heavy, broken water. Feed seemed abundant, and the fish disinclined to work hard to get it. The fly had to float right in the "window" of vision of the trout or there was nobody home. In the hot afternoons the fish napped, displaying more sense than the addled angler who flailed away to no avail. In the cool of the evening they rose steadily to hatches I could not imitate with anything in my fly boxes. But throw out a huge fanwing Royal Coachman, a fly that resembles nothing on earth, in heaven, or the other place, and the fish would give each other nasty digs in the ribs to be the first to come and skewer themselves on it.

Yes, the big fish were in the home river, but the nastiness encountered in luring them was sweetness and light compared to what happened after one was hooked. I lost two larger than any I have ever seen before in this river I think I know so well. Grounded for fly-casting by a heavy head wind and moved slightly by my own desperado instincts, I switched one morning to a spinning outfit. There was promptly a hand-to-fin brawl with a big one that the spinner had dared to come out from under a bush. As he slid over the rim of the net, a nasty look came into his upper eye and he knit one and purled two with one free barb of the treble hook into the mesh of the net, gave a mighty heave, tore loose, and took off.

An even larger fish committed assault and battery on a Joe's hopper, torpedoed downstream, and tied two half-hitches with the leader around the limb of a fallen tree. Instead of sitting on the bank savouring a chew of snoose while waiting for the fish to unwind, the addled angler waded out to net the fish and, in the clear water, frightened him into a dash upstream. My delicate fly rod transmitted to my shaking hand and heat-crazed brain the vibration made by each turn of the clinch knot unwinding as the trout absconded with the fly.

That gurgling you hear from the west is the trout in my home stream busting their guts laughing at the addled angler. But, as always with home streams, I shall return.

The Red Deer

Like most big rivers, the Red Deer gives up its secrets capriciously and reluctantly. In common with most anglers fortunate enough to live in a big city traversed by a big river, Red Deer anglers generally avoid the small effort involved in learning the secrets of their river.

Since I moved to this city, the work I have done in investigating the river has proved a pleasure in itself, and the secrets, when discovered, have been well worth the knowing. When I was knee-high to a tackle box, I knew of the many secrets of the Red Deer: when the walleye run in the spring and again in the fall; the locations of fine goldeye holes and exactly when the goldeye could be expected to hold open house. But all that knowledge applied many miles downstream from the city of Red Deer, so when I came to Red Deer, I started to "make book", to keep records on our river, to find the good holes, and to date the runs of the various fish.

The rains finally came two weeks ago, and out west the waters were muddy. So like a robin to the worm, I cocked my head to the rising, and allowed, like the veriest old-timer, as to how the rising water ought to bring the goldeye up. I even predicted the goldeye would already have reached a certain hole a few miles downstream from this city, and invited my neighbor, Dr. Jake Reimer—either a novice fisherman as he claims or an accomplished trifler with facts as I now claim—to come out and share my sport with the goldeye.

My eye was wiped by my own book and my own neighbor in my own fishing hole. There were no goldeye and no sport for the deep thinker of fish migrations. When I was not netting walleyes for my neighbor, my time was spent standing jowl-to-elbow with him, casting the same gold spinner he was using.

One fish Jake caught could not be netted. It was levered up on the beach with the handle of the net. It weighed 6 pounds, 12 ounces and, the last time I looked, it was leading the walleye class in every fish contest in town.

The doctor caught a fever either from the fish or the rain, because he tapped on my door bright and early the next morning. By this time, I allowed (to myself this time) that the goldeye must surely have reached the east bridge. O me of little faith! I left my fly rod at home, and the goldeye were there and rising to stoneflies with such concentration that only occasionally would they suck in even a worm. (Yes, I sinned, but I've sworn off again.) But we did catch a few, and the next evening I went back and proved once again that happiness is catching a goldeye on a fly.

Then there is my neighbor, full of the fever and thinking he knew something about the Red Deer, sneaking back to that first hole last Sunday looking for another big walleye. This time he caught nothing but goldeye. So I blush, and new entries go in the book. With the conceit of us of little knowledge, I explain that conditions this year have put a late run of spring walleye smack-dab on the usual run of goldeye.

I am certain the fishing is magnificent right now in our river, as certain as I am that the vast majority of local anglers will ignore that wonderful fishing. Perhaps this is for the best. A sombre note entered this week when a man whose opinions and observations I respect warned me that a government official had told him it would be better if fish from the Red Deer River were not consumed by humans this year. Apparently a mistake was made last winter with harmful substances which may have contaminated some of the fish in the river. My informant and I both wondered why a warning was not made to the general public. Such things are hard to track down, but I am trying. In the meantime, you do not have to eat fish to have sport. They can be put back in the rivers alive. Right now the river is alive with sporting fish.

Floating the Clearwater

Canoes and horses have at least two things in common as far as I am concerned: they both make me saddle sore. Both also have a following of fanatics who, as soon as they spot a novice showing interest, clamour to enmesh that novice in the darker mysteries of horse and canoe.

So I must make a couple of things clear. My presence has not graced the poop deck of a horse since I was swept from one by a low limb at the age of six. I'd as soon ride a rocket to Mars as a horse and, offhand, I can't imagine a set of circumstances that would compel me to do either.

Canoes, at least, I regard as legitimate means of transportation from point A to point B or somewhere in between when no other means will get you there. Mind you, there has to be a reason to get to point B. With canoes it is usually fishing, although I have been known to venture offshore for the sake of a duck hunt off some isolated point.

Saturday the reason was fishing, and there were many points B to be visited in 11 miles of the lower Clearwater River where I have long suspected huge brown trout loll in splendid isolation. (WARNING: I do not endorse or even suggest floating any section of the Clearwater other than the stretch between the Dovercourt and Rocky bridges.)

After the usual car juggling from bridge to bridge, we pushed off in Mac Johnston's 14-foot canoe which was purchased only slightly hump-bottomed after having been bounced by some canoe fanatic on a rock in the upper Red Deer.

It gives me great comfort to have Mac manning the stern paddle, as he is a practical canoe man, having taken his apprenticeship as a young skunk trapper, or something, in Newfoundland. Mac is also adept in the use of the setting-pole, an advantage if the object of the trip is fishing from the canoe. So adept is Mac that I only touched my paddle once, at the start, and he told me to forget it and stick to the fly rod. Iain, Mac's young son, sat in the middle, concentrating on ducking my back casts and speaking when spoken to.

Fly fishing rivers from canoe or boat is so beguiling an experience that I am astonished it is not practiced more often in this country. A dry fly generally floats along at the same speed as the canoe, so that drag is eliminated and natural floats can be achieved over water that could not even be reached from shore. When fishing for brown trout, fishing toward the bank is highly productive. Just after lunch, floating along one particularly fine cutbank, I picked up three browns not six inches from the shore and in water that could not have been much more than that deep. Most of the browns, however, came slashing up to take the fly from the slicks behind mid-river rocks.

Generally I was striking a pretty good stroke in spite of the slack line that develops when floating a river, but one I chose to strike out on was the only really huge brown we encountered. We were cruising along the bank of a huge hole when this one hove up under the fly from beneath the roots of a leaning spruce. He drifted under the fly for what seemed like hours and, just as I moaned he was not going to take it, he did with a gush and I missed.

Slack line is compensated for by the drag-free floats, the fantastic amount of water you can cover from the canoe, and the fact that even brown trout are not frightened in the slightest by a craft floating on the water. We ended up with a satisfying number of brown trout, but all were fryers which, surprisingly for their size, contained no developing milt or egg sacs. The indication to me is that the brown trout in the Clearwater mature at a larger size than in most of the waters of this area. That there are huge browns in the lower Clearwater, I know for a fact.

The trip is magnificent. Close as this stretch is to roads on both sides, there are virtually no signs of the hand of man on the river itself. We saw mink and deer and umpteen species of birds. The late August trip would have been little challenge for canoe fanatics. Only twice did we line the canoe through what we call rapids, but I am sure the sharks would call them riffles and ride them out. People who would like a canoe ride with perhaps a little fishing would enjoy this trip, particularly so when the leaves start to turn.

The only regret other than missing that big fish is not having stopped often to give some of those magnificent holes a real going over. In fact Iain proved to be a kindred soul. I heard him tell his dad he would come again, but next time we have to stop more to let him fish.

Exposure to the Bow

If you really think you are tough, go along for the ride sometime at the Calgary Hook and Hackle Club's fly fishing derby, generally held in mid-September. Unfortunately, at that time of year the weather can be a bit now-and-then, to say the least.

Last year the derby was on the honor system: contestants were to measure all fish caught and release them. This year, because Dennis McDonald, Calgary region fisheries biologist, is doing a study on the section of the Bow from the mouth of the Highwood River to Carseland Dam, the derby was to take place in that stretch, and all fish caught were to be turned over to a cruising crew of biologists for study. So I decided to attempt to move into the big time in outdoor writing by doing a feature story on this unique river and unusual fish derby.

Last year Calgary lawyer Hugh Douglas won the derby with a 23½-inch rainbow. This year Hugh kindly agreed to guide me in a manner that I would be able to take a variety of pictures of various anglers in diverse locations. On the Sunday morning we set out in two two-man and one one-man kayaks, Hugh, myself, and Ross, 14, Roger, 13, and Allistair, 9, three of his four sons. It was somewhat overcast, but the forecast was for fine weather.

Somewhat downriver we stopped to fish, Hugh and I each catching a couple of 10-inchers, two of which we killed and gave to the biologists when they hove on the scene. The biologists roared off downstream, promising they would see us later as they planned to run the stretch twice that day. If only they had!

We stopped for lunch. By this time Hugh had added to the bag three 15- or 16-inchers, and me, one 14-inch fish. Then a hatch of *Epeorus* mayflies came on with a pleasant drizzle of rain, and we fished and fished, adding numbers of smallish fish to the bag. I decided there must be a larger fish out there and put on a #6 Bird's stonefly nymph which was taken on the second cast by the hardest fighting fish I have ever had on a line. Twice he took the 30 yards of fly line and went 50 yards into the backing. He came in, a fish of only 17 or 18 inches and not the derby winner I expected.

Off we went again, and it began to rain harder, but it was still a drizzle. About 2 p.m., Hook and Hackle Club president Bill Rutherford hailed us from the bank. He was out of cigarettes and had beautiful 18- and 19-inch rainbows and the fattest 12-inch brown I have ever seen. Bill agreed with Hugh that we were about halfway to Carseland.

Kayaks are tricky, and Allistair rolled out of his before he got in it. Fortunately, Bill Rutherford came back from somewhere and took the sopping youngest member of our party off to a warm car. The three others were wet enough that I felt guilty that I had been the only one faint-hearted enough to bring a rain jacket. Then it pelted sideways, driven into our faces by a northeast wind.

I could paddle only in the safe stretches since I can see nothing without my glasses: in these conditions I could see less with them. From time to time I could hear involuntary moans from Ross behind me.

About 4 p.m. our kayak flipped in tricky water near shore. The only dry member of the party was soaked immediately and joined the others in being wracked by shuddering shivers and sudden weakness. On and on we went. It is a tribute to the construction of those little kayaks that they were not shaken apart by the shivering of their sodden cargo. On and on and never did the rounding of each bend reveal our destination.

It was getting dark about 7 when we heard a human voice on shore. Too proud to cry for help, we merely shouted "hello". The answer was a pair of headlights slinking away up the hills. So on we went, driven by the pernicious faith that it couldn't be much further. About 7:30 it was dark, and we landed where the cliff looked lower than it had for the past mile. At shore I tried to stand up, found with amazement that I could not, and over we went again into water that now felt beautifully warm.

Roger curled up in a sopping blanket on the rocks. Hugh decided he and Ross would climb the bank and look around and that I should stay with Roger. With hands that were little more than hooks, I peeled off the waders and poured out the gallon of water I could no longer afford to warm. I found my lighter would work, but noted there was nothing to burn down here on the rocks and probably even less up there on the prairie. I chose not to think of what the morning would bring if we stayed out all night.

Then Hugh shouted. There was a farmhouse a quarter mile away! The rest was slogging: four people who could not really walk, climbing a greasy cliff, marching in a trance over a wonderfully level field and falling anyway, ever toward the light that, to me, was only a bright splotch through the rain on my glasses.

The tradition of the unlatched door is wonderful, for nobody was home. It was only when I got stuck going through the door to the warm porch that I realized I still had my fly rod in my hand. Some kind people turned up who looked frightened and then concerned, and we were driven to the campground where the Hook and Hackle festivities were to be held and where Hugh's wife was to meet us.

In my emergency pack I had all the dry clothes I needed but a shirt, and Shirley Douglas was so relieved to see her missing family that she gave me the sweater off her back. Somebody else donated overproof rum. At that point, life was so beautiful that I'll not bother to list all my personal injuries and property damage. Suffice it to say that the outdoor writer moving into the big time took some amazing pictures which are probably, like the camera that took them, victims of exposure, which is something Hugh Douglas, his two fine boys, and I are not.

Skunking on the Bow

A couple of visiting anglers came a long way just to get skunked by the rabid rainbows of the lower Bow River. September 14th was Derby Day for the members of Calgary's Hook and Hackle Club, and a more perfect fall day would be hard to imagine. The last time I fished this derby I got caught by a September blizzard halfway to Carseland from the mouth of the Highwood and turned over twice in the kayak before giving up and crawling home. It has taken me three years to thaw out before risking Derby Day again.

This year John Lynde, author of *34 Ways to Cast a Fly*, came out from Trail, B.C., to train some casting instructors and to put on public casting demonstrations for the club and stayed for the derby. I came down from Red Deer to photograph the proceedings and perhaps catch a few of those magnificent Bow trout myself. Even during the blizzard three years ago, we slew the fish. Calgary lawyer Hugh Douglas and I nearly sunk one of the kayaks with the load of fish we caught. That year members were exhorted by the biologists to keep every fish they caught, as they were needed for research, but generally the derby is on an honor system: fish are caught, measured, and released, their lengths then being recorded on a creel card. The skeptical might suspect that running a fishing competition this way is akin to putting a sex maniac in charge of morals and conduct in a massage parlour. Perish such thoughts! I make no comment on their sexual proclivities, but Hook and Hackle members are honourable men.

Jack Lambert of Calgary, immediate past president of the club, was guiding, and he took us to the only flat-water, slow stretch in the Bow, no doubt because its huge finicky trout would prove properly challenging to such distinguished visitors as John Lynde and me. Unfortunately, no one informed the trout that it was Derby Day and they would be released. Jack did con a couple, one a beautiful 18-inch rainbow, into taking Jack's own version of a gold-ribbed hare's ear nymph, tied nervous style. From that point on Jack, too, was shut out.

John Lynde employed all 34 ways to cast a fly, with no result. Anyone would have forgiven him for noting, after watching Lambert and me cast, that he had discovered ways 35 and 36. But John Lynde is a gentleman as well as a superb caster.

I quit hiding behind my camera long enough to blow everything on the fish everyone was looking for and calling Jaws. The monster came back and engulfed a #4 pink Le Tort hopper going away. I was so afraid the fish was going to engulf me next that I was forgetting to strike, and Jaws ejected my fraud like a dud sunflower seed. The consensus of idlers in the vicinity was that they saw only half the fish, and that was 14 inches long. The lone dissenter said the fish was 14 inches between the eyes.

Meanwhile, current Hook and Hackle president Norm Walsh of Calgary spent the afternoon in a swamp umpteen miles downstream and horsed them in, up to and including a 19-inch brown trout, on a high-density line that drapes itself along the bottom and an indescribable fly called "Dave's Folly". Every time Norm released a fish a worm washer on the other bank would comment to the whole world, "Look there, he's lost another fish. I may not get much action, but when I do, I don't blow it!"

Whenever I fish the lower Bow I become convinced that we have there probably the finest trophy trout stream in North America and, as usual, we don't know what to do with it. The only unpleasant aspect of the day was the flotilla of idiots roaring up and down the river in motor boats under the guise of fishing. A big river like this could very effectively be fished from a boat, but a boat ever floating and required by law ever to float, downstream. Many Hook and Hackle Club members reported catching fish scarred and cut, obviously by outboard motor propellers. Allowing motors at all on magnificent fishing water like this is a hell of a way to run a river.

Back at the Carseland community hall from 7 p.m. on of Derby Day, the boys assembled to eat and turn in their creel cards. A quick tabulation revealed that the 50 or so club members who fished in the derby this year got 277 fish, virtually all of which were in the 12- to 21-inch category. Just to indicate the level of integrity, club members Cornette, Wallbridge, and Burchall tied for top fish with 21-inch rainbows.

John Lynde was off in a corner of the hall planning a new assault on the lower Bow for the next day. Me? I, too, shall return, whenever I get rid of this horrible red face—from all the autumn sun off the water, of course.

Cottonwood Creek

Seek the Holy Grail if you like or needles in haystacks if you are so inclined, but if you are really a nut, go looking for brown trout in cutthroat and rainbow country. Down in the deep south last weekend my fanatical brother-in-law hove on the scene slightly more than somewhat closer to lunch than after breakfast. Fishing went without saying, but as we loaded up his new old wreck of a truck he allowed that we were going brown trout fishing.

Now I knew that was not as ridiculous as it sounds, as 104,500 brown trout fingerlings were planted in the Crowsnest River below Lundbreck Falls last summer, and rumor had it even more were planted there the summer before. All this is in an effort, it is rumored, to establish the tough, tolerant brown in the Crowsnest-Castle-Oldman River system before pollution extirpates the resident bull, rainbow, and cutthroat.

But if you think we were going to the Crowsnest River, you just have not been a faithful reader and do not have the knowledge of my fanatical brother-in-law that past encounters in these columns would have given you. No, we would go to Cottonwood Creek and there seek out the browns that have been dribbed and drabbed in there in the past few years in an attempt to introduce the fish to the Belly and Waterton River systems.

Just to add the usual bouquet to the whole proceedings, we had completely failed twice previously in even finding Cottonwood Creek. Cottonwood Creek was alleged to flow through the domain of Andy Russell, author of *Grizzly Country*, so nothing would do but to consult him and to wrestle the wreck up the side of that young mountain to the Hawk's Nest, the magnificent home of the mountain man himself, set squarely on the very edge at the very top. On the slope in front of the house were limber pines that were just making it.

But first we gazed at the view from the porch across the "holler" from this, the last of the foothills west to the mountains, a view that explains a lot about Andy Russell and his work.

Most of what you read about the man deals with how he is tougher than a boiled owl, how he is as big as a grizzly bear, how he will stand in front of a charging grizzly armed only with his camera and commanding voice. All true, no doubt, but this was the Sabbath, and the mountain man was in his high-gabled living room in front of a fire in his fieldstone fireplace reading of the perils and pleasures of over-civilization in one of the racier novels on the current best-seller list. Scratch one illusion. Scratch still another when Andy said he had thought of going fishing, but it was just too cold.

The talk was stimulating, as always, particularly when it got on the subject of those who ruin many of the things that can be seen from the front porch and those who allow them to do it. For example, the sudden demise of every living organism in one of the creeks flowing into the Waterton dam, and now the mysterious death of fish in the dam itself. Of course many people know the cause, including the authorities, but in Alberta we do not rock the boat.

Down on the flat again we found Cottonwood Creek right where Andy said it would be. He said the cover was good, and this was obviously the reason we had been unable to find the Cottonwood before: you simply cannot see the creek for the bush. If ever there was a place in southern Alberta to make brown trout happy, then this is it: muskeg, beaver dams, and brush everywhere.

The word was that browns of a pound, pound and a half were being taken on worms. We decided the natives of the area must have invented a brush auger to bore down to water before lowering the worm. We were using tiny spinners, and the rule was that wherever it was too thin to walk on, that was the place to make a cast. We caught a fat little trout each and were surprised to find each was a bright little native cutthroat, a fish whose ancestors were probably negotiating this tangle when the ancestors of every brown trout now in North America were still lolling in the waters of Scotland and Germany.

Just as mountain men are not always in the character we give them, trout of any particular kind are not necessarily found where we think they should be. Now that we have found the creek, can the brown trout be far behind?

Rabid Rainbows

On past Labour Days the rabid rainbows of the Castle River had cleaned me out, as the saying goes in angling circles. Even so, this past Labour Day weekend my heart should not have been as full of vengeance as it was, for I was making a sentimental pilgrimage to the Castle. Although I had never fished the particular stretch before, I felt as though I knew it as soon as I saw it. And I had seen it before, in the photographs my father, on his return from trips years ago, would show to a boy too little to go with the men.

Here the Castle lurches through a deep half-mile canyon where the waters choke themselves down to 10 feet wide and 30 to 40 feet deep. In the dizzying green depths cruise bull trout reputed to live on mountain goats that slip on canyon walls and fall in. The river gushes from the canyon and sighs like the proverbial lady slipping out of her girdle as the water relaxes, spreads out to between 50 and 100 feet, becomes crystal again, and moulds itself over slabs, boulders, folds and faults in the strata, and snuggles up to the many rocky reefs jutting out in the channel.

In the deep, still waters before and behind these reefs lurk the rabid rainbows of the Castle River, huge fish of an evil disposition unmatched by any other fish awash in Alberta waters, jaws slavouring, teeth gnashing, waiting to pounce on #8 Len Thompson red and whites.

Why the rainbows of the Castle are rabid I do not know. Some people say they are really rainbow-cutthroat hybrids, so that perhaps they brood over their reputed lack of sex life or get enraged over the biologists who cannot agree about whether or not they have one.

Past Labour Days have found me minding my own business on the Castle, flipping a little spinner hither and yon for dainty cutthroats and Dolly Vardens, when everything would stop and four-, five-, even six-pound rainbows would cartwheel three feet out of the water and I would be disconnected before I knew I was connected. That sort of thing gives an angler nightmares through the long winter and engenders visions of revenge.

So this year I went with a new six-pound line and bushels of the brass and iron these brutes eat for breakfast. On the first long cast to a backwater in front of one of the reefs, the howling wind and raging current put such a great bow in my line that I felt nothing. But I saw the red-striped polaris that shuddered into the sunshine, scales rattling and clanking. Or was it only the sound of my spoon shaking loose and bounding off the rocks on that first jump?

Twice more it happened in the next day and a half. My only triumph was that I stayed with the third one to the third jump, but he was a wild joker and jumped twice in pure glee after the hook had gone. My companion, a man of unquestionable sanity, urged me to forget the rabid rainbows and dunk for Dolly Vardens as he was doing so successfully. I almost took his advice, but I left him as we were going up to the canyon. I wanted to get my fly rod and try the rainbows again in the hope that they would have more trouble shaking a fly.

Halfway back another angler was near tears. He had just lost two of the huge and rabid rainbows. "They're in the air too much for me," he said. But he was an old hand, and his eye took on an evil stare.

Claimed the way to beat these wild fish and the bow the wind and current put in the line is to shoulder arms with the rod at the first hint of a strike, about face smartly, and run like hell up the bank. This, he said, straightens the line, socks the hook home and, if everything holds, turns the fish over in the air and strikes fear and confusion into its evil heart by showing it who is boss right from the start.

But he had sworn off rainbows for the day, he said, and showed me a 12-inch Dolly Varden he had caught which he intended to use as bait for bull trout up in the canyon. I gulped at the thought of my friend alone up in the canyon with bull trout for whom 12-inch Dollies are bait.

The wind was too much for casting a dry fly upstream, so I decided it was about time to learn about fishing wet flies downstream. I was astonished to take a 15-inch cutthroat on the third cast on a Muddler minnow. About then my sane companion turned up and said he had gotten just one more fish, but it was "kind of a good one". Then I saw a tail like a scoopshovel and about 10 inches of a 4½-pound bull trout sliding out of his creel.

There must be a lesson in all this: a vengeful sport catches no fish, or the meek and the dunkers for bull trout shall inherit the earth, or something like that. Whatever the lesson, the score in the annual Labour Day match with the rabid rainbows of the Castle River is again nothing:all, with them getting all the hits and me making all the errors.

Clearwater Sidechannels

The fall fishing is just great—if you can stomach grouse fever. As an experiment into the fall fishing potential of the area and to plumb a few suspicions about the Clearwater River, I vowed this year to continue fishing and not touch a shotgun until the upland season was open all over the province on October 11. Last time out was rank exposure to an infectious disease, as the grouse season was open in the area of my experiment.

There is no accounting for grouse drumming in the fall, unless the young cocks are testing on hunters the arsenal of seduction they will employ on hens the next spring. As I strung up my rod, grouse in the woods were drumming and gunners gunning—almost enough to unstring me and the rod and send me for the shotgun I brought for self-defense only. But I remained staunch, even when I heard four ruffies flush during my walk to the sidechannel of the Clearwater: for me, it is not an attack until you see the bands of their tails.

It is generally the middle of August before the sidechannels of the Clearwater start to fill with spawning brown trout, and there they wait on into October. In late September I had fished a quarter of a mile of this sidechannel with no result until I came to one deep run along a fallen spruce. From tip to roots, about 60 feet, at least 10 fish were sipping, splashing, slushing, and porpoising. My own performance was less laughable than usual, and the result was one brookie and five browns, all in the 12- to 16-inch category.

This time, as last, the dry fly for the Clearwater seems to be the brown bivisible: no body and wings, simply a brown tail and a couple of brown hackle feathers wound up the shank of a #10 or #12 hook with two or three turns of a pure white hackle at the head. The fly is called bivisible because of its alleged high visibility both to fish and fishermen. The fish seem to have no trouble nailing it; for my myopic self, the collar of white hackle makes the fly extremely easy to follow even in the great turbulence of the Clearwater. The fluffy bulk of the fly makes it descend gently to the water on the cast, and it floats and dances on the water like thistledown.

I tied one on and, while straightening the leader with a small piece of inner-tube, noted that surely there has never been a fall like this, for color. It was as fine a fishing day as there has been this year and, as always seems to happen around here after September 1st, not another fisherman was in sight. Only that infernal grouse hunter getting off another quick two shots.

Water temperature was 58°F, not the best for dry-fly fishing. I wondered at what temperature the actual spawning would begin. The first few casts flick over the tail and body of a pool where I have never had a rise. Up in the throat the fly bobs over a jungle of submerged debris and is gone in a golden flash. A roll cast sets the hook and makes him think the trouble is upstream, so he swims down and away from his lair, and a 14-inch brown is landed. Beside the logjam in the next pool something keeps pecking at the fly but does not get stuck. Maybe a whitefish.

The first cast in a long run above the jam and another 14-inch brown comes arrowing back, hooks himself at my feet, jumps a couple of times, goes under the jam, but eventually comes out. Two more in the fast run come to the attack; the good one is too fast for me, and the small one gets put back.

In the run along the spruce tree, the 12-inch brown at the tip was closer than I thought and got caught on a cast being tried for size.

45

The next, halfway up the tree, is a 14-inch clown and flings himself sideways over the half-submerged trunk to nab the bivisible as it floats down the other side. Finally, up near the roots, the 16-inch matriarch takes in a gout of spray and three times flirts with the certain freedom of the submerged tree before she clears the downstream end of it and runs aground on a gravel bar.

A grouse drums as I clean the fish. The fish are obviously near spawning, and I feel the season should be over, even though sense says the progeny of a female brown are lost no matter what time of year she is caught.

Five browns over 12 inches on dry flies in late fall from the Clearwater: as good a way as any to end the season and a better way than it began. Now where is my musket, and where are those grouse?

4. Mixed Bag

Goldeye and Roses

Late June and early July is the time for goldeye and wild roses. There should be a song "Goldeye and Roses". Goldeye were the fish of my youth and remain the fish of my heart. As any Alberta lad knows who lives within a long cast of the silty sections of the lower Peace, Athabasca, North and South Saskatchewan, Bow or Red Deer rivers, this is the time to dig a can of worms or catch a bunch of grasshoppers and go goldeye fishing.

Chief Alberta Fisheries Biologist Martin Paetz reveals himself as much a prairie lad as a scholarly scientist in his excellent article in *McClane's Standard Fishing Encyclopedia* when he refers to the goldeye as "the best of (Alberta's) warmwater gamefish as far as sporting qualities are concerned".

Aficionados all have that favorite, secret goldeye hole. I well remember those days fishing my own goldeye hole behind a rock reef stretching far out into the Red Deer where it flows through the badlands many miles east of here. Oh the hard work, the suffering! Impale a worm or grasshopper on a #8 hook, 12 or 18 inches below a bobber, lob it out, sit back, relax and listen to the land erode. Very often the bobber plunges, and the twinkling flash in the murky water reveals a hooked goldeye who braces his broad sides against the current and exhibits his sporting qualities.

Part of the fascination of the goldeye comes from the appearance of this large-scaled, bright silver fish with the narrow back, the deep sides, and the shimmering gold ring around the eye. He looks like a fish that should be caught in salt water. The goldeye is also just a little risque, being one of the few fishes whose sex can be established from exterior features: if the anal fin is rounded, it is a male, and if pointed, you have a female.

An aura of mystery surrounds the goldeye as a result of the sparse knowledge of its habits and yearly movements. It has only recently been discovered that goldeye spawn their semi-buoyant eggs on gravel bars between May and July. Some biologists say that all mature goldeye do not spawn every year and that many mature and, for some reason, refuse to cast the eggs they carry. Other biologists say the problem is that goldeye do not spawn at all until four years of age and that large commercial nettings of immature fish is causing a decline in numbers.

They still exist in the Red Deer, though. Two weeks ago I held in my cupped hand, just for a moment before giving them back to the river, two tiny, newly-hatched goldeye scooped from a large school in a backwater near the Content Bridge.

Overfishing has sharply reduced the number of goldeye now netted in Lake Winnipeg, and the commercial market is largely supplied by Lake Athabasca and Lake Claire in Wood Buffalo National Park. Goldeye are not taken commercially in rivers, and it is in rivers that they will continue to delight sportsmen until pollution takes its inevitable toll. Being insectivorous in feeding habits, the goldeye are generally caught near the surface and can provide magnificent sport for the dry-fly fisherman using Black Gnats or grasshopper imitations.

Books say the goldeye averages less than a pound or 12 inches in length. The Red Deer has big ones: the 12-year records of one local contest reveal the average weight of the winners to be 2 pounds 4 ounces. So far as I can discover, the local record is a 3-pound 6-ounce goldeye caught by Bobby Nelson of Red Deer in 1962. This fish might figure largely in the current efforts of Alberta Fisheries biologist Dennis McDonald to establish provincial angling records for various Alberta species.

Last July 6th I was at the mouth of Waskasoo Creek doing my bit to rid the Red Deer of suckers, when the sudden plunge of the bobber instead of the sucker's bobbling, called up old memories. I knew it was a goldeye, and it was, a beautiful 16-inch male, the first I had caught for a couple of years. That started the fever again. Four days later my father and I stood to our hips in the water and to our shoulders in blooming wild roses and did battle with bright goldeyes galore in a flooded creek flowing into the Bow River.

Now, it is nearly July again, the roses are out again, and this prairie lad will try to get away to see if the beloved and mysterious goldeye can be found again.

"Pickerel" and Cotton

When the cotton blooms and blows, the "pickerel" go on the prod. When I saw the cotton pods forming on the poplars about 10 days ago, I decided the cotton was late this year and went to the mouth of the Blindman to see if the "pickerel" were running on time. I was hailed there by a couple of urchins: "Hey, mister, what kind of fish are these?" They looked a little like "pickerel", but not really like any "pickerel" they had ever caught before.

In this country two members of the perch family, the walleye and the sauger, are lumped together and called pickerel. What the two boys had were the less common sauger. The sauger is a slimmer fish than the walleye but has the same large, spined first dorsal fin and glassy eyes. The sauger is a dark olive grey with three to four dark saddle markings over his back and down his side and has well-defined longitudinal rows of spots on his spiny dorsal, where the walleye is a brassy olive on the sides and has only one large spot at the rear base of his dorsal fin.

Water conditions were perfect at the magnificent pickerel hole where the Blindman meets the Red Deer. The Blindman was the color of weak coffee and made a definite line where its clear water met the muddy Red Deer. Walleye should be feeding in the clear water of the hole just below the line of meeting waters, so I went for my rod and the battered lead jig with the green head and the bright yellow feathers that I have called "the sick canary" every since the evening I first used it. The first two casts I got into the proper place produced two nice walleye which I used to demonstrate to the kids the difference between walleye and sauger. The conclusive point seemed to be the silvery-white tip on the lower lobe of the tail of the walleye, which is absent in the sauger.

The abundance of pickerel make the mouth of the Blindman a very popular place, because pickerel are popular with anglers. Walleye and sauger hit readily, run in schools, put up a strong stubborn fight, and are excellent food fish. But many people catch neither walleye nor sauger at the mouth of the Blindman because they are not aware of a few fundamental rules. These fish are generally found feeding on the bottom in deep water, so that is where the bait or lure should be. Their diet is primarily other fish, so that is what the lure should resemble. Both walleye and sauger are slow and methodical about their dining, so the bait or lure should move slowly. They are generally nocturnal feeders; cloudy days, late evenings, or nights are the best times to fish for them.

The lure that seems best to fit the requirements for pickerel is the jig, a lure born in the salt water down east and adapted to pickerel fishing in the north some years ago. Jigs have a colored lead head moulded to a single sharp hook covered by a skirt of bright feathers, hair, or nylon. The lure is designed to hang with the hook point up so that it will not easily snag bottom. Simply cast into a likely looking hole, allow the jig to sink right to the bottom, and retrieve very slowly with up-and-down pumps of the rod to make the lure hop and skip over the bottom. Pickerel generally take the jig on the hop so hard that you think you are snagged until the fish moves off.

My discovery of jigs came on a late May evening in 1964 at the mouth of the Blindman. The many people there had caught not a fish. My frantic search of the tackle box produced "the sick canary", the jig with the green head and yellow feathers. I do not recall where, when, or why I purchased it, but desperation deemed I try it. The first and second casts produced fine big walleye. The total was half a dozen on about eight casts, much to the disgust of the multitude.

I could not find my rod after stringing the sixth fish, but soon saw it making a cast in the alien hand of my fishing friend who, on that one cast, promptly caught the largest walleye. When he returned the rod he sneered, "I just wanted to make sure it was the hook and not the fisherman."

Now that the cotton is really in the air, I think I'll try some serious pickerel jigging. I may even try it at night, if I can find someone who can see in the dark.

The False Grayling

I really don't know what to say about old *Prosopium williamsoni*. Within me rages a mass of conflicting loyalties and wildlife management theories. I am torn from stem to mainspring by all the mixed reactions you would get from a whole tangle of anglers on the subject of Rocky Mountain whitefish, which is what old *Prosopium* is when he's among friends or foes.

The first time I met him was the first time I fished my beloved Tay River. I stood right at the mouth and yarded these whatsits out one after another on a Mepps spinner while my bride applauded from the log atop which she was basting and simmering. I was happy to have caught fish, even when the sneers told me they were whitefish.

But consider two years ago when I embarked downstream on a three-mile stretch of Elk Creek, determined to find the planted brown trout. At the tail of every pool there was a rise. I slunk around behind every rise and dropped a #14 Joe's hopper on the button every time. Each time the fish took faithfully, and each time it was a whitefish. Dozens of them. The written word will not suffice to describe what I called Old Rocky that day, but it will suffice to say I did not call him "grayling" as so many do who do not know better.

This catching them when you'd rather not contributes to such things as the hatred anglers bear toward the Rocky in such places as Montana. Say you're fishing the Madison for browns and rainbows. You tie on a Sofa Pillow that cost you at least 75 cents, slaver gobs of fly oil, and take lots of time making it float just so. First cast, a big Rocky vacuums it in clean to a point that requires decapitation and disembowelment to get it out. You just know that fly will never float again without a shampoo and a sit under the dryer. Thus the origin of the Montana saying, "You release trout and throw whitefish back, as far back in the bush as you can." Montana is the only place I have heard the Rocky declared inedible, if not downright poisonous. In Alberta, they are delicious, but you do have to scale them.

Just last summer a Rocky of over three pounds took my fly in the Castle River and gave me the most frantic 15 minutes I have ever had with a fish. Enjoyed every minute of it but, you see, I was free to enjoy it. I saw that fish and knew it was a Rocky when it took the fly, so I was pleased, not enraged, when a Rocky finally slid up on shore.

Finally, for me, there is the suspicion, the nagging possibility that there would be many more trout if there were many less Rocky Mountain whitefish since they are generally found in waters also inhabited by trout. The biologists agree that the diets of the trout and the whitefish are so similar that speaking of differences is a waste of time. So they compete for food, and the biologists will tell you a given stream will support so many total pounds of trout, whether the total is made up of 4-ouncers or 4-pounders.

What about whitefish? Does one 3-pound Rocky take the place of a 3-pound or a 2½-pound trout? Nobody knows, and nobody but me even seems to care. I do know that river-keepers in England have regular campaigns against the grayling, which resembles our Rocky only in that it competes with the trout the keeper is paid to raise.

Before there is a hue and cry, let me hasten to say that I recognize there is a huge crowd of Rocky fundamentalists who love the Rocky Mountain whitefish, the maggots they catch him on, fishing for him, scaling him and eating him—who love everything about him. I understand just how they feel, because even though I do not fish for the Rocky in the traditional manner, I enjoy every moment of it when I purely and genuinely set out to catch one on purpose. (They gag in Montana when you tell them people up here do actually fish for them on purpose.)

If you are a fundamentalist you will know that late August is the time. You will have collected a good bunch of 6-inch spikes for weight and rotted up—or whatever it is you do—a bucket of maggots for bait. You will know that Rockies are now making their spawning runs by the millions in streams all over the west country and that with the spike, #10 hooks, and maggot rig, you can get them two, yea! verily, even unto three at a time.

Even I know that every evening from 6 to 8 the Rockies are rising like mad to flies in the big flat pool in the Red Deer right where the city stores its gravel. I may just go one evening, but I'm not really sure. Catching Rocky Mountain whitefish on purpose takes some thinking about.

The Holy Grayling

For a man who spends as much time fishing as I do, it is unaccountable how I have not managed to tangle lines with a grayling. For readers south of a line drawn east to west about at Edmonton, I want to get something very clear: I mean the genuine high-dorsalled Arctic grayling, not the people's fish, the ubiquitous Rocky Mountain whitefish so abundant in our streams and so erroneously called a grayling by so many people.

Oh, I have chased grayling and rumors of grayling. I have cursed and laboured through mazes of muskegs to little creeks, like Bogart in *The African Queen*, and cast to dimpled rises only to catch stunted brook trout or Rockies. I have plied northern Alberta streams that looked like canals filled with used dishwater or like the servant's entrance to a beaver lodge and have turned sadly away, believing I should catch my first grayling in the drink they prefer: clear, cold, unpolluted water.

My search for the holy grayling has not been single-minded, for I will fish for anything else along the way, but I have been known to grumble publicly about my terrible luck and utter lack of success in catching just one example of probably the most beautiful native fish that swims in Alberta's waters. Bob Tanghe of Edson, farmer and mountain man, heard of my plight and wrote, suggesting he could introduce me to a grayling sometime between the middle of August and the middle of September. So last weekend, with a sense of here we go again, I set out.

From Bob's farm north of Edson, we travelled in Old Jeep through a rabbit's warren of oilfield roads. With us was Carl Hunt of Edson, the only fisheries biologist I know who puts all that book learning and on-the-job experience to practical use by actually fishing on his days off. Bob Tanghe felt blindfolds were not necessary, as we would never remember where he was taking us. He was right, and after about 40 miles of utter confusion, he directed me down eight miles of sloppy clay and, after a bit, observed that Old Jeep "seems to handle all right". I began to recall that I was once told that Bob Tanghe believes if it is possible to get there by other than muscle-power, it is likely to be fished out.

Then it was waders, cameras, lunches, in packs on the back, and a 3-mile stroll down a couple of intersecting cut lines. For Tanghe it was a stroll; he is always in shape, particularly now that he has already been on a couple of sheep hunts. Eventually we got to wherever we were going, and Bob confided to us what Carl suspected, that it was the Berland River. It was beautiful: a couple of hundred yards of crystal water, a cold 50° F when we arrived, the only sound the syncopated slap-slap of a sweeper from a logjam moved back and forth by the current. The only other angler's tracks were days and days old. This far north the birches and aspens were already gilded and glistening in the sunlight of a perfectly clear fall day.

Carl and I had fly rods. Bob uses a battle-scarred telescoping glass spinning rod and prospects for fish with Mepp's spinners. Fly selection is a mysterious art and, for no other reason than that the trout sections of the river after which it is named are also wild and remote, I tied on a #12 Rio Grande King. By noon nobody had caught a fish. We perched like three bumps on a log beside a deep still run at the side of the current tongue at the foot of a rapid. I consoled the guide by telling him the fish would probably get active when the water got up to 55°F or so.

Then I saw the sudden wrinkle that shouldn't be there in the myriad wrinkles of the current in front of us.

"There's a rise," I said.

"There's a rise," I repeated.

"I saw it," Carl said, quietly.

"There he goes again," Carl said.

That time I saw it. Carl's was a different fish.

"If he does it again, I'll get him," I promised.

When he did and only I saw, I rose, parked my sandwich, and cast across and downstream for him. He came and completely threw me with what I now know to be the characteristic roll of a male grayling, about ¾ pounds, all purple, gold, and lavender with beautiful red and blue spots on the huge dorsal fin. About him was the odour of wild thyme that gives him his proper name *Thymallus arcticus*. I held him just long enough to look, sniff, and let Carl get a picture, then I released this example of our wildest and most delicate gamefish. Bob was surprised at having a grayling taken from under his nose, but relieved that I had come through. Then he settled down to take a few himself and a couple of Dolly Vardens on his spinners. Carl suspects grayling move around a lot and eventually found a willing batch in a deep flat-water hole. He returned glassy-eyed and late.

I caught only one other fish, our only rainbow, on a nymph beside a logjam. He was hard and slippery as a bar of soap, a native of the Athabasca watershed, much darker than the rainbows that have been introduced in all other Alberta watersheds.

That one grayling had me walking on air, albeit huffing and puffing, all the way back to the car. I wouldn't trade him yet for my own glory hole of grayling. After all, even the men who sought merely the holy grail would have been satisfied with only one.

Alberta's No. 1 Gamefish

If I had to choose, the man asked, what species would I select as Alberta's top gamefish?

Considerable of my time lately has been spent in the company of brown and brook trout and, if the crick doesn't rise much more, I will be devoting myself to southern Alberta's finest rainbows and cutthroats in July and August. My questioner, I am sure, expected me to name some form of trout or char, but I wouldn't think of it.

No, my choice as Alberta's finest gamefish is a species I like to call the people's fish, old *Hiodon alosoides* himself, the goldeye. My choice, I think, may be defended on many grounds.

Brook trout and brown trout are not native to Alberta, rainbows are native only to the Athabasca watershed, and I feel that our finest gamefish should be a native and available to many Albertans. The goldeye qualifies on this latter score, being found in the lower silty sections of rivers and streams in the following major river systems: Peace, Athabasca, North and South Saskatchewan, and Red Deer rivers.

Two factors endear the goldeye to his fans. First, he is a gregarious fish, a school fish. Find one and you find a million. Secondly, the goldeye keeps the faith: year after year, for centuries, his hordes have ascended the favored rivers about wild rose time. The roses are late this year, but I saw my first last Saturday and on Sunday encountered my first gibbering goldeye fanatics telling me the Red Deer is bankful of their favorite fish. Indeed, I parked for a time Sunday on a cliff high over one of my favorite Red Deer goldeye holes and watched the finny quicksilvers by the thousands heliographing their presence as they twisted and turned in the cloudy current.

The goldeye is a gentleman or a bum, depending on how the angler wants to take him. Put a gob of worms 12 inches below a float and he'll winkle the whole rig under with a lightning flash. Hardware? The goldeye will gourmandize your reds and whites and plugs and spinners like any old pike any day. But the goldeye will often turn gourmet and rise to the dry fly with a faithful finesse displayed by no other Alberta fish. The dry fly fishing provided by goldeye should be better known than it is, especially as it would make superb fly fishing available to thousands of Albertans in parts of Alberta where there is really little opportunity to fly fish.

One of my fonder memories is of a few years ago, wading through blooming wild roses to the channel of a muddy little irrigation drain near the site of the old Scandia Ferry on the Bow River to find the whole joint jumping with goldeye. I stood in one place for four hours in the Red Deer River and caught and released over 80 goldeye. There is no mystery. Just find a hole full of rising goldeye, wade out amongst them, and somehow chuck any old kind of fly at them, so long as it imitates a grasshopper. Don't worry about style; the goldeye has enough for both of you.

Goldeye are mysterious creatures, particularly regarding their travels. The prevalent folklore is that they travel thousands of miles each year. For about four years now, the Alberta Fish and Wildlife Division has been operating a tagging program on Red Deer River goldeye. Despite the fact that the majority of the fish must be caught by angling, a great many of the fish have been tagged. This summer (1975) the Edmonton Trout Club will be catching the fish within Edmonton's city limits to start the project in the North Saskatchewan system. Alberta anglers catching tagged goldeye should contact their nearest Fish and Wildlife Division office about the catch.

The proximity of goldeye to Alberta cities is another credit to the goldeye image. In July and August, fanatics will catch many goldeye within the city limits of Edmonton, Red Deer, Lethbridge, and Medicine Hat.

Goldeye fanatics are as mysterious as their quarry, particularly about thier favorite holes. My father and I have failed, to this day, to find one we heard about 20 years ago on the Bow river near Bassano. The Guv and I also have one of our own favorites on the Red Deer that we have only been able to fish three times in 20 years because we lose it so often. The first thing we do when we manage to get there is crack a sodie pop to celebrate our arrival. Somehow, to draw a map would ruin the flavor of the whole operation. Besides, a map might fall into the wrong hands.

The people's fish is a fighter. He will brace that slab side against the current and rattle your bait bucket. Encumbered only by a dry fly, he will jump with style. The most savage battle with a fresh-water fish I ever witnessed was fought by a stranger near the mouth of the Blindman. He had been fishing with a black jig which I saw drop out of the jaw of the largest goldeye I have ever seen, just before I was about to assist with the net. The stranger and I hardly cried at all.

Fresh goldeye have the taste and consistency of flannel that has been dipped in Hoppe's #9 and run through a few dirty gun barrels. If you can't smoke them, you might as well release the goldeye you catch. The pressure smoking process that turns goldeye into one of the world's great delicacies can be imitated by anyone in one of the small portable smokers, such as the Abu, being sold in many Alberta sport stores.

The bloom is on the bush and quicksilver runs in the rivers out there in wild rose country. Enjoy. Enjoy.

5. Booby Hatches and Bug Houses

Chasing Hatches

There are more, truly fine angler's insect hatches in Alberta than even our finest anglers realize, and perhaps it is all for the best. Anglers who fish Alberta's hatches will tell you that the old cliche "matching the hatch" is no problem; in these latitudes it is "catching the hatch" that will drive a man to rye without branch water.

The fact is that few mayfly hatches in Alberta are significant from an angler's viewpoint. No, in Alberta it is the caddis fly and particularly the stonefly that can, on occasion, cause even the largest brown trout in a stream to toss caution to the wind and feed in plain sight in broad daylight, tossing water hither and yon.

An angler who stumbles upon such an event acts much in the same uninhibited manner and is forever hooked on trying to be present for the same hatch on the same stream the next year.

Therein is the way to insanity, particularly if the hatch is stoneflies. The problem with stoneflies is that the best dry-fly fishing is not when they are hatching, when the adult insect emerges from the nymphal shuck, but when the adult females return to the water to lay their eggs. This process has astonished anyone I have been able to show it to. The female dips her nether regions into the water and flies upstream, allowing the surface tension of the water to pull the eggs from her body. Her wings beat a froth on the water and, if there are trout in the stream, it is a fortunate female stonefly indeed who makes 10 feet before disappearing to the strains of a satisfied slurp.

Catching the female stoneflies on their bombing run is the trick to drive men and fish mad. There seems to be a standard time each year when the nymphs climb up on the rocks, their nymphal cases split, and the adult insect emerges and flies away to the trees, but there is no sense at all to when the mature females return to the water. I have seen adult stoneflies hang like grapes on streamside bushes for days while slavering trout stared themselves crosseyed in the water below.

Five years ago I stumbled onto a hatch of huge stoneflies. That day I took five brown trout, 19 to 22 inches and had the foresight to capture a few of the insects and have them keyed out by an aquatic entomologist. These creatures were 2½ inches long with a wingspread between 3 and 4 inches. Their bodies were beautifully marked with salmon pink. Sure enough, they turned out to be *Pteronarcys californica*, the same insect that gets such press as the famous salmon fly of Montana. An Alberta stream with a salmon fly hatch? I didn't believe it, but next year I caught it right on the button again, and five fish ranging from 18 to 23 inches fell to me and a friend.

That year as well I confirmed an excellent June salmon fly hatch on the Oldman River downstream from the Gap and got highly suspicious that there is a superb hatch of the same insect on the Bow. The next two years I haunted my home stream and managed to miss the hatch both years. A man does have a job and human obligations, after all. The first year I missed, I decided I would go home for a shower and a change of clothes. That night about 11 p.m., my fishing buddy Mike showed up, grinning like a donkey eating thistles, with a beautiful female brown of about five pounds. Those contrary stoneflies got at it while I was away.

Last year I missed it and knew it. I just had too much work to do and hated every minute of it. When I finally got to the stream again, it was at an unaccustomed time, and I found the fish lapping up a new stonefly. One brown trout of 24 inches and six pounds on the nose lapped up my imitation. When the scientists reported, I found I had a

58

new stonefly hatch to haunt me, this one, *Acroneuria pacifica*, or the willow fly of Wyoming and Colorado fame.

This year I was determined to catch that salmon fly hatch and arranged my work schedule so I could go at a moment's notice during the critical two-week period. But this was an unsprung spring. Everything came three weeks late, including all that undone work. I just had to put in a couple of days in Calgary, and when I got back and saw Mike, he said, "You blew it again. Tuesday was the day." He and a friend had found the hatch on an entirely new stream and had cleaned up on big fish.

Last Saturday I got out to my favorite stream. The empty nymph shucks on rocks and streamside vegetation with no adults whatever in the bushes showed that the bugs had hatched, and just the odd adult on the wing showed I was at least three days late. Sadly, I bent on a #8 Bird's stonefly nymph and started the eternal labour of yarding out one of those infernal weighted monstrosities in a high wind. I resolved to get off the hatch-catching circuit, it being no way for a mature adult to conduct himself.

Umpty-ump casts later, something over near the rock wall on the other side took the nymph going away, and I had the first good workout of the year, ending up 30 minutes later and 200 yards downstream with a 21-inch brown. It took about 20 minutes to revive myself and that fish so I could release him, and in the process of doing so I discovered I am hooked again.

Now those *Acroneuria pacificas* ought to be hatching in about 10 days, and if I just move this job forward and postpone that other one...

Fly-Tying Diatribe

Judging from the number of inquiries I have had on fly-tying since the snow blew, there have to be as many nuts per square inch in central Alberta as on any other patch of God's ground. In fairness, I must number myself among the nuts, as my fingers are cramped and I am bleary of eye after a marathon two-day orgy in which I tied eight dozen of one variety of fly, the only novelty being that I tied them in four different sizes.

Now there are many blessed nuts who tie flies as a hobby

sufficient unto itself, glorying in the perfection of their art and product, as well as experimenting constantly with new patterns and materials. Sadly, I am not among the ranks of the truly devoted, and you cannot understand the extent of my dementia until I tell you that I, a man who would tie eight dozen of one pattern, am also a man who despises fly tying with a true passion.

Why do I do it? I wondered, as I whip-finished the head of the 96th of that infernal eight dozen. Economics might be the answer. The fly I use about eight dozen of per year in four sizes, #8, #10, #12, and #14, is the Le Tort hopper, a fly that is ideal for waters in these parts, as it admirably imitates grasshoppers, stoneflies, and caddis flies, all insects that will be found on our local waters more frequently than the dainty mayfly imitations favored by most local anglers, but not by trout. So all I was doing was subjecting myself to the misery of tying the eight dozen Le Tort hoppers I expect to cast upon the waters from about April 1st to October 30th of the current fishcal year.

The only place I can buy Le Tort hoppers tied better than I can do it (which is really terrible) is from Orvis in Manchester, Vermont, U.S.A., at 85 cents each or $10.20 per dozen. Thus, eight dozen would set me back $81.60, and the approximately 30 per cent customs duty would add about $24.40, for a total of $106.00 for my year's supply of one pattern of fly. I doubt if all my fly-tying tools, materials collected over the years, eyedrops, and shattered nerves can come to a total like that.

But even such a saving is not enough to make me like the process of tying the things. Tying flies is a bit like butchering hogs: it may save you money, but you do not have to like it. No, I am even tighter than that. The only other thing that keeps me at the repeated tedium of tying is the fact that no matter you are a mediocre tier, you can often produce better flies of a given pattern simply because you seek out and employ the very finest materials. It is only the very finest and most expensive flies, from a very few of the finest suppliers, that will use better materials than can be purchased for a song by a home tier.

You do not tie for very long before you know such things as that Orvis puts out a superb 2X long, 3X fine wire hook that cannot be purchased anywhere else, that Dan Bailey has cream Angora spun yarn just the right shade for Le Tort hoppers, that a new outfit in Michigan has polypropylene, a new body material even better than flesh, and so on.

The much-touted thrill of catching fish on a fly you tied yourself is a once in a lifetime thing. Soon you realize you can also catch a fish on a fly tied by a machine in Japan that retails for 5 or 10 cents, but that is about all you will catch with it before the brittle hook breaks, the dyes in the material run, or the whole thing unwinds like a home permanent in a steam bath. No matter how it looks, the materials used and the durability possible to build into your own flies are valid reasons for the misery of tying them.

Some things defy explanation, such as my angling companion Mike Burrington, who caught his first fish on his own tie last summer. The fish, as I recall it, was a 21-inch brown. Prior to that, Mike was a superb fly finangler; that is, he was expert at getting me, for example, to supply him with the fly that was currently catching the fish. Generally all Mike had to do was let a little tear course down his cheek—much simpler than tying the 100-odd he told me he was at about a week ago.

A man soon learns the angles. On one of those days I was tying the eight dozen Le Torts, nine-year-old Iain Johnston came for lessons, set up his vise beside me, and was soon tying adequate hoppers. There's no flies on Iain, and he realizes his dear old dad is one of the truly great fly finanglers in the business, his method being to roar and threaten. To avoid a life of servitude tying flies for father, Iain sat Mac Johnston down last weekend and showed him how to tie a hopper.

"Iain told me the first one was probably good enough to catch a fish," Mac proudly told me on Monday morning. Which is truly the most that can be said for the whole process.

III Wind and Mayflies

Occasionally you will encounter an Alberta fly fisherman who can count on the fingers of one hand the times in his career that he has encountered a genuine "fishing hatch" in Alberta. His eyes will take on a glazed, almost crazed, expression, and his voice will shake as he recounts the glorious fishing produced by each rare hatch.

Hereafter the tone of this column is crazed and shakey, since last Sunday I encountered the finest hatch of mayflies I have ever seen anywhere, on a small stream in the vicinity of the town of Pincher Creek in southwestern Alberta, a stream I have fished an average of 10 days a year for the past dozen years. This year is unusual in that the creek has been running clear all spring, owing to a local drought, and was low and clear for the July 1st weekend when, in other years, it has been bank-to-bank mud, fit only for a marathon bridge game held in warm quarters as far from its banks as possible.

Most days in this area this spring it clouds up and huffs and puffs and perhaps produces a couple of drops of water per quarter section, and that is what it did Saturday as I caught a limit of fryer rainbows and released about 30 others in ridiculously easy fashion, using only a #10 white Le Tort hopper. The next morning was also cloudy, but the wind was at barn-roller velocity, so that the suggestion that I take son John, 3, out of herself's hair for a while tempted me to the creek.

Me and my little shadow did a mean sneak on a deep little pocket in a rapid and floated the hopper downstream. There came such a wallop that John turned the proceedings over to me. Together we landed a 14-inch rainbow, above average for the stream and much larger than anything I had taken the day before. This I took as a good omen, deposited John and his fish in the safekeeping of mother, set up my anti-wind outfit, and went off down the creek.

Long ago I learned that if you do not fish in southern Alberta when it is windy, you do not fish in southern Alberta at all, and I obtained an 8½-foot Berkeley para-metric glass rod that takes a #7 double taper or a #8 weight-forward line. With this outfit I have a chance of casting the fly upon southern Alberta waters into the teeth of all but the most offensive gale.

It became apparent that the fish were just not enthused about the hopper. They would look at it, come short to it, jump over it. Yet I began to see more rises than I have ever seen on the stream. And such rises! The fish were good fish, feeding with purpose on something they liked. As the trout porpoised, the wind flung the spray from their slippery backs. Everywhere I looked the air above the water was punctuated by these apostrophes of spray.

This is a plunging little freestone stream, and a man is hard-pressed to see anything on the surface, but eventually I came to the smooth, long flow of an ancient beaver dam. Sailing along its surface like an armada of sail boats were hundreds of just-hatched duns of a species of mayfly. Occasionally the gusts would rudely capsize a few and tumble them over the water.

It was a handsome insect, the body of light olive green with slate-blue wings. Now that I have had some time with the books, I would bet it is *Ephemerella flavilinea,* the western slate olive dun, one of the super hatches to anglers on the spring creeks of Idaho and Montana, but generally wasted on Alberta's freestone creeks that are high and muddy at the time of the best hatches.

But here I was, July 1st, up to my withers in a clear Alberta stream afloat with succulent mayflies and alive with rising trout, and the closest I could come with my fly boxes was the Light Cahill, tied in imitation of an entirely different species of mayfly.

It was close enough. I had been fishing over a rainbow that persisted three times in letting my hopper float by, turn, chase it, and then turn away. He took the Cahill head—on its first float. From then on it was fish after fish, and most of them were above-average size for the stream. A really heavy hatch of any insect the fish savour will generally put all the best fish on the prod.

Every year a family of beaver construct a dam, which goes out with the ice. This year's dam is high and narrow and causes a flow of about four feet deep along an undercut bank. Roots and brush wave gently just under the surface. The first cast fell about a foot short of the cutbank about 20 feet upstream of the dam. A form met it as it fell, and the fly disappeared in a wrinkle of water. There was no spectacular struggle as, for 10 minutes, the fish dogged it in midstream where I had pulled him before he could break the momentum of his rush at the Cahill. I stood with the rod bent as far as I dared. Finally the fish came, but spent another five minutes in 30-foot rushes until he swam himself ashore.

He was a rainbow of 18 inches and over two pounds, a monster for this tiny stream, and the largest of the hundreds I have taken in the stream over the years. It took drought, an ill wind, and an unforgettable hatch of mayflies to do him in.

Flies for Alberta

Fly fishermen are dogmatic, but never so much as when they are talking about the only fly to use. Three years ago in one of these columns, I held forth on a list of what I considered to be essential flies in this area.

I have stuck a lot of flies in my ears since that time, indicating my casting is no better now that it was then, but I think I should test the proof-rating of my own dogmatism on flies by playing a little trick on myself. Without looking at that earlier column, I am going to suggest what flies I now consider to be essential for this area, then I am going to look up that old column and either praise my faithfulness or explain away my lack of constancy.

The damp weekend has given me the opportunity to catch up on some work at the office and, incidentally, to tie nearly four dozen Le

Tort hoppers. I have not had time to tie flies this past winter and have been getting a little desperate over where I will get the eight dozen Le Tort hoppers I will need this season as I have for the past two. Ninety per cent of my trout are now taken on the Le Tort hopper, and it is the fly I would choose if I was restricted to only one dry fly pattern for the rest of my life. Its secrets are its great buoyancy, the way it floats low in the surface film, and its silhouette, which resembles three major items of trout food in these latitudes: first the grasshopper, then the stoneflies and caddis flies which also carry their wings horizontally over their bodies.

The hatches of mayflies are not great in this country, but occasionally the fish can be found sipping a few of them, at which time the trout can be maddeningly selective. To solve such occasions, I find myself more and more delving into the works of Theodore Gordon, Preston Jennings, and Art Flick. The result is that I would not be without a few of the traditional favorites in sizes 12 and 14: the Quill Gordon, the Light Cahill and, that most ancient of patterns, the brown hackle peacock.

In this area there is one fly that is occasionally the only fly to have, particularly when there is a hatch of caddis flies doing their peculiar running over the surface, and that is the Adams, a traditional old favorite that has saved my bacon on more than one occasion.

I always carry a tiny fly box that comes out on those occasions when trout are rising like mad, apparently at nothing. Chances are that such fish are slurping tiny midges, and the fly box contains eye-straining confections in various colours tied on tiny #18, #20, and even #22 hooks. The trick here is tying the things on the leader and then hooking and holding the fish that will lap them up. There is much very fast water around that calls for a fly that is a good floater and highly visible. I always carry a supply of grey and of brown bivisibles and some of the Wulff-style flies, the white and blond Wulffs particularly.

Then there are occasions when the stream is dead, and something must be done to drive the fish mad with desire and bring them up out of nowhere. Nothing is better for this than either a fan-wing or a hair-wing Royal Coachman, not the standard, unless it is one of the huge, fluffy, and dancing spiders or skaters on a short shank #14 hook with hackles the diameter of a half-dollar.

All the flies mentioned so far are dry flies, reflecting the fact that I prefer to catch trout on dries and that I know little about the deadly arts of fishing wet. Every year, however, I catch a few good trout on the various Black Beetles so popular in this area, on the Royal Coachman streamer, and on the Muddler minnow.

I have read that old column and Oh, McGinty, how I have forsaken

64

thee! That was my favorite then. The McGinty is still an excellent fly for brown trout in this area, but the Le Tort hopper is better. For the man who does not tie his own flies, however, the McGinty is better, as they are now readily available in the stores, while the Le Tort hoppers are not, a situation which soon may be remedied.

I have also forsaken Joe's Michigan hopper, my second favorite in that old column, but this is for practical reasons. The deer hair on the Le Tort makes it more buoyant than Joe's, and it also floats with its belly in the surface film like a hopper should, instead of fraudulently up on tippy-toes like Joe's. You also get more for your money with the Le Tort, as it is much more durable than Joe's, which can be a 70-cent basket case after only one encounter with a trout.

Other than the change of major choice and change of style of tie for my new major choice and my new liking for the traditional ties for mayfly hatches, the rest of this list is much like my old one. Of course, I included the black gnat on my old list and left it off this one, as I never use it. Strange, I know excellent fly fishermen in this area who never use anything but black gnats. We must be talking to a different class of fish.

Fishing the Hopper "Hatch"

If you are a farmer or any other well-balanced individual, the grasshopper is the scourge that annually plagues the land. If you are an angler, the grasshopper is a source of fish food that annually drives the trout to orgies of feeding in their constant search for protein.

Thanks to the efforts of Ernest Schwiebert, Charles K. Fox, and Vincent Marinaro, three stream wizards of the famous Le Tort in Pennsylvania, grasshopper season can be the best time of year for the fly fisherman. These three anglers noted that in late summer and early fall the trout kept rising but could not be tempted with the well-known imitations of the water-born spinners, duns, and nymphs. They observed that in late summer and early fall the hatches of the water insects fell off and the trout were feeding on land insects, terrestrials they called them, ants, beetles, grasshoppers, and so on, that had accidents and fell or were pushed into the water.

These men are also skilled fly tiers, and their discoveries resulted in a swarm of imitations of terrestrial insects and new methods of fishing them that together form the most exciting advance in fly fishing knowledge in many years.

Most important of the terrestrials for anglers in this area is the grasshopper. Ordinarily skilled fliers, on breezy days grasshoppers are blown into streams in great numbers and the trout wait to lap them up. Grasshopper imitations should float in the surface film, but definitely on the surface of the water, so that the fly imitation should be treated with silicone to make it float, and it should be palmer-tied with short, stiff hackles so it will float low.

Hopper imitations are simple things, generally tied on 2X or 3X long hooks, with a yellow wool body, a brown palmer-tied hackle, and mottled turkey wings tied horizontally and tent-like over the back. A good and simple variation is the yellow wool body again, with grey deer hair spun horizontally around the hook, laying along it for wings, and tied at the head so that it splays out, forming a short hackle effect. The leader should be 9 feet long, tapered to 3X to beguile the trout in the low, clear water generally associated with grasshopper season. Excellent commerical flies available locally are Joe's grasshopper and the Muddler.

The best hopper fishing is found on a breezy day along trout streams near grass flats or pastures. The angler should walk upstream, keep low, and watch for the small waves made by hopper-feeding trout at the edges of the stream near the grass or along cutbanks below grassy flats or hills. The rises should be cast to straight upstream or, preferably, quartering upstream. Deadly tricks are to cast the fly onto a grassy bank and twitch it off into the water or to crawl to the edge of a cutbank and dap the fly on the water.

Quiet, careful casting is not as necessary when using grasshopper imitations as it is with other flies. A fly splashed on the water will sometimes provoke a vicious strike, perhaps because it imitates the splat a natural grasshopper makes when he miscalculates.

The naturals kick and twitch in the water, and the occasional twitch of the imitation as it floats back will often bring sudden results. A dragging fly seems to be no problem when using grasshopper flies. I have seen even brown trout rush savagely at a dragging hopper imitation and miss two or three times before finally catching it.

The angler will be amazed at the variety of rise-forms he gets to a hopper imitation. If there is one form more common than another, it is the beautiful one where the trout fins back with the current, the hopper fly seeming to be balanced on his nose as he inspects it; then finally, when the angler can stand it no longer, the fish tilts slightly and sucks the fraud hopper in with an audible smack of his lips.

Build a Better Hopper

Build a better grasshopper and fishermen everywhere will beat it over to see you, and fish of many species will lock fins for the privilege of being first to gulp your creation.

In the past few years fishermen in this area, whether they throw it out there with a fly rod or with a spinning rod and bubble, have discovered that a fly pattern called Joe's Michigan hopper is cordially received by many species of our local fish: cutthroat, rainbow, and brook trout particularly, but also goldeye and Rocky Mountain whitefish. Even the Dolly Varden, hitherto thought to spurn the fly, especially the dry fly, will rise to the occasion of a Joe's hopper floating overhead.

The pattern, of course, imitates the common yellow-bellied grasshopper, the entree that is number one, particularly on the menu of trout in mid-July. That the grasshopper is a desirable mouthful of protein indeed, becomes obvious to anyone who has seen the vicious, slashing rises of trout to foundered and struggling natural grasshoppers or a carefully fished imitation. One of the problems with the Joe's hopper is that it is always very expensive, probably because it is extremely fiddley to tie. Also it seems to be quite fragile, so that a large number is required. Notwithstanding these problems, many local anglers have been sobbing greatly because Joe's hoppers have also become scarce.

An extra problem for me was that while the cutthroats and rainbows gobbled Joe's hoppers as fast as I could heave them out, the brown trout around here never got very enthusiastic. The trouble seems to be that while a natural grasshopper afloat is a sorry sight, struggling fitfully awash in the surface film, the Joe's hopper rides high and dry on all that bushy hackle, its body seldom touching the water. Brown trout seem suspicious enough to know the difference and, when bent on meat and potatoes floating awash, are not likely to be distracted by hors d'oeuvres in the form of some base canard floating on tippy-toes like a common mayfly.

Ernest G. Schwiebert, Jr., is an American architect who is expert angler enough and amateur entomologist enough to have written an excellent book called *Matching the Hatch*. He noticed the defects in the way common grasshopper imitations floated and proceeded to build a better grasshopper. His solution, gradually becoming famous, is called the Le Tort hopper, after the magnificent Pennsylvania limestone stream on which it was developed.

I read the recipe for tying this fly some three years ago, but such is my poverty of knowledge of fly tying, that I simply could not comprehend the tying method. The problem was solved on my recent trip to West Yellowstone when an excellent fly tier explained it in words even I could understand, and then gave me a sample to use as a pattern.

The materials are simple. The fly is generally tied on 2 or 3X long dry fly hooks in sizes 10, 12 and 14. A simple body of yellow or cream fuzzy wool is wound on, and a single section of lacquered turkey wing is tied tent-like over the top of the body. A hank of deer hair is then tied like a bucktail wing on the top, and short hanks of deer hair are spun and flared around the hook from the wing base to the eye of the hook. This flared hair is then trimmed to form a bulky head. That's it! No expensive materials, no complications, no hackles. The pattern is available from only a few commercial suppliers in the States, but any reasonably competent amateur tier could produce them a bushel an hour at a moderate cost.

In fact, I botched up a few sorry looking specimens recently and then took a trip to Stauffer Creek, where the brown trout are notable for their disdain of the creations of us mortals. I found that the fly hits the water with a satisfying, juicy splat, as a grasshopper imitation should, and then floats along on that hollow deer hair with body and hook submerged. The browns were pleased, too. I hooked and lost a nice one on the second cast and then lost three more in rapid succession. Then I discovered the trout seem to like to chomp this crisp number fairly thoroughly and that a delayed strike results in better hooking.

For the time being I am content with the Le Tort hopper, but such are the joys of fishing in the grasshopper season that I am always willing to listen to anyone who thinks he has built a better hopper.

The Waspe Flye

The first outdoor writer in English, Dame Juliana Berners, in her *Treatise of Fishing with an Angle*, written in 1450, describes a popular fly used in July by fly fishermen of her day: "The waspe flye, the body of blacke wull and lappid abowte wt yelow threde: the wings of the bosarde." I will not presume to translate this early recipe for brown trout medicine, except to say that the wings were made of the flight feathers of a buzzard.

A translation into more modern English, and an indication that the pattern stood the test of time, is provided by the words Charles Cotton used in his 1676 addition to Walton's *The Compleat Angler* to describe an excellent fly to use in July: "We have likewise this month a wasp-fly; made either of a dark brown dubbing or else the fur of a black cat's tail, ribbed about with yellow silk; and the wing of a gray feather of a mallard." In those long-ago words, Dame Juliana and Cotton both were describing the July food preferences of brown trout in England, the ancestors of those same immigrant brown trout that now infest various waters of central Alberta.

Two points: brown trout have not changed much in the 500-odd years that have passed since Dame Juliana wrote, and a fishing companion and I had a lot of gall about three years ago in thinking we had made a discovery in the fatal craving of local brown trout for the "waspe flye".

It had all the earmarks of a great discovery in that it was an accident. My companion and I were both steeped in the tradition that brown trout flies were, above all, sombre in hue. So it was as much to decorate the various national disgraces he calls fishing hats as for anything else, that he purchased from Les Rhodes at Caroline a couple of ridiculous, gaudy, bee-resembling flies.

The fish were rising on Alford Creek that day, but to the birds for all the success we were having. In desperation my companion plucked one of the monstrosities from his hat and promptly discovered that it and no other fly was meat and potatoes to the brown trout that day. Naturally, he did not tell me about his discovery until he had lost one of the flies and only had one left. Until he lost the second, I had the agonizing pleasure of watching him slay the browns. It probably did not occur to us to go back to Caroline for more of those flies because we were ashamed to ask for more so soon after the ribbing we gave Les Rhodes about the two monstrosities he sold us.

Since that day we have discovered that that fly outfishes all other flies we use in late June, July, August, and into September. I believe it is more than just a question of confidence—admittedly, an important factor in fly choice. Experiments prove to me at least that there are days when that old "waspe flye" is simply what our hippie generation brown trout are stalking.

Now it is nigh onto July again, and before various black cats sacrifice their tails and buzzards their flight feathers, let me hasten to assure anglers that fly patterns and methods of production change even if brown trout and fly fishermen do not. The modern version of the "waspe flye" is called a McGinty and, yes, I am trying to find out why. For those who roll their own, the body is alternate bands of black and yellow chenille, the tail is of grey mallard topped with scarlet hackle fibres; the hackle is brown and the wings are either white-tipped blue mallard sections or white-tipped turkey quill sections. Oh, it is a painted hussy, fit to knock your eye out, a fishermen-getter that gets fish as well. They can be purchased, of course, but not yet at enough stores in the area. Sizes 10, 12, and 14 work best.

On the past two weekends I have fished five different central Alberta streams with the McGinty exclusively and have caught brookies, browns, and rainbows. Last weekend, my McGinty-discovering companion took a two-pound rainbow on one.

Actually we may have made at least a rediscovery, for the modern angling world seems to have forgotten the "waspe flye" of late. Even Ray Bergman, in his monumental work, *Trout*, has these lukewarm words for the McGinty: "While this isn't generally a popular fly, it will often produce nicely in the summer months. I find only occasional need for it when fishing for Browns...It is a good Canadian ...pattern."

Barnacles to Bergman! Get a swarm of McGinty's, oil one up good so it floats well, sneak it up along a likely looking cutbank or overhanging bush, and stand ready to sting invaders.

The McGinty

A personal observation from a couple of trips before the deluge is that the browns out west have developed a fine taste for honey. At any rate, using a McGinty, a fly tied to imitate a bee or a wasp, I recently had the unusual experience of defrauding vast numbers of browns on two streams well distant from each other on trips two days apart. An angling friend found this fly to be very successful on another two streams on an earlier weekend.

Search as I might, I can find no mention in the learned books of the McGinty being fished as a dry fly, nor can I find any suggestion that the McGinty is a good fly for brown trout. Dealers in this area say the fly has never been popular, and many do not stock it. I mentioned the fly to a grizzled veteran of at least 30 fishing seasons in this area, and he jerked as if stung, then smiled slyly and admitted he had used the fly and found it to be good at this time of year.

An earlier column dealt with the fall-off in aquatic fly hatches that occurs in this country at this time of year and asserted that a large proportion of the trout diet in late season is made up of such terrestrial insects as grasshoppers, ants, beetles, spiders, and now bees and wasps. As many an angler has found to his pain who has poked too industriously around logjams in August, wasps and bees abound at this time of year. Many are blown and many more are washed by showers into the streams where they become succulent morsels though not the chocolate coated gourmet kind—for trout.

The McGinty should be well soaked with silicone, dried to make it float, and used in the smaller sizes with a long leader tapered to 4X. Browns often take this imitation of bee and wasp as though they expect to be stung. Roderick Haig-Brown, the fine B.C. angling writer, makes the same observation about steelhead taking a Wulff-style dry fly he ties to imitate a bee.

The browns often seem to snatch the McGinty down, back off, and run at it again, so that you sometimes miss if you strike too quickly at the first swirl. Often the first suggestion that there is a fish anywhere in the vicinity is one jumping crazily with the McGinty in his soon to be bee-stung lips. Three times on one of my recent good days, browns came to and were hooked on a McGinty I know had pricked them on the previous cast. It is unusual for a brown to come again immediately after feeling the hook in other flies; it almost seems as though they find nothing unusual in being stung by a fly that looks like a bee.

I, for one, can understand the snatching approach and sudden jumps of the fish. Two years ago, either by design or ill fortune, my wife constructed for me a ham sandwich, on a picnic, and it contained a wasp. I had I known before what I knew after that first bite, my leaping and roaring would have started much earlier than it did!

Despickable Doings

The first time I ran out of magpie tailfeathers and used eight strands instead of peacock herl for the back of the black beetle fly so popular in this area, the green, shimmering effect nearly blew me across the room. Since then my beetles have always been tied that way, and they have always been tied for other people.

Vern Caddy was struck by the effect of the herl back the first time I showed him one. "It's marvelous," he gasped. "It's despicable." So Despickable became the name of the fly, and I have tied hundreds over the past 10 years, but always for other people. My problem has been that I simply could not catch fish with the beast, for reasons that were only too obvious to me.

The fly is tied on a regular-length, wet fly-weight hook and is nothing more nor less than a bulky black chenille body and a black hackle palmer-wound from tail to head and clipped top and bottom. The strands of peacock herl, previously tied in at the bend, are then pulled over the top and tied down at the eye. Despickables are most effective when fished upstream and slightly awash in or just under the surface film of the water, so the fly is designed to sink just slightly.

The standard procedure of real beetle hotshots is instructive, the group being almost equally divided into the school that anoints the creature with saliva and the one that dollops it with mud before sending it out among the trout. Whatever, the object is to get it down, just under the surface where the fish can really get a look at it and where I cannot see hair nor herl of it, peer though I might.

The best fishing with the Despickable is by casting to a peculiar, quiet, circular rise form on such waters as the Raven and Stauffer Creek, where there is no apparent break in the surface and where there certainly is no residual bubble left by a fish expelling the air he gulps when inhaling a dry fly off the surface.

At countless such rises have I hurled the Despickable, with no apparent result. At how many such rises have the likes of Vern Caddy flung my Despickable with the immediate result of a good trout? One afternoon I even stood behind Vern as he caught fish after fish; another day I spied on Cec Grove as he caught fish on his version of the beetle, but always, like Schultz, I saw nothing. Nothing.

In angling you can catch what you can't see, but only if you have some way of knowing it is there. With more heavily weighted nymphs that run deep I soon got onto the idea of using a floating fly line and watching where line joins leader for the twitch or pause.

As I recall, the only fish I had ever previously caught on the Despickable had been so butter-mouthed as to cause the line to twitch. All others came and kissed the bug just under the surface and ran away just as I became aware they were there. Then, a couple of weeks ago, I was having one of those days on Stauffer Creek. Not many fish were rising, but here and there would be that sudden capital "O" on the quiet surface, repeated over and over. The trout would take nothing I could cast them, and I would not cast them what I knew they wanted. Still, I was determined to prove to the cantankerous but gentlemanly anti-electro fishing faction that at least I could catch fish in Stauffer Creek.

Finally, the herl backs of my last six Despickables winked at me so despicably that I chose one and a new leader. So unsure am I of this method of fishing that I did not smooth the coils out of the new leader with a piece of rubber as carefully as I usually do. What is more, late May's mosquitoes were boring in, so I applied some dope and then handled the leader with those smelly, greasy hands.

Came one of those quiet rises over a shallow gravel flat, and I false cast once and cast just upstream of the fading rings. Eureka! Those ungainly floating coils sprang forward as something mouthed the fly, and I struck a nice brook trout wearing a tag of the previous summer's elecro-fishing. Five times more did the same thing happen on four other brookies and a decent brown. Not once, so far as I know, did I miss a strike.

Fishing a kinky floating leader may be bad form, and fishing the beetle this way may not be cricket—in fact the whole process is, well, despicable—but at least I now can say I have had one period of success with a fly I tie for others by the dozens. The next week I went back to do it again, but the beguiling trout of Stauffer Creek were not slumming. No sir. They were sitcking their snoots right into the air and churning up the runs as they picked off one after another of a species of mayfly dun that was hatching in great abundance.

What they wanted was a Light Cahill, dry, blond, floating on tippy toes at the end of a leader straight as a parson's alibi, and I served them up in abundance, grateful that I did not have to see whether I could produce again just the right combination of curly, doped leader.

Invisible Hatches

The law of contrariness must have been drafted by brown trout. This is the law that explains such things as why a slice of bread always lands butter-side down and asserts that if anything bad can happen, it will, and so on. Brown trout sometimes will not eat anything they can see and often will slurp with gay abandon that which is invisible.

Saturday I went to a big river that has been an obsession with me ever since I first saw its voluminous pools, massive boulders, and endless runs along cutbanks. The hangup is that I do not catch fish there—well, four in the last six years—and when I do they are always over two pounds. In addition I have seen browns caught by other people out of that very same water, most in the three to five pound category.

I was first astonished Saturday by the number of what looked like hummingbirds buzzing the stream. Hummingbirds, however, do not flutter across the surface, dipping their posteriors into the water to lay their eggs, and when I caught one of the creatures so engaged it proved to be a stonefly at least an inch and a half long with a bright salmon-colored underbody. Such a creature, I thought, does not exist up here, but in Montana and Wyoming, where it is known as the salmon fly or the willow fly, it exists in abundance and turns usually cautious brown trout into blithering gluttons.

In an old fly box I even had a supply of a devilish Montana fly pattern called the Sofa-Pillow, a magnificent imitation of the salmon fly. All day I let fly with it and other patterns and not once did I see a fish rise to gulp one of those hundreds of huge sources of protein and polyunsaturated fats that were skittering everywhere over the water.

Once a fish rose to my imitation that day. At the time I had my hand down inside my waders to fish out a quid of Beechnut from the package in my hip pocket. The rise startled me so much I nearly got a pound of flesh instead.

I did, for a fact, get gloriously skunked on Saturday. Sunday I went to redeem myself at the South Raven, shrine of local fly fishermen. The sun was glaring and the water had that crystal quality that makes it difficult to decide where water leaves off and air begins. But the fish knew, and everywhere were punctuating the surface with the commas of their rises. Trouble was, I decided, they were doing it for practice, because there was nothing whatever visible that they could be eating.

So I tried every fly I had in sizes 14 and 16. Nothing. Then I decided the sun was throwing a ropelike shadow of my 3X leader on the stream bottom. So I tied up a 12-foot leader tapered down to 5X. This brought on the balancing act. Trout would drift back almost to my feet, tilting themselves vertical in the water, with the fly balanced on their nebs, looking crosseyed at the fraud. Then they would come to with a start and squirt off into the sunset.

This performance generally means the fly is too big, but still I did not get the message. Finally a couple of little fish struck at the knots in my leader. Then I got the message, went to seek out a shady spot, dipped the tip of my nose in the water, and saw them. Humming just over the surface everywhere were billions of what American anglers call midges. The fish were doing what British anglers call smutting.

Last winter I purchased a number of size 18, 20, and 22 hooks after reading an article about tying tiny midge imitations. I managed to tie one on a size 22 hook before I had to apply for a blind pension; a simple thing, a peacock herl body and a whisp of a tiny black hackle. A size 22 hook is so small you would have to melt down about five to get enough steel for a size 16. I decided no self-respecting trout would even see, let alone consider, such a tiny fly.

Sunday I had with me the only one I tied, and it took almost as much time as in the tying to poke the leader through the eye. From the time I tied the midge on until I quit for the day, I got some kind of action from every rise I cast to. There was no hesitation from any fish, particularly the large Rocky Mountain whitefish, but even the browns took the tiny imitation with such confidence that they were invariably hooked inside the mouth rather than in the lip.

So the law of contrariness governing the brown trout last weekend was: Eat what you cannot see. What they will do next weekend is anybody's guess, as the umpteenth subsection in the brown trout's law of contrariness is: Be contrary even in how you are contrary. By the end of every season brown trout have driven me happily nuts. A measure of how good this season is that it is only May and I am there already.

Stoned on Stoneflies

No fisherman knows what being high is until he has slipped into a river full of brown trout, every mother's spawn of which is stoned on stoneflies. In these latitudes it is a fortunate angler who runs into a real "hatch" of stoneflies once or twice in his lifetime. Not that we do not have stoneflies, but generally they are not abundant, and the large varieties are not common in our streams.

My hatch came recently when I least expected. I was bone-weary, wind-broke, and bug-bit from 12 hours hard slogging the day before on a tangled stretch of the Raven. What is worse, it was raining to a chorus of thunder and lightning, and my waders were inside out in my garage, forgotten and purging themselves of the condensate of my toil the previous day.

So I put on a rain jacket to keep the top half dry and strung up a spinning rod so I would not have to get the nether regions wet, at least not by wading. I was half-heartedly flicking a spinner over the first pool when I noticed a remarkable number of large stoneflies lumbering ever upstream in their peculiar clumsy flight, dipping their posteriors in the water from time to time to lay their eggs. One did this not seven feet upstream from me, and I was poised to catch her for an examination. She did not keep the appointment. There was a whoosh, and a gout of spray hit me as a big, protein-crazed brown trout dropped another stonefly.

Big fish and fishermen throw caution to the winds when the stonefly is "hatching". My left leg wanted to take me to some rocks for a close look at the insects, but my right leg won and nearly tore the gusset out of my drawers in taking me back to the car for a fly rod.

Back at the stream I examined the rocks, and two varieties of stonefly were emerging. So help me, some were the genuine salmon flies of Montana, over two inches long, with the pink body, but more abundant was a stonefly of a little over half this size with a yellow body. My Sofa-Pillows, tied to imitate the salmon fly, were doing me just as much good as my waders back home, so I fumbled on a #8 Le Tort hopper, a fair imitation of the smaller fly, and promptly forgot about dry drawers as I jumped in with those hopped-up browns.

In cool, wet weather, browns love to snuggle up to the bank and scoff the stoneflies as they fall off the bushes. The first fish, a 17-inch brown, took with a gush in a little pocket at the side, and it took me 15 minutes and 75 yards downstream before he gave in. Then there was a quiet, sneaky rise in the tail of a pocket alongside a log at the other side. Two sloppy casts resulted in a missed rise, then I lucked a good one up alongside the log just to prove I could do it. At the downstream end of the log there was a dainty sip, and I almost shook off what I thought was a tiddler. If I knew then what I know now, I would have shook and shook.

Whatever it was, it went under the log. I reefed on that four-pound leader and loudly praised my own stupidity as the fish cruised out from its lair, obediently as a poodle on a leash, directly to the other side, jumped once, then tore off downstream. Unaccountably, I heard a ruffed grouse drum and looked at my watch. Then I snugged my hat down and started to wade downstream after the fish, which was just pulling the last of the fly line and the first of the backing out the top guide of the rod.

Twice I came within 20 feet of getting below the fish, and twice he jumped, then bolted the 30-yard length of the fly line downstream. Finally I got a little below him, and he lounged behind a rock. Five minutes I pulled to the side, and five minutes he gave not at all, not even the slightest indication that he was as tired as I was. Then he started to let his head come around and would have to fight the current to get it straight.

Exactly half an hour after hooking and about 300 yards downstream, a 19-inch three-pound brown trout slid over the rim of the net, a fish as gold as the autumn that spawned him. I was soaked, even under the rain jacket, but I did find a couple of dry cigarettes and smoked them before my hand stopped shaking enough to tie on a fresh fly. Then there was time enough to take three more browns in little pockets at the side, two 16's and a 15½, before the "hatch" stopped as mysteriously as it appeared.

Five browns totalling just a shade under 10 pounds can keep me high enough to wait and watch the one, two, maybe even three years necessary for the stonefly eggs that were deposited that day to go through many nymphal stages until the new adults emerge, and until bigger brown trout and a slightly older fly fisherman can indulge again in a spell of madness.

The Salmon Hopper

If you tie flies, three years is a long wait to try out your latest invention, so I was fumble-fingered a week ago as I tied on my salmon hopper. It had been devised after the last time I managed to be present for a *Pteronarcys californica* hatch on an Alberta stream. The creature of the strange sounding name is actually a giant stonefly famed in such places as Montana under the name of the salmon fly. The creatures are generally 1½ to 2 inches long with wings in repose and have a wingspan of 3 to 4 inches while in ungainly flight. The fly gets it name from the salmon-pink markings and underbody color.

Few Alberta anglers realize this important hatch takes place on many Alberta streams and drives men and fish every bit as mad here as it will do when it takes place in July on Montana's famed Madison River. Then the great and near great anglers from all over the world will be on hand to fish over the largest fish in the Madison, every one of which will be out, exposed, in broad daylight, acting like a dummy, stoned on stoneflies for this brief, glorious period each year.

Stoned on stoneflies is what I have been ever since I blundered onto my first Alberta salmon fly hatch in 1970. Miraculously, I calculated everything right and caught the hatch again in 1971. That was the year I decided the Sofa-Pillow and Bird's stonefly patterns used to imitate the hatch in Montana were too hard for the angler to see on Alberta waters, their brown squirrel-tail wing too closely matching the brown stain of so much of Alberta's prime trout water. So I tied up a batch of the easy-to-see deer-hair Le Tort hoppers in sizes 4, 6, and 8, using salmon pink polypropylene or phentex yarn, frayed out to form a rough and very buoyant body.

Not one did I cast upon the waters in 1972, 1973, and 1974 as I went through the stream-watcher's ultimate hell of missing the hatch. Last year I missed, for example, because high water seems to have delayed things to a day when I had to be in court. The year before that everything was so mysterious that I am still not sure the creatures even hatched at all. So it goes, and it drives an addict crazy.

I described my stonefly spotting to a hunter friend formerly of the Hanna area, and he said the whole process sounded exactly like goose hunting. "That's why I had to leave," he said. "Either that or starve." Precisely.

Long ago I decided I'd starve first, but it was not hunger that caused me to tremble when I saw the tell-tale nymphal shucks on the rocks of my favorite stonefly stream a week ago. I was too late that day, but a 12-incher who took a Quill Gordon after flirting with four other patterns was stuffed with 37 of the huge flies. Then the tapered line, longer and stronger than the grapevine, gave up the word that a friend had taken nine fish during the hatch that afternoon, releasing all but the smallest and the largest, a 12- and a 21-inch brown trout. I decided to stay overnight.

Next morning I prospected a good pool with a Sofa-Pillow, then with a Bird's stonefly. Nothing. But I knew the pool had more than one good fish in it, so I tied on the salmon hopper. Seldom do our bright fishing ideas work out at all, but a 16-inch brown saluted my first cast. That one I sacrificed for science. He had been feeding all night on salmon flies.

The thick of the hatch moves upstream about a mile a day, and about 2 p.m. I found it. The next two hours were an addict's dream of angling utopia. I released browns of 23 and 21 inches, a brookie of 18, kept a batch of friers, and was absolutely wiped out by a half a dozen fish bigger than my two largest.

Pteronarcys californica hatches on a number of Alberta streams between the end of May and the mountain-melt high water period. I have seen them in the main Castle, the Oldman downstream from The Gap, and in Fallen Timber Creek. I suspect they will be found in stretches of the Bow, in Cataract Creek, in the Little Red Deer, and in the Waterton River. Any good run of pure water with lots of huge boulders should be watched.

Even if you miss the hatch, as can so often happen in this land where even the anglers have not developed their lore yet, the first part of June is a rewarding time to be out in Alberta. Everything is green and bursting. New green on the aspen could break your heart, and often the drum of ruffed grouse harmonizes with a heart set beating by big fish. From time to time last week I paused to pick morels, the finest of the wild mushrooms of the aspen parkland. At one point I looked downstream to see bears going by, a black bear swimming my river with three cubs. I wanted to go and play with them, but I was not that far gone. Not quite.

No other time of year would I trade for it. The opportunity for fishermen to get stoned on stoneflies is just an additional fringe benefit.

6. Flora, Fauna, and Fungi

The Beaver

Something strange has been happening at Billy Beaver's pond down at Smiling Brook. Every spring some early wormers return from the west country highly irate, cursing the mysterious dam-blasting "they" who have been destroying beaver dams again.

Beaver trappers have been getting the blame, but I have news for all concerned. Recently, a nervous Alberta fisheries biologist reluctantly admitted to me, after making sure there were no sweet old ladies within earshot, that the government Fish and Wildlife boys often remove beaver dams. A good thing too, the angler in me says, although as a loyal British subject I still love old *Castor canadensis canadensis* and feel the urge to salute the popular concept of him as "nature's engineer".

I think the beaver can ruin a stream as effectively as any dam-designing engineer, and I have returned from my last trip to my favorite stream cursing the amphibious rodents who have, since September, constructed a dam that has flooded three of the troutiest runs in the stream. We anglers are the greatest beaverites of all, but some of us might agree, if we think about our own observations of beaver dams, that the periodic destruction of dams is beneficial to the streams and to the fish.

Beavers, like human engineers, think one dam calls for another, and they do not remove an old one after they are finished with it. The first dam goes in and the bottom of the pond is littered with sticks and dead brush, and silt immediately begins to cover the spawning gravel. Year by year, there are more and larger items of brush and debris, and the silt builds up foot by foot. The water, slowed by the dam, made shallow by the silt, and now unshaded by the brush and trees the beaver have felled, gradually becomes warmer and warmer, and slimy green ropes of algae form. Somewhat before this, the beaver have run out of brush to gnaw for food and move upstream to build another dam, gnaw more brush, and have babies. The abandoned dam becomes a silted, near-stagnant pool, its denuded banks an eyesore.

Soon there is a series of dams and, in the ponds between, the trapped trout cannot spawn on the silted gravel. As no new trout can get over the dams from the river below or down from spawning beds further up, trout numbers in the ponds are restricted to those originally trapped. The rest of the stream is, of course, robbed of the progeny the trapped stock might have produced but for the silt. Trout in the ponds sometimes grow to a good size, but the angler who has found a series of ponds better get at it, as there are only so many trout in each pond, and they will die when the water inevitably becomes too warm for them. At best, beaver ponds provide good fishing for a couple of years, the value of which is questionable because of the harm caused to the rest of the stream by the discharge of warm water from the dams into the lower stream and through the destruction of spawning beds by the dams.

In fairness to the beaver, the biologists say he is a great water conservationist on the headwater streams and provides the opportunity for the stocking of trout, thereby making angling possible on streams that have previously known neither fish nor fishing. But on the lower, larger, "good" trout streams, the ones most of us fish and the ones wherein the trout are able to reproduce naturally, to allow a beaver dam to exist too long or to allow a great series of old and new dams to remain, according to modern biologists, is to invite the ruination of the fishing.

Some big brookies were taken from the Stoney a few years back. Fishing fell off. Somehow the dams went, and last season anglers told me there were small brookies in the stream by the thousands. Fish and Wildlife officials say the cycle is coming again: beaver are back at work and some large fish should be coming out soon. Eventually, however, the dams will have to go again.

A huge beaver dam behind which fish were becoming scarce went out on the Raven last year. A cistern inspector would gag at the vista of mud and dead brush left when the water lowered and began to gurgle gaily along its ancient channel, clearing from it the silt of antiquity. But grass and brush will grow again, and last season I personally saw a dozen fine browns taken on a fly from the channel.

We should live and let live with the beaver, but when he goes too far or when he moves on, steps should be taken to get the water moving again. Cool moving water lets the trout live and lets anglers live a little, too.

Martins and the Coys

Whether or not it was the anti-hunters who got to me or merely the fact that I thought it might be interesting for my son, is irrelevant. The fact is that one mid-May evening I found myself raising a 12-suite martin house on a custom-built, folding steel pole.

My innocent thought as I drove the last bolt home was that Red Deer's humans should only have the housing surplus to which I was contributing. I was ready for the heartbreak familiar to the owners of new martin real estate. Latest statistics indicate there are now 30,000 rooms available for Red Deer's 5,000 martin couples. Seems to me we need a zoning by-law restricting martin houses to single family dwellings, in the interest of more equitably distributing the tenants among the available landlords—that is, if anyone is interested in an encore to the cat-belling by-law.

Next there was the balmy Sunday afternoon I was out mulching my onions when I heard that familiar "peent, peent" becoming ever louder. I looked up in time to see a black dot become a male martin swooping down that celestial roller-coaster right at the blazing orange roof of my bird house. He circled twice, uttered a couple of avian razzberries, and never set foot on the premises. I collapsed in my onion patch, a pitiful bundle of rejection.

But we had been noticed. A bull sparrow moved in and commenced building nests in every room to provide for the fruit of the drumsticks of his not inconsiderable harem. Then some martins noticed the sparrows and every morning would buzz the joint, routing the bull sparrow and every chippie in that lofty brothel. The martins would even enter the rooms and toss straw and feathers to the four winds like an industrious vice squad, while the sparrows sat on the garage roof and mourned monotonously as only they can do. I thought this was a little raw for a child, and sent him in to view "The Untouchables".

The plot thickened when some tree swallows began hovering around the martin house, uttering their polite queries about the size of the entrance holes and, eventually, their obvious objections to the communal living. Back to the workbench I went and soon nailed a spanking new tree swallow house to the eaves of the garage. At 3 p.m. next day the hot line rings. Herself: "You had better not come home without another swallow house. Six of them like this one so well there is blood, feathers, terrified children, and a cowering bird dog in your back yard." So I whomp up a gawdy little confection, which I may have to get patented, from a coffee tin, and peace reigns, for a little while.

Three big black brigands of cock martins take to visiting the martin house in the mornings with their ladies. All of them absolutely vanish in the afternoons. Where do they go? To while away the afternoons of their days in some great beer parlour in the sky? "What good are male martins?" Herself muses one noon.

Five minutes later my martin house is swaying violently as two of the shameless creatures make love on the roof in a high east wind. "That is what male martins are good for," I point out, and Herself claps her hands over the eyes of our two-year-old and glares.

Now I know the truth. My house is not home to these critters; it is merely a *pied a terre* in the air, so to speak, for the casual affairs of these vagabonds. But I got all mushy when I discovered a nest abuilding in the first swallow house, until some serious observation the next morning revealed it was that bull sparrow that was building it for the newest addition to his harem.

"I'll kill him," I ranted, sighting down the barrel of the new, single-shot 12-gauge that Winchester had just shipped to me for testing. "Another will take his place," her that lives with me said, primly. This is the first time my non-hunting bride has admitted even to the existence of the theory of game management on which I, from time to time, justify the potting of the odd grouse or pheasant.

I was ashamed of myself. Never before, engaged in any pursuit, have I permitted myself to display or even feel hatred toward a wild creature, not even starlings, buzzards, or mealy bugs. But now I have fallen among birdwatchers and find I cannot stomach gentle nature at its gentlest, which is to say, at its rawest.

Too bad I have to wait at least three months until a hunting season opens and I can pacify my mind by becoming a part of nature again, instead of a mere observer.

Gophers

Gophers take a man back. Especially if the man is a small-town prairie boy at heart. By early April the local Pee Wee or Bantam hockey team had always been taken out of the provincial playoffs by Pothole or some other worthy community and, anyways, the local outdoor rink was too slushy even for 30-man shinny. The air was still too cold to throw a ball around—mustn't risk bonechips—and natural disgust still won any fight with the seasonal attraction toward girls.

Any little prairie town worth its name has, just on its outskirts a whole world of prairie and gophers. After school about the middle of March, during this in-between season, armies of urchins would form and march on the local gopher supply. Old paint cans and buckets could be found, and water existed in abundance in every depression on the prairie. There was always one kid, just one, with hands faster than the speed of light, who stopped at a willow thicket on the way to select just the right willow stob with which to dispatch each gopher that invariably fizzed and sloshed out of that hole currently receiving the attention of the bucket brigade.

At least one after-school expedition of "drownding out" gophers was a spring tonic, the beneficial qualities of which could not be destroyed by the many tongue-lashings handed out around supper-time for getting soaked and catching a death, or even just for overlooking the chores.

You can take a prairie boy out of the small town, but no matter where he goes, man or boy, you'll never really take the prairie out of him. There are lots of us, steeped in a curious ennui about this time of year, waiting for the Stanley Cup to add some spice to a long old hockey season and anxious for some moving ice to bring on a new fishing season. Too cold and miserable to go fishing, we say, and too nice to hang around the house all Saturday afternoon waiting for six o'clock and the umpteenth battle for the fourth and final playoff spot in each of umpteen leagues.

This area is not exactly prairie, but add to its list of attractions the abundance of gophers that love to gnaw their way out of their dens about the middle of March each year. They blink for a while in the weak spring sunshine, stagger around a little on rubbery legs, and then cavort and chase madly over the deep but rotting snow, as though they realize there is a lot of living and loving to do before new snows blow.

Red Deer is also just small enough that you can count on hearing on some Friday afternoon about the middle of March, as I did about three weeks ago, some farmer telling somebody in a local store: "The gophers are out." The next day, if sunny, the former small-town prairie boys are out, too, to get taken back a bit. The convenient puddles of water are still around, but nobody stops for paint cans, and not one former prairie boy among them stops to cut a willow stob. Time has passed; times have changed. These are big prairie boys, and the weapons are different. Gone even is the single-shot Cooey .22 with the rear sight filed out of a bit of the tin band off a nail keg; the gun which, if you aimed two inches low and three to the right, and, if your hand was steady and your eyes clear from drinking your milk and always thinking pure thoughts, would dispatch one gopher in five.

At the very least now, we have smooth-functioning .22 longs with 4X scopes zeroed in at 75 yards, or .22 Hornets, or .222 Remingtons with 6X scopes dead-on at 150 yards. I even know a few nuts with .243's with 3X to 9X variable scopes who can shoot flies off a fence post at 400 yards. Then there is the one I know who hunts his gophers with stealth and a hunting bow.

Take away the equipment and things are pretty much the same: feet get wet and legs rubbery from all that plodding through the snow, the ordinary .22 and bow an' arrow types stalking forward to get close enough and the higher-power rifle types stalking backwards to see how far back they can get and still hit what they can't see with the naked eye. Some seats get wet from the sitting position, and the odd complete soaking results from the necessity of making a prone shot. Many gophers are spared by the hard breathing of riflemen conditioned by a winter in front of the tube.

Once is about enough, but once is essential. Next day, stiff, sore, and sniffling, the prairie boy can make up his mind that he couldn't possibly make himself any more miserable plodding through even deeper snow and falling in icy streams. So the next Saturday that is exactly what he'll do. But it's the gophers that have taken him back.

Death of a Coyote

A sudden chinook intrudes on a prolonged cold snap, and all manner of wild creatures prowl again. A lone coyote roots, digs, and snuffles under the snowy swathes and gleefully slashes, snaps, and gnashes at the tiny scurrying punctuation marks on the dazzling snow.

Five minutes before, he was gorged on the mice he was evicting from their homes under the swaths. Full after the long famine, now he plays at hunting, carefree and careless in the balmy air. The coyote does not soon enough hear or heed the dull, sputtering sound coming from below the hill.

When the snowmobile tops the rise, its explosions, unmuffled by the hill, vaguely resemble the less frequent explosion the coyote fears. Home is a brush pile in a dense stand of poplar and spruce at the head of a gully that slopes down to a large slough. A dozen bounds through the belly-deep snow, then he has to make that pause and look back over his shoulder.

Two family men ride the machine, anonymous city boys in dark glasses, ending a pleasant family outing with a cross-country jaunt to the next road where wives and kids will meet them with truck and car. The man at the back pounds the driver and points. The driver grins, the machine comes around slowly, skims over the snow, catches the coyote easily, and drives him away from that brush pile and out onto the slough.

Where the snow is not deep on the ice, the coyote runs easily; in the drifts he wallows and founders. But it is all the same to the tireless machine and all in good fun to the men who ride it. The machine goes ahead of the animal only when it appears he will make cover and turns him out onto the slough, again and again.

In no time at all, or so it seems to the men, the coyote cannot bound high enough to clear his legs from the deep spots, and he wallows, staggers, and stops frequently. The machine pulls up too close, a hesitant foot probes at the coyote and he strikes, like a snake, ripping to the sock the driver's expensive sealskin boot.

A little panic, a little exhilaration. The tone changes. The driver gets turned around and comes up to where the coyote is again foundered and stops to consider. The coyote is collapsed on the snow, eyes glazing, sides heaving, lips curling up from a lower jaw resting on the snow, foam and blood breathed from nose and mouth tracing harsh red etchings on the snow. Something has burst inside the body that was healthy and fluffy and that now is small, thin, and mangy. Death is the answer and death the judgment.

Even the civilized are primitive enough to know that you must make a hole to let the life drain away. But it was all in fun, and these men are not equipped. As a makeshift, they try to spear the coyote with the front runners of their machine and end by running him over; turn and over, turn and over and over and over. It is amazing, then frustrating, then embarrassing. Death will not come; at least it all takes too long. Finally, in a turmoil of churned snow, blood, and fur, the mangled form is still. The family men, the city boys, the mercy killers, turn their machines back on schedule for the rendezvous with wives and kids.

These are civilized men, and there are many like them. They earn good livings. They are deeply pained and mystified by what men do to men in places like Viet Nam and the southern States. They regard fun with the family as a sacred duty. Hunting and fishing, being inferior as family activities, are also just a little primitive and uncouth. Respect for the quarry is just a rationalization of the "blood sports". So they really do not have much to say to each other as they load the snowmobile, and without having talked it over, they say nothing to wives and children about the coyote.

Among "the boys" they do tell of conquering the wily, savage, and probably rabid little beast, this despised predator, this coyote. Some listeners allow that the only good coyote is a dead one, and this is satisfying. But from a few others they get a blank look, stiff formality, sometimes an outraged protest, and these reactions they pretend not to understand.

At first I was an unbeliever. I felt that even if I did not know coyotes as some claim to, at least I knew my fellow men. But three times in four months I have read just such a story and twice been captive at the telling of just such a tale. I, too, just do not understand.

Calling Coyotes

The gunrunner stopped just inside the fringe of bush around a large clearing. He exhaled a measure of breath straight up and studied the action of the vapor in the frigid air.

"Not much breeze, but the direction's wrong," he said.

Then we hunkered down; he drew a walnut instrument from his pocket and blew as heart-rending a lament as has ever echoed and re-echoed through these old hills. It sounded so much like a human infant in acute distress that the instincts of the ages raised my hackles. About every two minutes the gunrunner played a brief, subtle variation on his theme.

"If nothing shows in 20 minutes," he said, "you move on."

Ten minutes after the first blast I saw a few quick flickers in the bush on the other side of the clearing. Soon the shape of a coyote resolved itself, sitting, suspicious, just inside the fringe on the other side, wondering how something that smelled human could possibly make such appetizing sounds. With a rifle I probably could have got him; for the camera he was kept just too far away by the wayward little breeze.

The gunrunner had to get on his way, so we headed back to the jeep. He is an importer of firearms who regards his anonymity highly and had merely been delivering a rifle to me when the talk got around to coyote calling. He used a type of call I had never heard before, and I talked him out into some parkland coyote pasture for a brief demonstration.

"It would be a different game around here," he said. "Hard to see them. Back home you can see them get out of their bed three miles away and start to look for that wounded rabbit."

For the gunrunner back home is an area of Saskatchewan where you can see farther yet see less than anywhere else in the world. He started calling coyotes five years ago, and this winter expects to get his 1,000th coyote by calling.

I have called coyotes for about three years, but the high-pitched call I use is so hard to blow it bids fair to give me a hernia. The gunrunner says that the call he uses (made in Texas) is easy to blow, and the human baby sound seems more effective in his area than that high-pitched squeak of some calls. Coyote calling is highly competitive in his area, and he would never sell a call close to home. But he decided I was far enough away to risk and let me have a couple. I can now confirm that the crying-baby call is more successful in my area for calling coyotes than the squeak I formerly used.

I did discuss with the gunrunner all the other creatures that will come to a predator call, and his experience has been the same as mine. I have had lynx, magpies, ravens, mule and whitetail deer, great horned and snowy owls audit my concerts on occasion.

The gunrunner kills the coyotes that answer his call. I try to photograph most that come close to me, although I shoot them in the vicinity of my Stump Ranch, where a neighbouring sheep rancher often finds himself so hard-pressed by coyotes that he spreads poisoned chicken heads. I would rather do my neighbourly duty by some coyotes than see all the other creatures done in that also partake of that poisoned bait.

I guess I am saying that I am a tender-hearted but practical man, familiar with all the arguments pro and con as to whether anything should be called a predator and whether it should be controlled. That is said to protect me from readers who wish to engage me in a protracted debate on the subject by mail.

The unprecedented high numbers of coyotes this winter unaccountably occur at a time when the price for the hides they bear has also reached unprecedented heights. It does not surprise me that the coyote is being hunted hard this winter and that I am receiving many inquiries for suggestions on how one might shoot a coyote without seriously damaging the pelt. That is a nice trick indeed, when most people believe that wily animals like coyotes must be shot, if at all, with modern, flat-shooting, high-velocity rifles. Trouble is that that kind of rifle, with standard ammunition, shoots right through a coyote at almost any range and makes a horrendously big hole going out. Those who have tried solid-jacketed bullets tell me the entrance and exit holes are gratifyingly small when they get the animal, but most of the time a wounded animal escapes, a result that is unacceptable for the people who have the problem, not to mention for the coyote.

The answer, for whatever rifle calibre being used, is medium-jacketed bullets with powder loads reduced sufficiently that the bullet expends all its energy inside the coyote and does not exit. The people I know who use this system invariably say the problem is in getting close enough to the coyote. These people will have the whole answer when they start watching the wind and letting the coyote come close enough to them by using a good predator call.

Mushrooms and Prickly Pears

There must be thousands of former boys in Alberta who have been taken from the prairie but from whom the prairie could not be removed by all the magic of medical science. Displaced though I may be, there is still enough of the prairie in me that I was deeply hurt at the editorial remarks *The Calgary Herald* made lately concerning the efforts being made to turn a large area near Suffield into a national prairie park. *The Herald* asks, in effect, "Who needs a virgin tract of barren prairie?"

Last weekend I travelled to Brooks to collect wife and son, who had been visiting with my parents, and was greeted by Herself, one of Alberta's hill people, bubbling over with enthusiasm for something she had never seen before, the beauties of the Alberta prairie in June.

To the truly converted, the prairie is beautiful at all times; those same heavy spring rains that can turn our gentle west country streams into torrents can unleash unusual torrents of life and beauty on Alberta's prairie.There is nothing on earth that smells cleaner than the prairie after a long rain; the air is pure vitamins with a slight scent of sage.

Saturday afternoon, brisk winds tore the low overcast into chunks of fleecy cotton scudding across sunny skies, so an expedition was raised to a long arm of prairie jutting out into Lake Newell, about 10 miles south of Brooks. A serious bird watcher could spend his life on this peninsula. Saturday it was curlews upstaging all other forms of life. They marched in regiments through the grass, then simultaneously would leap into screaming flight, the underwings of the young flashing white.

The springing shoots of tender grass tempted even the Canada geese inland and, at our arrival, a low-necked goose led her brood of at least 10 fuzzy goslings back to the water while the gander brought up the rear, head proudly erect. Pelicans, truly whiter than white after the rains, sailed back and forth over the narrow strip of land.

The purpose of the trip was cactus. Everywhere were the large succulent lobes of the prickly pear, crowned by the yellow and orange flowers that seem so exotic as to be ridiculous on the "barren" prairie. Less frequently, you could find the low-growing pincushion cactus, topped by its brilliant red flower. The object of the exercise was to find sufficiently small and youthful specimens of each that they might acclimatize themselves to the blazing hot desert that is my patio in Red Deer.

My attention was taken by a foolish young gopher, and I decided to get his portrait. Four feet he would abide, but not three, and then I noticed three bulbous growths behind the mouth of the burrow where the little rodent had been crouched seconds before. Mushrooms, in the button stage! The books call them meadow mushrooms, but no meadow was ever like this sage and cactus peninsula teeming with wildlife.

From that point all hands fanned out, for it is well known down here that a little sun after a good rain will cause the germination of one of the greatest gifts of the gods. We found a few pounds, mostly under sage bushes. The next day or two of sunshine would cause the springing of fungus I have seen as far as the eye could see. We found two or three of the ridiculously large 8- and 10-inch diameter specimens and marvelled anew at how they grow so quickly without disturbing the earth from which they spring.

Time means nothing on a prairie full of life, but eventually we had to haul our harvest of cactus and mushrooms back home. On the road I was delighted to see four lads carrying an empty beer box over to what was once my favorite and secret mushroom hunting ground. Apparently one of the products of the prairie is still prairie boys who know something about the prairie.

Stalking the Wily Morel

For a number of years I had been convinced that buck deer were a figment of the imagination of doe deer and wind-broke outdoor writers. So the first time a buck deer actually sauntered by the stump to which I was frozen "on stand" has to rank as one of the greater hunting thrills I have experienced.

My greatest hunting thrill, however, came unexpectedly last spring when I was fishing. It was late in May and I was pussyfooting up to what I hoped was a very large brown trout indeed who was intent on assaulting female stoneflies, much as we humans scoff cashews: one by one as they come along, with gusto.

As I made my final approach the last six feet to within casting range of my quarry, I glanced down at the gravel bar over which I was skulking and all thought of that brown trout vanished. There at my feet was the first actual specimen of a trophy I had been hunting for six years, a quarry so elusive and wily that I truly did not believe my eyes when I saw that delicate light-tan creature shining as only something that is newly-minted can. It was a *Morchella esculenta*, or, in a word, a morel, the one-species grand slam for the mushroom hunter, the nectar of the gods for the mushroom eater.

Here, on a sandbar, when I had been scouring mixed aspen and evergreen woodlands for five years in fruitless pursuit of this elusive quarry? I spread myself out, deployed all my forces in the immediate vicinity, and came up with half a dozen others in the same thin, sandy soil. As so often happens when the ice is finally broken, I found quite a few more morels during open season last year and confidently expect to find a few this year.

Mushroom hunting has become a popular outdoor pursuit among a growing number of fanatics in the past 10 years. Most current practitioners of the sport will admit they started with the excellent pamphlet published by the Canada Department of Agriculture, "Mushroom Collecting for Beginners". The pamphlet is still in print and is available direct from the Queen's Printer or from the many Queen's Printer outlets sprouting like mushrooms in many Alberta communities.

"Mushroom Collecting for Beginners" says that the morel "grows on the ground, usually singly or in groups in open woods, orchards and pastures during May and early June". Severna Nash, a Red Deer bookstore owner, is a mushroom maniac. When I was in her store the other day seeking a more advanced guide to mushroom hunting, she allowed that the morels were late, along with everything else this spring. Generally she agrees that mid-May to about mid-June is morel time in Alberta and says that she prefers mixed aspen and evergreen forests for morel hunting. Mrs. Nash kept the conversation on generalities, as mushroom hunters are even more secretive about their hunting spots than anglers are about good fishing holes. Like so many things in nature, morels are creatures of habit and appear in the same locales year after year if the habitat is not disrupted.

In her Red Deer store she has the finest collection of books on mushrooms that I have seen. She sold me *The Mushroom Hunter's Field Guide*, revised and enlarged, by Alexander H. Smith as a reasonable way for a mushroom hunter and eater to keep himself out of intensive care. This book notes that the morel may be found in a variety of habitats; one of the other books I looked at indicated morels are often found on sandbars in rivers and streams, so I guess I will not write up my discovery for the learned journals after all.

Most mushroom guides indicate that you'll not mistake morels even for the poisonous false morels once you have seen the true morel. All that, of course, is relevant to the many delights and the only potential hazards of eating wild mushrooms.

Tom O'Keefe of Calgary, immediate past president of the Alberta Fish and Game Association, is one mushroom hunter who claims never to have seen a morel. Actually I know this is a falsehood concocted to get me to show him some of my favorite morel hunting grounds. Tom says that whenever he gets a batch of a new species of mushrooms that he has positively identified, he will still eat only one. The next day, if he is still alive, he and his sons will eat the whole batch. The morning after the feast, O'Keefe's daughters, who do not indulge in mushrooms, check to see if the governor is up and around. Makes me feel a little less silly about that single succulent morel I cooked and devoured about a year ago.

The morel is the harbinger of the season for the mushroom hunter. Already my favorite native scout down Brooks way has reported that the excellent *Agaricus campestris* or meadow mushroom, is starting to show up in harvestable herds. Too soon fall will be upon us and with it the bushels of *Coprinus comatus* to be gathered along central Alberta roadsides. But the Shaggy Mane Story will be the subject of another column.

The Pronghorn

It was probably on the third pass rechecking the mileage on the east-west road near Schuler that we determined the 16 rocks in the two strips of winter rye were really pronghorns basking in the October sun. Red Deer lawyer Mac Johnston and I spent most of the Sunday before the October 20 opening of the antelope season looking for our camp set up earlier that day by John Horn and his son, John Jr., both of Red Deer.

Oh, we had found John's post marked with surveyor's tape and his note saying "7 miles due east", but we assumed that a land surveyor means 7 miles when he says so and not 9.5, and we were not prepared for the pipeline activity that has everything in this country over 6 inches tall festooned with surveyor's tape. Young John found us eventually, and led us to our camp at the bottom of a deep coulee in prime pronghorn country. There we found John Sr., drawn and white and taken to his sleeping bag, felled by bad water or questionable quantities of Ukranian sausage that is as impossible to digest as it is to spell.

The four of us had drawn an antelope licence for area F, and the first order was to get young John his first big game animal and back to school. John Sr. had spoken to the rancher about the 16 in the rye, and the rancher allowed we could have a crack at them.

The next morning we thought we were late when the good shooting light revealed empty strips of rye. Then we spotted the 16 in the stubble on the horizon to the south. Around we went, and as they so often do, these ghosts of the plains vanished. Assuming that they were going to the rye, Mac and I headed up a deep draw to peek over the saddle at its end overlooking the first rye strip, and the two Johns decided to come in from the other side.

I had nearly topped my end of the saddle when Mac waved me over to the nest of rocks at his end. Sure enough, on our bellies, peeking through grass, we could see ears but no horns. One of the ear owners saw us, however, started over, and from the dead-on view neither of us could see horns. Just as the animal turned sideways, revealing herself as a huge old doe, John Jr.'s .257 Roberts Improved spoke, and I heard the bullet hit. The kid had his first big game animal, a nice 13-inch buck, and was on his way back home by 10 a.m.

The fact that the herd ran right past where I would have been if I had not come over to Mac started the ifs. Mac and I had never hunted pronghorns before, and now realize that if we had immediately stood up at the shot we would ourselves have had excellent shots at the other good bucks in the herd. Mac put it all in perspective: "If only we had dug goose pits in the rye".

John Sr., on the departure of John Jr., forsook his Ruger Model 77 in .257 Roberts and repossessed his prized custom .257 Roberts Improved. By afternoon of the first day the yahoos that chase antelope in vehicles and fire at herds two miles away had made the ghosts even spookier. John decided he knew where we were and that he and Mac would gumboot it back to camp. Shortly after they got started, John stopped a running herd with the piercing whistle he uses on laggard rodmen, then missed a standing buck at 200 yards, a most uncharacteristic development for an excellent rifleman.

The next day we decided to let things settle down and took a trip half way around the zone to Atlee without seeing anything but three does, one herd at a full gallop, and trees full of sharptails. Then and the next day when I went after those sharptails, I saw the national disgrace: the huge burned-out strip of over 8,000 acres from Drowning Ford on the east of the Suffield Military Reserve to the Suffield-Jenner road on the west side. Other hunters tell me they observed the bloody British Army finishing the burning job.

We topped the rim of our home coulee at about 2 p.m., and five completely calm pronghorns were drinking at the slough behind our cook tent and tent trailer. We glassed them from the ridge above our camp as they munched their way from patch to patch of buck brush and then lay down about half a mile away.

I saw horns, but the vote was 2 to 1 against me, and so I, the lone dissenter, picked my way in Old Jeep down lease roads, pipelines, etc., to the base of what I thought to be the right ridge. I finally crawled near the top of a hogback between draws and could see nothing. I fought the temptation to stand only because, with binoculars, I could see Mac still hiding and watching from the ridge above the camp. Finally I could see only ears again and even tried waving the hanky, but these pronghorns were not going to be done in by that old clinker. After about an hour of the slither bit, these old bones said it was now or never, and I rose to sitting position with my Husqvarna 6.5 x 55 braced by elbows on knees. My impression was of small but legal horns on everything but one old doe, and I collected the best buck I saw at 125 yards.

That evening John Horn sat down, took aim at a fine buck at a little over 100 yards, and was already apologizing to the departing spirit of the dead animal when a sharp click both announced that the magazine had fed nothing to the bolt and saluted the fleeing buck.

The next day the animals were spookier than spooky. The only shot missed was by John at 350 yards, for which nobody should have to apologize, but it was starting to get him down. Mac and I had to leave that evening, and we left a woebegone John Horn as sole survivor. Thursday morning he decided the .257 Roberts Improved, sighted in by young John, was not for him, and chose instead the new Ruger .257 Roberts. That evening at 5 p.m., just the other side of our home coulee from where I had taken my buck, with one shot at 250 yards John Horn took a respectable buck indeed, with 12½-inch horns.

7. Tips, Hints, and Help

Putting the Tackle in Order

For an angler, any February is the cruelest month, but particularly cruel is a February blowing hot and cold like this one. A week ago there was a tonic in the air strong enough to start the sap running in sundry fishermen but not strong enough to loosen the bowels of the earth and start the streams flowing. For the trout fisherman the desire is there but the streams are not, leaving only impatience at nature taking her own good time warming the earth.

Clearly, an antidote is needed for the premature tonic in the air. Ice fishing? It is surprising how few devoted anglers are that far gone in their dementia. The tackle catalogues that are arriving now? No antidote at all. Initially they provide diversion but ultimately induce in a man a melancholic awareness of his own poverty.

The ideal would be a trip to B.C.'s burbling coastal streams up which mighty steelhead are running. A man can dream of rivers with magic names: the Cowichan, the San Juan, the Campbell, the Bella Coola, the Kispiox. Rumor has it that some Albertans are actually long gone. But the expense, the time off! For most of us the ideal antidote for that early tonic is to put our fishing tackle in order. One look at the porcupine's nest that is our tackle is enough to discourage any thought of using it for at least three weeks.

I have been devouring those righteous articles that appear in outdoors magazines about how a little time spent now untangling the old tackle will pay dividends later out on the stream and so on, *ad nauseum*. It's all true, too. So, as the fruit of my studies, I offer a summary of how best to fiddle while the world warms.

First find the tackle. This will generally kill a week a man would otherwise waste mooning around the house cursing the slow arrival of spring and the rapid arrival of the income tax deadline. Try looking in the trunk of your car under the gaily entwined duck decoys and their anchor lines. While at it, remove and cremate the half-decomposed but mercifully frozen mallard that was the forgotten trophy of the last hunt. Every community has an expert or two in Chinese puzzles who, in a day or so, should be able to separate your wretched tackle into its component parts.

Next strip down all reels and give all parts a good sloshing in a can of some sort of grease solvent, being careful not to spoil the bouquet of your cigar by smoking it in the vicinity of the solvent fumes. Try and try again to assemble the reels, then take the whole mess to your dealer and ask him to lubricate the machine properly as he puts it together.

Hang your chest waders by cinched-up suspenders on the shower nozzle over the bathtub and fill with water from the shower. Mark the locations of obvious leaks. If non-obvious weak point suddenly succumbs to exhaustion and deposits wader contents—generally 18.4 imperial gallons—on wife's clean bathroom floor, leave immediately for urgent two-day business trip to Pothole, Saskatchewan.

Line guides on rods should be examined for those little grooves that slice monofilament like egg noodles just when old Scarbelly is coming to net after a 90-minute battle. This is what the line guide manufacturers say, and naturally they also say that guides with deep grooves should be replaced.

You will probably be among the 90 per cent of glass rod owners who discover that the first time they try to do the beautiful silk thread winding that holds the guides on most glass rods, it is either the eyesight or the rod. Glass rods are not very expensive anyway. Remove any guides left on rod, snap rod smartly against a tree just above the handle—most anglers are good at this—and give the result to your wife to prop up her hollyhocks this summer. Then head for the first dealer you hear of who is displaying his new stock of rods.

But why go on? All fishermen know how to care for their equipment and know also that a trip to their sporting goods dealer can cover a multitude of sins. In fact, the crowds you see in some sports shops during those fine but not fine enough February days indicate that most anglers consider equipment browsing to be the best antidote to the treacherous tonic in the air and the best cure of all for tangled and tattered tackle.

The whole discussion becomes academic when February turns cruel, as it has the past week. Tonic gone, antidote not needed. All anglers can hibernate for another six weeks.

Getting in Shape

A combination of circumstances leads me to belabour a labourious subject. First, through what must be a masterpiece of misinformation, I get invited to address a genuine, athlete-type Sportsman's Dinner. Along with making my mental notes to be brief, I mentally re-suffered the real agonies and anguishes of the torture known as getting into shape during my own brief and undistinguished athletic career.

Now comes to hand a book purporting to tell the sportsman all he needs to know about getting into shape to endure the various lunacies he calls outdoor sports. The sap rose in me to such dizzying heights the past couple of March weekends that I actually found running water and fished in it, and I have survived to tell all who care to listen that all books on getting into shape for outdoor sports are—as the young say so often today—irrelevant to the whole question of early season fishing in this country.

Here follows a practical regime of exercises, designed by me, guaranteed to prepare anyone to meet, though not necessarily to survive, March and April conditions in the west country. For starters you should don a heavy, itchy suit of old unshrinkables, at least one pair of pants, a flannel shirt, a sweater, an eiderdown vest, and a windbreaker. Next, and this is the important warmer-upper, you should stuff the whole mess, including self, into a pair of chest waders. After pulse and respiration return to normal, stage two can be undertaken. Still dressed as in exercise one, take at least three offspring down to the tallest building in town and, putting one offspring astride your shoulders and carrying one under each arm, proceed to climb all the stairs to the top of the building, three at a time. If you can prevail on the piggy-back child to stuff snow down your neck and the under-arm ones to whip you in the face with willow wands, you will exactly simulate the blissful streamward trudge of the equipment-laden angler through the snowy March and April woods.

If not taken into custody or to the emergency ward, go home, put on thick woolen mitts, and untangle the worst mess of hooks and line in your tackle box. No cheating! Choose *the worst*. Every tackle box has two or three. This important exercise prepares one to handle casting with spinning reels, with gloves on, using frozen mono-filament line that should have been replaced last July.

Then call up faithful fishing buddy, have him dress in waders, etc., and waddle over. Buddy or self should brace hands on the sides of your house with feet on the worst patch of ice on the sidewalk under the worst leak in the eavestroughs. Partner should stand directly behind while you run as fast as you can on the ice, kicking as high as you can behind. If you lose your grip completely, skin hands and face on the stucco and kick partner in the face, so much the better, as you will then be prepared for the joys of climbing icy stream banks or pushing the car when the invariable March or April blizzard happens along.

After the bleeding stops, fishing buddy and you should take turns draping the rubber cord of a landing net around each other's neck, backing off about 19 feet behind and letting fly only after you have made partner turn around, by some evil ruse, so he gets full benefit in the teeth. This exercise prepares you for fishing at any time of year.

Now, still in waders, etc., waddle off to a nice tub filled with only the coldest water steeped in at least six good grain scoops of snow. Make sure water is no more than 38° F, as that is what it will be out west. Stay in and get a good soaking. Tossing, fumbling, and squeezing a bar of soap previously frozen solid in the deep freeze is optional, but it does prepare a man for the unlikely event that he might actually catch and have to unhook a fish in March and April out west.

Stand up from time to time and do a little dance in the tub. If you should happen to step on that soap bar from time to time, wonderful! A man wading icy streams should know how to fall. Falling makes it unnecessary to do what you don't want to do anyway. How can you tell where the leaks are to patch waders if you are soaked inside?

Finally, probably still in waders, sit down and drink two dozen beers and smoke a pack of cigarettes. Not as frivolous as it sounds, this is in fact the most important exercise, as it prepares you for what most anglers do when they get one look at the actual conditions all the other exercises are designed to prepare them for.

Depending Dependants

One pair depends from my hips, two pair depend from my shoulders. I refer of course to waders, hip and chest. Waders are expensive, a trait they have in common with dependants of all kinds. Little did I realize what a time of bliss it was for a couple of years after my arrival in Red Deer in 1962, possessed only of my high school graduation suit, a 1959 *Criminal Code*, a law degree that would be forwarded upon payment of my library fines, and a zeal to bring the law to the frontier.

Instead I took to spending much of my time out west of the 5th where everyone knows there is no law, but there are considerable fish. Not being able to afford waders, I did without them and waded wet, as the saying goes. Now that water is cold, and I learned to do an excellent tippy-toes when the waters approached crotch level and developed a passable soprano when I ventured beyond that depth. Unfortunately I also developed a chronic dull ache through the hips, and my doctor, after a very skillful cross-examination, put the nix on any more wading wet.

So I took out a small bank loan, giving back a chattel mortgage on what was left of my Volkswagen that the finance company didn't own, and purchased my first pair of hip waders. Scarcely had I become fully aware of the true miseries of owning hip waders when I took up fly fishing and absolutely had to have chest waders. From that time on, I have always owned at least one pair of each. Like any other dependants, they eat money and break your heart. Unlike most dependants, the average life span of waders seems to be two years, so that each year I am obliged to purchase more misery by replacing one pair or the other.

As some people do with children, I attempt, right from the start, to bring up my waders in my own image. Before they are worn once, I take them to a tire shop different from the one that handles routine wader repairs for me and have tire studs put in the heels and the treads ground off the soles, the better to install indoor-outdoor carpeting. The whole procedure is for safety and better traction in the streams; however, the honest workman *knows* I am crazy. The honest workman at the tire shop that does my routine repairs just suspects I am crazy, so never the twain shall compare notes.

Routine repair? There is no such thing as a routine wader repair, mainly because of the difficulty in finding the leaks. So exasperating is this procedure that I once happily patronized a tire shop where they knew I was crazy and said so, but patched my waders free, provided that I had first found and marked the leaks.

The last resort that generally works is to fill the whole thing with water after hoisting it, of course, to a strong floor joist. Currently, my left hip wader defies analysis of this kind. Step into four inches of water and immediately there is four inches of water in the boot. Fill the thing up, hoist it to the ceiling for a week, and not a drop appears.

Last summer my dependants embarrassed me in Pincher Creek, of all places. At the start of last season I vowed that the one hip and two chest waders I then owned would last me two further seasons. So on each day of my two-week fishing trip to Pincher Creek, the pair that had sprung a leak the previous day had to be sent into town with a member of the family.

Gradually, the family took to sneaking off to town without telling me, and I had to take my wetting urchins in by myself, endure the exasperated sighs and wisecracks as long as I could at one shop or another, and then seek out ever more obscure shops.

This was good for me since, besides learning humility, I also learned much of the techniques for wader patching. I learned that most of the little kits sold for patching waders really are useless, as I had suspected. The secret is buffing, but wader material is so thin you just make more holes if you buff too much. I could buy a whole new set of dependants right now if I just had a dime for every hole I have buffed in myself. Then one day, eureka! One slicker did not buff at all, but used Liquid Buffer. His patches stuck and he did not manufacture holes.

So I have turned pro. I went to an automotive supply firm and purchased a supply of professional cement, professional patches, Liquid Buffer, and even one of those little wheel-jiggers that "stitches" the patch.

The last three weekends I have spent staunching the wounds in my three pairs of dependants, and I predict I will have at least one pair finished by the time all snow goes. I may even refuse to buy a new pair of hip waders at the end of the season as I had planned and pay off the mortgage on the house instead.

Wade or Swim

So far I have remained afoot in Montana's Madison River, but I have been washed slightly more than somewhat downstream in Montana's Bighole and B.C.'s Campbell rivers. They are all noted for their treachery to wading anglers, but in this department I will stack our own Clearwater up with the worst of them any day.

Sunday the Clearwater nearly stacked me up. Throughout a tough afternoon of fishless prospecting I had waded the river a couple of times just to see if there were any fish on the other side. Each time I plotted my course carefully and used a stout limb for a wading staff to provide that valuable third leg. No incident, and each time I reached the other side, I experienced that exhilaration I always feel in wading fast water. Then I saw a fish rise beside a logjam on the other side and broke my cardinal wading rule: never cross a good-sized stream on impulse.

The other rivers I have named are dangerous because they are fast and because their big rocks are slippery with moss. The Clearwater is dangerous because it is faster and its good, unslippery gravel bottom lulls one into a false sense of security. But that fast current will wash that gravel out from under foot and did just that on my impulsive crossing. As I went down, I had time to reflect that I had never passed on to the readers of this column some of the things I have learned about wading from just such bad trips as the one I was about to take.

This is going at it backwards. The suggestions I have are designed to prevent all this. But I am awash in the Clearwater, and when this happens don't panic. I didn't. You will float. I did, on and on. You may be able to get your feet under you, or you will soon be pushed into shore. I got my feet under me and stood up. I would have preferred to be elsewhere than the rapid I was in. Nevertheless, I wallowed ashore and, just to keep my nerve up, waded up and caught that fish. Only then did I discover that only my hat was dry.

Of first importance in preventing such debacles are the soles of the waders. The slipperiest substance in the world on slippery rocks and logs is the rubber that makes up the soles of the waders universally sold in this country. Felt is what you need to provide bite on slippery surfaces. In this area, in the absence of any waders sold with felt soles, the only answer is to obtain a pair of rubber waders, *not* vinyl, some rubber contact cement, some continuous fibre indoor-outdoor carpet, a sharp knife, and a hammer.

Using the glue as directed, cover each sole with a piece of the carpet, pound it into the cleats with the hammer, cut it to sole shape with the knife, and let set for a few hours. If you can talk your tire man into applying half a dozen tire studs into each heel, so much the better. Then purchase good polaroid sunglasses. Only with them can you see the bottom properly, and if you cannot see the bottom, you should not wade there. The polaroids will also improve your ability to spot fish, but do not let this make you lose sight of reason, as it did with me.

A wading staff makeshifted from an old ski pole is handy, but essential only in very fast water. A nylon belt to snug the waders around the chest is a must, as the drawstring on most waders simply puckers the fabric and allows the water to flow in quickly if you go over. And forget that old fishwidow's tale you always hear about always wading upstream or facing the current when crossing fast water. That is the surest way I know to capsize and to tire yourself out so badly beforehand that there will be no strength to do anything about it. Pick out a point on the opposite shore and downstream and wade down and across to it. The strength of the current will help you gently along.

So why wade, you ask, if you need to worry so much about equipment and safety? I, too, fought it for the first couple of years after I arrived in central Alberta. Then I gradually became convinced that, around here, no matter whether you fish flies, hardware, or good raw meat, wading will get you more and better fish—and I do not mean paddling in hip boots. More often than not there is one most effective way to present the lure to a particular fish or likely spot, and this often means standing in a particular spot, very often sunk to the withers in the water.

Wading is also good exercise, and there is that exhilaration I spoke of earlier which may have something to do with the intimate contact with the river, constantly feeling its power, that Roderick Haig-Brown writes of so often. Besides, wading just plain gets you to the other side and is refreshing on a hot day, even if you do not capsize en route.

Facing Downstream

Not so many years ago, trout season started for me any time after I had shaken off my New Year's hangover. Back in those days, from the first day on, my *modus operandi* was the same every fishing day until grouse season started and my fly rod went up on the rack the shotgun had just vacated.

But let an old friend with a lyric gift for invective describe it: "He wades in to the withers, jams that foul old hat down until you can barely see his polaroids, lights up a cigar, and chugs ever upstream belching smoke like Albert the alligator."

That's what I did all right, casting a dry fly as I went through fair weather and foul, an absorbed, dedicated purist to my chilled marrow. Of course, things were a little lean, as Alberta trout just do not really get to looking overhead for their vittles until about June 15th. But never mind, I was out, wasn't I, getting all that exercise and casting practice?

Five years ago, I started out up Pincher Creek from the town and did not desist until six miles of nothing convinced me that particular April day was not a dry-fly day. Next day was absolutely nothing as I was too sore to heave my hulk from its nocturnal berth.

This year I started the season on May 17th, in keeping with the resolve I made a few years back not to venture forth until the green is on the aspen and the crop is in. That is revolutionary enough, but in the past five years I have also become a wet-fly man. It was snobbishness that done me in. I had heard that nymph fishing was the most difficult of all forms of fly fishing. So for a couple of years, as I steamed ever upstream, I pegged those infernal weighted nymphs into the eternal downstream wind, occasionally being felled to my knees when a wayward gust would direct the lead-weighted nymph to the base of my skull.

As I say, I became a wet-fly man, and that accomplished the revolution to the extent that I myself revolved 180 degrees and proceeded to fish my way downstream in the time-honoured method of our forefathers with their cast of two or three wet flies. Last Saturday I mused the whole conversion over and decided to give my method to the world.

The warm spring sunshine was producing the light that drives painters mad. The wind was so slight that the ruffed grouse could be heard to drum at midday. I picked out a goodish run of water about 100 feet wide and full of boulders, got right out in the middle, and poled myself downstream with a wading staff fashioned from an old ski pole with the basket amputated.

The cast of wet flies is passè, and as I went I cast, quartering downstream to likely lies near either bank, a single size 6 weighted Bird's stonefly nymph #2, the brown and orange one. From time to time, when I would run aground or heave to alongside a boulder, if I had the energy, I would change flies and tie on a #8 Bitch Creek.

As I drifted along, the sights and sounds of spring were with me. In one streamside clearing a sandhill crane strutted for a hidden beloved. Frequently my progress would flush a school of spawning suckers. At one point I moved to the bank and sat down. May waters are cold, but on this day May sunshine could warm my old bones even through the waders. While sitting, I noticed the tapered cases of the *Brachycentrus* caddis fly pupae ranked like infantry on every underwater rock near shore. When these hatch in about three weeks, *then* I'll become a dry-fly man again and clean up.

In February, while going through the new catalogues, I flirted with the idea of buying one of those inner-tube, suspender, and didy contraptions U.S. anglers use to float and fish through land on which they dare not trespass. But it just isn't logical. After ballasting myself with sufficient equipment to keep my feet on the bottom, should I now add something to buoy them up?

The water-walking method has proven itself absolutely deadly for large trout the past couple of years, especially just after a summer rain has raised and slightly discolored the water. The waters last Saturday were low and clear. Nevertheless, my reveries were twice rudely interrupted when brown and gold lightning struck from beneath the bank as huge old soakers of brown trout tried and failed to nail the swinging nymph. Each nipped it but did not stick, nor did I stick them; the fish were no more in mid-season form than I was.

A good thing, too. Prolonged tussles with large brown trout would have broken a pleasant spell of spring fever. Besides, we former dedicated dry-fly men know May is much too early to take trout on a fly.

Nymphomania

There are forms of human activity more challenging, beguiling, and downright pleasureable than even dry-fly fishing, but before I have the vice squad hammering my publisher's portals, I should hasten to explain that nymphomania refers to fishing the nymph.

I should also explain that in this context nymph means a fly tied to imitate the underwater stages of various aquatic insects such as mayflies, caddis flies, and stoneflies. Unlike dry flies which are fished floating on top of the water, nymphs are fished sunk. But, like dry flies and unlike standard wet flies, nymphs are best fished upstream.

The lure to the angler is that most authorities agree that trout feed on the adult stage of the aquatic flies on the surface only about 10 per cent of the time; from 80 to 90 per cent of the time they feed below the surface on the immature underwater stages of these flies. This fact has given rise to many inflammatory squibs in angling literature concerning the effectiveness of nymph fishing in catching large numbers of very large trout. One famous squib often quoted for the inspiration but seldom for the warning it contains is from Edward R. Hewitt's *A Trout and Salmon Fisherman for Seventy-five Years:*

It is only because nymphs are not used properly that our streams are not depleted of trout. It is fortunate that few have acquired the necessary skill and knowledge to fish in this way well, and those who have are men who never take many trout from streams.

Most of these angling writers are strangely reticent, none more so than Hewitt, in explaining how to fish the nymph properly, which leaves the fisherman pretty well on his own, as I have been for the past five years. Time after time when no fish were rising, I have switched to nymphs from dry flies and then back again since, if I am going to catch no fish anyway, I would just as soon do it by means I understand.

At the start of this season, along with my resolution to make a nymph fisherman of myself, I acquired a copy of Charles E. Brooks' *Larger Trout Fish for the Western Fly Fisherman.* Reading it, I learned something of the wonders of using a large nymph and the dead-drift method of fishing it. The methods applied to the streams this year showed me the fish were interested, but generally they spat the fraud out before I knew they were there.

Because the nymph is best fished upstream, there is generally some slack line and this, coupled with the fact that the nymph is underwater, gives nymph fishing its greatest difficulty: simply knowing when a fish has taken. Despite the fact that I had read of the slight pause in the floating line, a bit of a boil on the surface, a flash of the side of a turning fish, or a spot of white of an open mouth, or even the "sixth sense" possessed by some fishermen and countless other indicators of fish taking the nymph, I continued to see and hear nothing until the fish themselves gave me a recent lesson.

The water was not high, but was cloudy after a recent big storm and, although I flailed valiantly away with dry flies, I saw no rises whatever. Half-heartedly, I tied on the only weighted Bird's stonefly nymph I owned and started flipping it up a likely run. On the umpteenth flip a great boil came up from where I thought the fly had drifted downstream from me. I struck. Nothing. Three drifts later the boil came again, and this time there was something that 35 minutes of give and take later proved to be a 22-inch male brown trout.

A few minutes later I was drifting the nymph back to me under a bush where I knew was the home of a worthwhile fish. Nothing. Then, behind the bush and tight to the bank, I thought I saw two wrinkles far apart, the wink that would be made by a big fish turning his head to take a natural nymph and flicking his tail to recover his position. Over went the imitation. I know I saw nothing, but I struck anyway when the nymph had drifted only six inches. There was the most frightful uproar and brouhaha. The eventual result was a 21-inch female brown.

In the next very fast run upstream, my floating line merely paused on its float back to me, I struck, and a very indignant brown hurtled into the air, a mere sprout of 14 inches. The next was easy. I felt I was not properly fishing a backwater across a fast current from downstream. Nymphs, I had read, could sometimes be fished straight downstream, so I let the line extend downstream and started to cross the fast water at the top of the pool. I had nearly made it when there was a hefty pull of a fish that had hooked itself against the taut line, another female brown, this one of 18 inches.

I have a tendency to like to quit while my hand is hot, and I was somewhat disheartened by my failure at reviving the second two big fish so I could release them. It was also very hot, I was a long way from the car, and those fish were heavy. Besides, that Bird's stonefly was the only one I owned, and I was mortally afraid a really big fish was going to take it away from me.

So back to the car I went to savour a cold beer and what I had learned from the fish, and then home to rush off an order to Dan Bailey in Livingston, Montana, for a couple dozen of those marvelous nymphs.

Accidental Fish

A mighty nice run of fish has been coming my way this summer, most by accident. It is a thundering comedown when all you catch on purpose run six to the pound, and a strain on the nonchalance to fabricate the illusion that the accidental brutes come to net only through the exercise of unspeakable skills earned through hours of neglect of family and employment.

Earlier this summer of 1971, Mike Burrington and I were wading an ordinarily heavy run of water that had been swollen and discolored by rains. The result had been fresh air and plenty of exercise.

Three or four years ago, an excellent guide on Montana's Madison taught me that you do not reel up your line before wading up to a new casting location; you just let the fly trail along straight below you on the extended line. "Saves time," he said, "and you never know your luck." A few moments later a violent pull from behind that nearly separated my shoulder signalled my first fish from the Madison, a 17-inch brown.

The trick has become a habit, and resulted in a 15-inch brown that morning with Mike Burrington. Then came the piece de resistance when, a few minutes later, a 3-pound brown of 19 inches met his demise by scoffing my Le Tort hopper as it dragged far behind me. Mike was first incredulous, then indignant, then suggested I tell no one lest it ruin the reputation of large brown trout for faultless judgment and my own reputation for at least purposeful fishing. "They laughed when I sat down at the piano," the saying goes, and I did notice Mike Burrington making like human troller the rest of the day, plowing ever upstream and dragging that fly behind. As I recall it, neither of us caught another fish all day.

You just cannot catch big fish on purpose if you ignore the little things, and I have long known a fly fisherman ignores to his sorrow the slightest unusual resistance on the back cast. This generally means the fly has ticked a rock or a branch and that the point and barb will have broken off. If you complete the cast, the law of contrariness decrees that the largest fish of the season will take the hookless fly.

A few days after the accidental fish taken by trolling, I ignored the resistance on the back cast and completed the cast. A brown trout I still do not believe rose under the fly and took it. I struck and felt weight, then the fly came away. Without hesitation, I cast again immediately, the brute came again, and again the fly came back. I cast immediately to another part of the run, hooked a 14-incher, and was ready to net him when the fly came away.

Still without looking at that fly, I cast over the lie of the big one and I had him on a third time. I do not know how long it was, but Carl Hunt stood by with the net for some time before the fish finally saw us, shook once and the fly, sans point and barb since that tick on the back cast, came skittering back to me. Such things happen often to me and have made me a philosopher and given me the fortitude it took to staunch Carl's tears.

Upstream I forged, stood in the lee of a big rock, and made a cast into an incredibly fast run of water. The surface was broken; the sun was bright. I saw nothing and heard nothing. All I knew was that I was snagged. Snagged? A floating fly in a deep and heavy run of water?

Having nothing better to do, the snoose being in the other jacket and the fruit juice in the cooler in the car, I set the hook in the obstruction. It moved and moved and moved, ever and onward, downstream to where Carl finally netted a 21¼-inch brown for me. It was foul-hooked, the fly caught in the muscle of a pectoral fin. I did not release the fish to be caught fair another day, as the British would have you believe they do.

Carl was still hiccoughing through his tears and politely allowed it was a nice fish but not nearly as big as the one I had just lost. Privately, I am here to tell you that lost fish was 21¼ inches from ear to ear. That one had better look out lest I have a real accident near his hole one of these days. After all, I nearly had him on a hook without point and barb. Next time I will not be so careful.

Angling Ethics

One August a while back I had a brief but brisk encounter with a big rainbow trout. I made a long cast upstream to the head of a riffle that ran along a cutbank and then stripped in line feverishly as the Michigan hopper bobbed along the fast current back toward me.

When about 15 feet of stripped-in line was trailing in the water behind me, the fly was taken by a big fish in a lightning head-and-tail rise. The fish surged upstream, making the loose line hiss as it came off the water. The fates were not kind that day, for the loose line tangled and caught in the lower guide of the rod. Everything twanged like a tortured G-string, and the fish kept going, along with the fly and about a foot of leader. May the fates forgive me for what I said.

After a month of plotting revenge on that fish, I once again stood at the foot of the same riffle and was concentrating on getting my line out to drop the fly in the right place. Suddenly another angler appeared, a stranger, strode up to the head of the riffle not two feet from the spot I was casting to, and plopped in about seven ounces of lead and worms. He hung his face over the water as he inspected the riffle and announced to the sprout with him, "This looks like a good spot, son."

On that occasion I said nothing, for the fish was obviously long gone and the boy seemed to be learning enough bad habits from his father. I reeled up and headed far downstream.

In four years of fishing that particular stream, that man was the first other angler I had ever encountered. But more and more anglers are being encountered on streams these days, and many seem completely ignorant of angling ethics and etiquette. It is not that these people are basically evil and selfish; most of them are simply new to the game and do not realize that angling is a sport where the competition is with the fish and not with other men and that angling, like most sports, has a few rules that improve the enjoyment for all.

An angler should walk carefully and quietly along a stream and stay out of sight of the water as much as possible. To do otherwise is to give the trout no credit for his sharp vision, his ability to detect vibrations, and his quickness to take fright and ruins the sport for the clumsy angler himself and any other angler in the vicinity.

Never, ever should an angler approach and fish a pool being fished by another angler. An angler coming to an occupied pool should either stop and wait until the other angler is finished or go around, giving the pool a wide berth, and not enter the stream again for at least 100 yards either upstream or down, depending on his direction of travel. I suspect that a rifle rather than the written word should be used on the type of person who rushes himself all day to keep just one pool ahead of a downstream angler.

Completely aside from consideration for other anglers, there are considerations that will go a long way to ensure the continued existence of sport for anglers to enjoy. There is no general size limit on trout in Alberta, but more and larger trout would be available if anglers would voluntarily return alive to the stream all trout they catch under eight inches. This is a relative thing, for in some streams an eight-incher is a large fish and the population should be thinned out. But on most of our central Alberta streams, an eight-incher is a joke on the angler who kills it and an irreparable loss to the stream and future sport.

In this area there is much ignorance and cynicism about bag limits. The limit is 10 per day with a total of 15 in possession, and that includes the deep freeze back home. Essential to angling as a sport is recognition of the bag limit as a mark never to be exceeded, not a mark that much always be shot for. Anglers who fish for food rather than sport can't afford this sport and would be better off to try something else.

111

As more and more people take up angling, more and more will need to be said and written about the rules of streams and angling ethics if the old-timers and newcomers alike are to enjoy the same pleasant days of magnificent sport many of us now know. Like so many things we humans do for pleasure, angling can be made more enjoyable by the thoughtfulness and courtesy of those who participate in it.

Roderick Haig-Brown, in his book *A Primer of Fly Fishing* puts it on the basis of generosity: "The generosity I am thinking of is an attitude, a whole approach to the whole subject. It implies generosity to other fishermen, to the fish themselves, to the water and the surroundings in which they live."

On Letting Them Go

Among the attractions of angling, especially to the older, more thoughtful sportsmen, is the fact that you need not necessarily kill anything to enjoy the sport. There are anglers who have had red-letter days, catching many times their limit, yet who have carefully released every fish so that it can grow and provide sport on another or many other occasions.

On any given day, particularly on streams, most anglers catch numerous small trout that they wish to release as a matter of course. As the number of good streams decreases and the angling population increases, the necessity of increased size and decreased bag limits will arise if good sport is to be available. It is important now and will become more important for anglers to know how to release fish so that they will survive the experience of having been caught. If, after all, a fish does not live after its release, the whole point of releasing it has been lost, and less waste would have resulted if the frying pan had been its end.

The key to high survival rates for released fish is not to land fish at all that are to be released. In many cases the fish can be brought close in shallow water, and you can grasp the hook and shake it loose without even removing the fish from the water. Small trout, particularly if caught on the fly, can be lifted briefly from the water, the hook grasped between thumb and forefinger, reversed, and the trout shaken off just above the surface of the water. It is important

112

not to drop even little trout too great a distance to the water, as the impact can seriously injure them.

Sometimes a trout is deeply hooked or hooked in such a way— under the tongue or in the roof of the mouth—that the hook cannot be grasped simply to shake the fish loose while it is in or just above the water. In such circumstances, the fish must be handled. Grasp the trout firmly and quickly over the back and below the gills, lift it out of the water, keeping a firm grip, decide quickly what has to be done to get the hook out, and do it fast.

The wet-hand or dry-hand controversy over handling fish rages unabated among anglers, but every reputable angling writer I have read prefers the dry hand because the firmness of grip it affords reduces the chance of internal injury to the fish. Internal injury is far more serious than the loss of the small amount of protective slime the hand removes and which a healthy fish quickly replaces anyway.

Pressure should never be applied between the pectoral fins because of the danger of damaging vital internal organs. The gills and gill covers should never be used as a handle to a fish that is to be released. Fish have a very small blood supply, and it flows through the gills; almost any injury to the gills means death to the fish. Generally, if there is any blood flow, you might as well keep the fish for the table.

Another fish that is a fryer is the one that has been dropped or pulled onto a gravel or sandy beach. The thrashing of a trout on such a surface will likely cause cuts and scrapes that will not heal.

Research has shown that the stress and exercise of the struggle to get off the hook cause chemical changes in the blood of a trout from which he will take some time to recover. Careful handling can improve his chances of recovery. One aspect of careful handling of an exhausted trout is to balance him on your hand upright in quiet water facing upstream. The fish will rest quietly there for a while, getting his wind and his bearings, then finally dart off with a powerful flirt of the tail.

There are angling films—you know the type—where fish after fish is yarded in, then held up and turned this way and that for the camera by his beaming captor who generally has a hand deep in the gills. Then the fortunate fish is thrown far out into the water as the commentator solemnly drones on about another one gone back to live and fight another day.

Having seen such films, suspicious local anglers have asked me how many fish handled and released in such a way will live, let alone fight again. The answer: not 10 per cent.

Goldeye on Fly

The goldeye keeps the faith.

On June 8, 1968, I fished from the north bank of the channel around the island just upstream from the east bridge and caught goldeye. Exactly a year later, I stood in my footsteps of the year before and hit a bonanza of faithful goldeye, right on schedule. What many veteran goldeye anglers will find hard to believe is that on both occasions all fish were caught on artificial flies.

Various official Alberta government publications dealing with sport fishing have noted for years that goldeye can be taken on flies, but say little about what fly to use and how to fish it. A handful of river rats in Red Deer, down Content Bridge way, and further on down at Steveville claim to have taken goldeye on flies, but beyond the bare claim all is mystery.

The majority of Alberta's anglers, particularly in our big cities, live just a hoot and a holler away from good goldeye supplies but just do not realize they are living exactly that far from excellent fly fishing. Such sport is too good to keep secret and, in the interest of popularizing fly fishing for goldeye, I am willing to share what little I know of it.

On that first June 8th, the river was fairly clear, and I used a size 8 Muddler Minnow, a bucktail fly with a silver tinsel body and grey wing of deer body hair. On June 8th the following year, the river reminded me of the way it always was during my youth down Steveville way: too thick to drink and too thin to plow. No matter. I long ago learned that goldeye feed avidly during such conditions and, unlike other fresh-water fish, seem to have no trouble spotting their vittles in the murk. I chose a size 8 bucktail with a silver tinsel body, bright scarlet wool tail, and jet-black wing. The often-proved theory is that in murky water fish see black better than any other color. The flash of the tinsel helps, of course.

On the Red Deer I use an 8- or 9-foot fly rod with a #8 floating, weight-forward line, because even channels around islands in the Red Deer are big water and I like to get the fly out as far as I can. Whatever the fly, the form in early-season, muddy-water goldeye fly fishing is to heave it out there, straight across the current or slightly upstream, and let the current swing line, leader, and fly around until the works straightens out below the angler. The floating line helps keep the fly from sinking below the top two feet of water, the area, I will argue with anyone, where most goldeye are caught. Once the fly is straight or almost straight below, it should be drawn back agonizingly slowly along the shoreline and right to the angler's feet.

114

In muddy water the goldeye often lie in pockets and eddies right at the edge.

My first goldeye in the murk came on the second cast, when the fly had been drawn to within 10 feet of me, and signalled herself by a brilliant flash, visible even in those cloudy waters, as she took the fly and turned a quicksilver side to the sun.

Of course, I stayed right where I was, because you soon learn that goldeye run in schools and when one comes, the second is not far behind. My second came on the fourth cast and took with the peculiar, hesitant pluck of the goldeye, just as the line straightened below me. The third took just after the cast had been made, out in the fast current; I struck when the line started moving upstream instead of down. After the second, I released them untouched, just flipping the fly out. My smoker holds about two fish; unsmoked goldeye are unfit for human consumption.

All fish put up the characteristic, unsophisticated but vigorous battle of the goldeye: much skittering over the surface, jumping and turning end for end, which was made much the better by the light lure and light leader.

When the river clears up, the goldeye take to surface feeding and can be caught fishing traditional dry-fly fashion, upstream with dry Black Gnats, grasshopper, and stonefly imitations. The problem in this later season is that the goldeye spread themselves over the river, and the largest always seem to be rising just beyond wading depth and the range of the longest cast. I remember last August, standing on a cliff overlooking the river just four miles from this city, watching dozens of huge goldeye rising in cadence, making rings the size of a bathtub right in the middle of the river.

For this August I have a plot. The faithful goldeye will be there then. In fact, the goldeye have been there snapping natural flies for centuries and will continue to be, so long as the works of man do not too much interfere with their family planning and extensive and mysterious travel plans. The angler needs to be only a little unfaithful and change his style to fly fishing for goldeye to experience excellent sport right near home.

Smoking Witchcraft

Judging from the number of inquiries I get and the amount of equipment and supplies sold by local dealers, in central Alberta the home-smoking of fish and meat is second in popularity only to home-brewing.

For many years the only smoker available, other than various home-built types, was the small Abu Swedish portable smoker fired by an alcohol burner. For a number of years, an Abu smoker, has infallibly produced small quantities of excellent smoked fish for me in the eight minutes flat it takes for the flame to consume all the alcohol the lamp will hold.

Goldeye particularly turn out excellently in the Abu smoker, as it employs a quick, hot, pressure-smoking formula similar to that invented by a culinary genius named Firth who gave the world one of its delicacies, the famous Winnipeg Goldeye. The trouble with the Abu smoker is the very uniformity that is built into its design and smoking formula. The result is the same every time, and flavour variations are nil.

A couple of years back, I got into a real sale in Spokane and stole one of the cabinet-type Luhr-Jensen smokers fired by a built-in hot plate. Thus did uniformity go by the boards, and I was initiated into a dark art bearing more than a superficial resemblance to witchcraft and into using fish-smoking formulas that contain more variables than the so-called formulas by which fish are caught in the first place.

The Luhr-Jensen smoker is capable of cold or hot smoking. You can use as much smoke as you like, and when you stop is up to you. These are only a few of the variables involved in smoking food by the traditional method. Add to these variables the type of brine used, the length of time in the brine, and the drying time, and it becomes obvious to me that my smoking experiences must be very similar to those of the many people who have purchased Luhr-Jensen smokers since they became easily available in Alberta.

Flushed with the success of two perfect batches of smoked salmon in a row, I will pass on my experiences before I have another of the disasters with which I am even more familiar. Last June I returned from Campbell River with some fresh salmon and found an ancient Scots recipe for a brine for salmon—which I have since found to be superb for trout.

1 2/3 gallons cold water
4 cups pickling salt
1 1/2 cups blackstrap molasses
3/4 cup lemon juice
1 tbsp. liquid garlic
1 tbsp. liquid onion
1 tsp. dill weed

I had filleted five pounds of coho, skin on, and then cut the fillets into pieces about six inches square. The brine must be kept cool in an earthenware or china crock; you simply stir and stir till the dry ingredients dissolve. The fish is placed in the brine and the crock kept in a cool place. For salmon pieces of the dimensions described, three hours in the brine is long enough; for fillets of a two-pound trout, two hours in this brine is long enough.

Once out of the brine, the pieces of fish must be washed quickly in cold water, dried on paper towels, and then placed on the smoker rack in a well-aired room until the hard, dry, glossy pellicle forms on the flesh side of the meat. Sometimes this stage takes as long as 12 to 14 hours, but fish should not be placed in a conventional smoker until the pellicle has formed. I made that mistake with about 20 pounds of goldeye once, and the result was not unlike biting into kerosene-soaked cotton lamp wicks.

About noon of a 70° F clear, sunny June day, I fired up the smoker in the garage, placed the fish in it, and left my father to add hickory dust as needed. Four hours later it was done, and the Guv and I found it to be as insidious as popcorn: we got into the cycle of cold beer to stop the thirst and make us hungry and smoked salmon to stop the hunger and make us thirsty.

Books on smoking, especially *Home Book of Smoke Cooking Meat, Fish and Game* by Sleight and Hull and published by Stackpole, emphasize that you must keep records if you are to achieve uniformity in smoke-cookery: type of brine, time in brine, time in smoker, even the direction of the prevailing wind and the location of the smoker.

So when I decided smoked salmon would be nice for Christmas, I did everything the same as in June except for using thawed frozen salmon and up to the time, about two hours into the smoking process, when I discovered the smoker was puffing away but stone cold owing to a temperature of 20° F in my garage. At that point I hauled the whole contraption into the house, plugged it in, set it on the hearth, and let it puff up the fireplace chimney. It smoked up a very satisfactory heat for about an hour and a half, then I shut it off.

The result? If anything, better than the superb June batch made from fresh fish, indicating that while much is to be said for record-keeping in smoke-cookery, one should never under-estimate the importance of luck and witchcraft.

How I Took up Deer Hunting, Became a Gun Nut, and Blew the Works

Last fall I took up a new outdoor sport. For an outdoorsman, such a decision is akin to a lady deciding she needs a new handbag: ultimately, what you wind up with is a whole new "wardrobe".

The first step was when I purchased my first deer licence ever. Next, of course, I got involved in the question of what would happen if I actually went deer hunting. I knew that deer hunting involved stumbling around in the woods at peculiar times and that a man better have a rifle to avoid having his sanity questioned by those who might see him. Indeed, even a wildlife officer might see you, should said officer be up and about at such ungodly hours, so the rifle had better be a lawful arm for big game hunting, just in case one was forced to admit one was deer hunting and not sneaking home the long way from a tryst with the widow Flathammer.

All this involved me in a very vexed question indeed: which rifle is the best deer rifle? Having never hunted big game, you see, I was burdened neither with a rifle legal for big game nor with prejudices. So I promptly set out to weight myself with all the prejudices of anyone who had any. I read Jack O'Connor, Frances Sell, Lawrence Koller, and Rollo Robinson. I consulted every deer hunter possessed of the power of speech. I even had a chat with the individual I shall call Tub of Guts Tumpline, the greatest poacher in east central Alberta, if not the whole civilized world.

Then I went out and did exactly as I pleased. I traded my beautiful Anschutz bolt-action .222 Remington with 6X crosshair scope, with which one can pit cherries at 200 yards, for a .243 Winchester bolt-action with 4X post and crosshair scope. My choice was dictated by the fact that, while I knew I was fond of target shooting and dispatching the odd magpie and gopher, I had not the slightest idea whether I would care for thing one about deer hunting. So I wanted a calibre light enough to continue with what I formerly did with the .222 Remington. Also, as those who know me will attest, I am puny and do not need a rifle with a heavy recoil to keep me regular or to clear my sinuses.

The trouble turned out to be that the manufacturers do not load .243 ammunition in the very lightest bullet weights I wanted for gophers and the heaviest bullet weights I wanted in the event of deer. The answer, apparently, is to load your own. So I spoke to Santa about a loading tool for Christmas, and he came through. Then did the plot thicken inversely as my finances thinned! Ball and shot, as they say in the old westerns, primers, plastic mallets...I even—and I don't believe it myself—built a bench strong enough to take all that pounding.

Out to the range I went with my first box of reloads and, after I became convinced they wouldn't blow up and quit flinching, I sealed my fate and shot better groups with them than I ever had with factory ammunition. That started for me the syndrome familiar to hand-loaders that makes a mockery of any economic advantage to rolling your own: you can't wait to get out to the range to shoot up all the shells so you can get back to the bench to load them up again. You don't save money loading your own: you just shoot more.

Meanwhile, back in the willow tangle, I was getting quite fond of deer hunting and decided that what I really needed was a faster-handling, lever-action rifle in an out-of-production calibre that has less velocity than a .243. So I fell among the gun nuts at a gun auction and came away shell-shocked and a little wiser. What I was looking for, precisely, was a... But no, there may be gun nuts reading this column, and one of the things I have learned is never to let a fellow nut know what is your heart's desire in the way of a rifle.

Then I think maybe the answer is to get a 6.5 X 55 Swedish Mauser army rifle, of which there are millions—well, hundreds —available, restock it, install receiver sights, etc: the amateur gunsmith bit that can't possibly mean less than a fortune in tools.

While I dream of a lever action.........in.........calibre and of customizing Swedish Mausers, I load and shoot targets, load and shoot targets, burn up gas back and forth between home and the range and scandalously neglect the tying of next year's quota of 13 dozen Le Tort hoppers.

After one full season I have yet to fire my first shot at a deer, which of course doesn't matter in the slightest.

Deer Rifles

Deer seasons are starting in various areas of the province, and early reports are of excellent deer numbers.

In early October every year there is a recruitment of novices to the ranks of deer hunters, a fortunate few of whom have the benefit of experienced fathers or friends they can go to for answers to the dozens of questions that loom immediately for the person who contemplates hunting deer for the first time.

Virtually the last question always comes first. The novice ignores completely the intricacies and woodcraft involved in the best deer hunting and first wants to know what rifle he should use. Humbled as I am after my first two deer seasons, I do recall that the question of firearm choice was the one I asked first, so I will set out here the benefit of what I have learned so recently.

I found out initially that every veteran deer hunter is strongly opinionated about the best deer rifle, so I hasten here to say that my conclusions will not recommend the best deer rifle, but only make some general and perhaps unusual suggestions obtained from my observations. Actually, the fact that veteran deer hunters are so opinionated on their choice of deer rifle indicates that they have arrived at the point I suggest novice deer hunters must arrive at in their choice of rifle: what is more important than anything else is that the deer hunter shoot a rifle with which he is completely familiar, with which he feels comfortable, and in which he has complete confidence.

For myself and, I suspect, for 80 per cent of all hunters, the feeling comfortable requirement rules out virtually all magnum calibres, most firearms of the .30 calibre family, and even the excellent and justly popular .270 calibre. The horrendous recoil of most magnums and .30 calibres is simply too much for most humans to bear. It is a pure question of physics, not of manhood. While the recoil of the .270 is not bothersome to me, its terrific muzzle blast bothers me and many others.

My view of recoil will not make me popular, because it is a rare man indeed who will admit he is terrified of the punishing blow of his own rifle. But I see them every day at the range I haunt: hairy-chested, grown men hunching up like shivering dogs as they try to squeeze the trigger on their 7 mm Remington magnum or even on their 30-06. Tensing up, flinching, and blinking are all enemies of accuracy, and the man who cannot shoot accurately with his rifle—indeed, who even hates his rifle—will have no confidence in it. A deer hunter sporting such a rifle and such an attitude to it is unlikely to hit a deer even from the inside and would be wise to lower his calibre sights somehow.

Thus I decided that a deer rifle for me would have to be below .30 calibre and that I would have to exclude the fine .270 calibre. In going smaller, one must always remember that it is unlawful in Alberta to hunt deer with a rifle of less than a .23 calibre or loaded with rim-fire cartridges or non-expanding bullets or with any cartridge case measuring less than 1.75 inches long. That rules out all .22 calibres and many of the larger than .23 calibres that have short cases.

One .30 calibre I should mention that is pleasant to shoot is the venerable 30-30, an excellent choice for deer in many parts of North America. In Alberta, however, all deer hunting is not in dense bush for close-in whitetails. Our terrain is such that one often gets shots of 200 yards and longer, even at whitetails, and in certain areas of the province shots at mule deer will invariably start at 100 yards. With its looping trajectory, the 30-30 is a 150-yard rifle at best and simply is not adequate for the overall deer hunting situation as it exists in Alberta.

A first choice for beginners who do not know whether they will like deer hunting could be a .243 Winchester or a 6 mm Remington. I know a controversy rages over whether the .243 and 6 mm bullets are adequate for deer or not, but the fact is that they are pleasant to shoot, are accurate, have tremendous velocity and flat trajectories, and kill hundreds of deer in Alberta annually. A major problem is that in brush the very fast bullet can be disintegrated entirely by a collision with a twig. One of the best brush-busting whitetail hunters I know carries and swears by a bull-barrelled Varmint model 6 mm Remington. The beauty of this choice, if a man does not like deer hunting, is that the .243 and 6 mm calibres are excellent for varmint shooting at long range.

One of the great whitetail hunters, Lawrence Koller, in his classic *Shots at Whitetails*, has nothing but praise for the .250-3000 or .250 Savage calibre on deer, a fact that has caused many of his readers to gnash their teeth the past few years, as no production rifles were being chambered for the calibre. I am happy to report that in the past couple of years popular demand has inspired Savage to introduce a pretty little lever-action Model 99-A in .250-3000, and Ruger chambers its fine bolt-action Model 77 in .250 Savage.

Another great deer hunting author, Francis Sell, champions the Swedish 6.5 X 55 mm because it is so pleasant to shoot and because of the stability of its long, heavy bullets in the brush. There are many Norwegian Krags and Swedish Mausers around in this excellent calibre, and now Husqvarna is producing beautiful sporting rifles with stronger actions than on the military rifles, so that the cartridges can now be loaded to higher velocities for excellent long-range performance.

Jack O'Connor, former guns editor of *Outdoor Life*, was a fan of the .270. He also advocated the 7 X 57 mm Mauser round as a superb all-round big-game cartridge. The 7 mm is just a shade smaller than the .30 calibres that are too much for me. I have shot creaky old military carbines and slick custom sporting rifles in 7 X 57, and I must say they are very pleasant to shoot, having no muzzle blast or recoil noticably greater than that from the .250 Savage or the 6.5 X 55.

Perhaps sportsmen are getting the message about rifles that are pleasant to shoot as opposed to those whose only virtue is that their heavy recoil clears the sinuses of the user and keeps him regular. In any event, Brno produces a superb but expensive 7 X 57, and now Ruger is chambering the fine and economical Model 77 in 7 X 57.

Those are my deer rifle calibre suggestions for Alberta. All are available, all are pleasant to shoot, and all are capable of superb accuracy and of clean kills on game of at least deer size. The final word to the novice is that, whatever rifle chosen, it should first be taken to a range and properly sighted-in at 100 yards with the actual bullet weight and powder charge weights that will be used when deer hunting.

Sighting-in Old Betsy

I was associated with the Red Deer Fish and Game Association in acquiring and building its fine new rifle range in time for its first use during Alberta's 1975 Summer Games. I had time to hang around another range or two as hunting seasons approached, have snapped a few caps myself, and have watched numerous hopeful hunters sighting-in Old Betsy.

While I have never observed the traditional sighting-in scenario of a rifleman aiming at a white rock on the hillside an undetermined distance away, touching off a couple that raise clouds of dust in the rock's general vicinity, and proclaiming "that's good enough", I have seen enough in the field and at various rifle ranges to know that at least half the hunting rifles in the field are not sighted-in at all and that very few people know what it is they are trying to do when they sight their rifle in. In addition, there are the more advanced questions: how accurate should a sporting rifle be and how good a shot is a good field shot?

Most modern rifles in modern calibres as well as their owners will be best served by sighting-in to the Rule of Three. That is, most modern high-powered rifles should be sighted-in so that they put their bullets three inches above the point of aim at 100 yards. The rationale of the Rule of Three is that most modern big game rifles are flat-shooting, and by sighting-in to the Rule of Three, most hunters will be able to deliver killing shots from the muzzle out to a distance of 275 yards by holding their aim dead on and not worrying about holding over. For most of us this is simple perfection, as more shots over 300 yards are made with typewriters than with rifles.

To save a lot of time and ammunition a person can, for a small charge, have a gunsmith adjust his sights with a collimator to ensure that the first shots land on the paper of the target. Then, to save even more ammunition, the rifle can be shot first from a solid but padded rest at 25 yards and the sights adjusted until the rifle is putting the shots right in the bull. This is Jack O'Connor's fast way of sighting-in and takes advantage of the fact that a bullet from a modern flat-shooting rifle crosses the line of sight twice, once at 25 yards and once at about 250 yards.

When a rifle is sighted-in at 25 yards, it should always be checked from a padded, solid rest at 100 yards. Generally, the bullets will be printing three inches high, but probably some small sight adjustments will be necessary to make the bullets print precisely three inches above the bull at 100 yards. Old faithfuls like the 30-30, 32 Special, and other acknowledged deer-killers that do not have flat trajectories are exceptions to the Rule of Three and should be sighted-in to put their bullets right in the bull at 150 yards.

There is a tendency in this day of ready availability of absolutely superb rifles and of a proliferation of gun writers, for even occasional hunters and average shots to scorn a hunting rifle that will not routinely produce the "minute of angle" group. The magic minute for hunters is produced by a hunting rifle that, shot from sandbags from a bench by a competent shot, will print three bullets on the target in a one-inch group, centre to centre, at 100 yards. The fact is that I have two hunting rifles that will occasionally do just that, but only if it is nice and calm and I am feeling up to snuff when I am doing the shooting, and provided that I am using handloads I have carefully and individually developed for each of these rifles.

Jack O'Connor, former shooting editor of *Outdoor Life*, perhaps went too far in scorning the minute of angle criterion that many writers made to seem essential for hunting rifles. O'Connor did a service to all ordinary hunters, however, by pointing out that no man need be ashamed of a bolt-action hunting rifle that will produce 1½-inch groups, lever-action rifles that will produce 3-inch groups, and automatics that will produce 4-to 5-inch groups, all at 100 yards from the sandbags and with factory ammunition.

Given ownership of such a rifle properly sighted-in, what standard of marksmanship constitutes big-game shooting accuracy? How can you test yourself? Two of the finest big-game shots in the sense understood by most men were Larry Koller, author of *Shots at*

123

Whitetails and Francis Sell, author of many books on big-game hunting. Sell states it best, perhaps, in his *Advanced Hunting on Deer and Elk Trails*:

Can you put a "hunter group" of three shots in a twelve inch circle at one hundred yards off-hand, fifty yards, twenty-five yards? Can you get your first shot off in a second and a half at those shorter ranges, within two seconds at one hundred yards? Can you put three shots in that size circle at one hundred fifty yards from a sitting position, or standing, resting your forearms against a tree for rifle support?

We are all inclined to become bench-bound, and I try to make it a practice never to leave a range without trying one or two of the tests Sell suggests. Sound easy? Try it, over and over and over.

The least result is that you will very quickly find what you can and cannot do, and you will gain confidence in what you find you can do. You will also become a better game shot than all but 10 per cent of the hunters you see out bruising the browse with you during the season.

Patterns for Mediocrity

The average shotgunner—and that takes in a lot of men who hunt in Alberta—is a lousy shot. Unfortunately, the category includes me, first and foremost. One of the greatest tributes paid to my wing-shooting was by an excellent shot who said that my own performance was, well, ah—erratic.

Erratic indeed! I will admit there are one or two days a season when my whole being magically accommodates itself to the idiosyncracies of my shotguns and I cannot miss, but the rest of the season I am steady and consistently conserve game by touching not a feather.

Most riflemen would not think of going hunting with a rifle that was not at least sighted-in, if not modified somewhat to fit them. Most shotguns, however, go straight on a hunting trip from the rack in the sporting goods store. The new owner has not the slightest idea if the gun fits him, where it shoots, or what loads it handles best. But shooting he goes, always, well—erratically.

Standard shotguns are made with stocks of standard dimension to fit a fictional average man and actually do not exactly fit more than 5 per cent of the population. A good shot can decently accommodate himself to most gun stocks, but most of us are not good shots. The stock should be modified.

Patterning the shotgun can provide the diagnosis of many shotgunning ills, but patterning is a mysterious practice most gunners have only heard of and never indulged in. I partook of the vice for the first time last weekend, but only with the ulterior motive of checking up on a gunsmith I had asked to bore out the full choke barrel of my 20-gauge Browning over and under to improved cylinder, and thus turn it into an improved modified, ruffed grouse gun. Just for fun I took my barn-blaster of a sawed off double 12-gauge Ithaca to confirm the worst.

Six shots in all were fired, four with the Browning and two with the Ithaca, at six sheets of 4 X 3 brown wrapping paper with an aiming point marked in the middle. Because both guns are ruffed grouse guns and ruffies are seldom shot at more than 30 yards, I shot from 30 yards rather than the 40 at which shotguns are routinely patterned. A glance at each pattern showed that all the shots centred slightly high, which is good for a gun intended for rising game, but five of the six were also centred slightly to the left, which is bad and confirms what I long suspected, that the standard shotgun stock is a mite too long for me.

At home I armed myself with the information from the *Upland Game Hunter's Bible* that there are 350 pellets per ounce of #7½ shot and 585 pellets per ounce of #9 shot and made the necessary conversions for the number of pellets in the total weight of each kind of shot in each shell I was using. Then I drew the traditional 30-inch diameter circle around the heaviest shot concentration on each pattern, counted the pellets that had struck within the circles, and then computed the percentage of the total shot in each shell that struck within the 30-inch circle.

The accepted standards are that at 40 yards a full choke barrel will put 65 to 75 per cent, a modified choke will put 45 to 55 per cent, and an improved cylinder choke will lay 35 to 45 per cent into the 30-inch circle.

With my new and hopefully improved cylinder barrel of the Browning at 30 yards, I put 58 per cent of the #7½ shot in the circle but, strangely, only 44 per cent of the #9 shot. Thus, at 30 yards with this barrel I am getting tight improved cylinder patterns with #9 shot and almost full choke patterns with #7½ shot. The disparity caused by shot sizes showed up also on the alleged modified choke patterns of this gun, where I put an alarming 90 per cent of the #7½ shot in the

125

circle and 71 per cent of the #9 shot.

The patterns from this "modified" barrel are just too tight for a grouse gun and are perhaps recognition of the often heard allegations that the shotcupping wads in the new ammunition will turn a modified choke into a full choke on any gun. The front trigger of the Ithaca put 63 per cent and the back trigger only 43 per cent of the #7½ shot into the 30-inch circle at 30 yards. Thus, at 30 yards I am getting great ruffie-finding, improved cylinder patterns from the second barrel, which I seldom fire, and tight modified patterns from the first barrel which I often fire, sometimes even resulting in the odd grouse.

This season I shall have to make an effort to pull the back trigger first on the Ithaca. Next season I will have about a quarter of an inch taken off the stocks of both these guns, and I will certainly have to have that modified barrel of the Browning bored out to improved cylinder.

Right now I shall fire off an irate letter to everyone's favorite ammunition firm about their discontinuing this year's shells loaded with #9 shot. After all, a man should spare nothing in his efforts to improve from an erratic to a mediocre shot.

Prairie Boy Duck

November is the time of the year in Alberta when the harvest of ducks is a feast: bushels of big northern mallards with bright orange feet just begging to be the feature presentation at a banquet. Unfortunately, the feedback I get from various former prairie boys, to paraphrase Auntie Mame, is that if the ducks are a banquet, most of the world is starving to death.

Many were the mothers, apparently, who could cook duck fit to drive wild their sons who now have wives who drive their men wild by refusing even to touch a duck, let alone cook one. In her day my own late mother served up duck to dozens of hungry hunting men and even converted a few unbelievers who felt they had been permanently turned off duck by one or more of the following popular schools of duck cookery:

1. The hang-by-the-neck-until-high-and-dropped school;
2. The infuse-with-vinegar-and-baking-soda-until-it-tastes-like-Draino school;

126

3. The wipe-its-nose-and-let-it-fly-through-a-500-degree-oven school.

Now probably many people enjoy ducks done in any one or combination of these three schools, and this column is not for them. My mother rejected the three schools and evolved her own methods. To spare me the research and because she believed a man did not have to starve if there was no woman around, she passed her methods on to me. Since that time I have had the opportunity to serve duck to some of the jurymen who partook at mother's table. The verdict? "Not proved. Call us next time you are having duck. We need more evidence."

Should the following recipes seem detailed to the ladies, remember, I am writing so that a man who does not know the difference between a pinch of salt and a half-cup of heifer-dust, could, if necessary, cook himself up a mess of ducks.

The ducks I prefer are mallards, pintails, canvasbacks, or redheads, not necessarily in that order. They should be plucked and cleaned out as quickly as possible after being harvested. Get all those pieces of lungs out! Those who believe game birds must be aged could then permit the cleaned birds to repose in the cool of a refrigerator for a day or two. I believe that ducks are ready for the pan or the freezer promptly after cleaning.

So take two to four fresh, cleaned ducks or thawed, frozen ones. If you do only one, you'll be sorry. Resolve on stuffing and roasting them in the old-fashioned manner.

First the stuffing. Chop two medium onions and a couple of stalks of celery and simmer the works in about a quarter pound of butter until onions and celery are transparent and yellowish. Then turn the heat off and throw in a good handful of fresh parsley or a couple of tablespoons of dried parsley. Add sufficient very dry breadcrumbs or cubes to make up in volume approximately what it will take to stuff the ducks you have ready. Core and dice into the mixture a couple of tart green apples with skin on. Finally, add at least a tablespoon of a good poultry seasoning or more to taste, depending on how many ducks you are stuffing. No plug is intended, but mother preferred Spice Islands poultry seasoning, and I agree. If you have some really good dried sage, the addition of a couple of pinches or so is all to the good. Mix the dressing and spices well.

Rub each duck inside and out with a quarter of a lemon and then stuff fairly firmly with the dressing. Skewer or truss, or both, each duck at the opening so the dressing will not come out as it swells. Place the ducks backside down on a rack in a shallow roasting pan so they will not swim in the pan juices. Put one cup of boiling water in the pan and place the uncovered pan full of ducks and water into an oven pre-heated to not more than 300° F and roast in this slow oven for not less than three hours. I repeat: *Uncovered!*

The ducks should be basted every half hour or so with a couple tablespoons of a good dry sherry, orange juice, or apple juice. If the basting is not enough to keep up the level of liquid in the pan, it does not hurt to add another cup of boiling water to the pan half-way through the cooking. If, toward the end of cooking, the ducks appear to be brown enough, a loose covering of aluminum foil over the pan will prevent any further tanning.

If duck gravy is desired, wait until all the liquid has evaporated and only fat and drippings remain in the roasting pan. Then remove the roasting rack and pour off and discard most of the fat. Place roasting pan over one or two stove burners, if a large pan, and, over a low heat, melt about three tablespoons of red currant jelly, and then add one can of consomme. Scrape up with a fork and dissolve the flavor-packed pan drippings as the jelly-consomme mixture simmers gently. Finally, add a couple of tablespoons of brandy, salt and pepper to taste, and remove gravy to a saucepan and let simmer. It is by no means against the law to add a small can of mandarin orange sections to this gravy, nor does a couple of scrapes of orange peel over a grater hurt at all, but such frills are not absolutely essential.

Mother always contended duck gravy was an impossible dream and was green with envy the first time she tasted this one. In fact she called me an ungrateful child for the minute or so that I refused her the recipe.

To serve duck you need only snip each one in half lengthwise down the breast and backbone and give each customer one-half complete with its one-half of the dressing, for starters. Purists say you should have mashed potatoes and a vegetable that can stand on its own roots: turnips, for example, or braised red cabbage.

There is also little harm in a glass or two of a California Cabernet Sauvignon or Pinot Noir, many brands of both of which are now available courtesy of an enlightened Liquor Control Board that knows something about both wines and pocketbooks.

Last Road Hunt

Old buddy Don Towers, county inspector, seems to have had me in hot water for allowing him to be quoted by his old buddies of the press as saying that the president of the Alberta Fish and Game Association approved of the no-shooting by-law passed November 20, 1973, by the County of Red Deer.

What I actually did, once again, was commend our county council for their modest and reasoned approach to problems and allow that Red Deer's no-shooting by-law is so reasonable, compared with the ridiculous efforts in force in other areas of the province, that I see no reason to take court action to quash those portions of the Red Deer by-law that are beyond the powers given to the county in Alberta's Municipal Government Act.

Having said that mouthful, I should hasten to explain I was encountering heavy flak even before the by-law passed and Don Towers turned me in to my tormentors. I was not aware of it, but it appears that there is a sport known as road hunting, and that the practitioners thereof fear the Red Deer County by-law was aimed primarily at them, insofar as it restricts the discharge of firearms along, from, or across developed highways.

A Red Deer professional gentleman cornered me at a party the other night and allowed it was the duty of a good citizen to ignore unjust laws and that he would road hunt nigh unto the Supreme Court if necessary. A lawyer friend moaned that the hunter is a vanishing species and he was going to take up pushing the cart in the supermarket on Saturday mornings and downhill skiing in the afternoon. Compatible activities, I would say; I saw him in full avalanche once, and he looked like a runaway hogshed with two staves loose.

The only poacher in North America who has a factory training certificate from the Cibie spotlight people, Pile O'Guts Percy, phoned from a booth and fulminated that the by-law was discriminatory. "It's getting so," he screamed above the roar of traffic, "that unless you own land in the county you can't even jack the odd deer or snare the odd grouse."

Anything that arouses such passion arouses at least my curiosity, so I went road hunting the evening before the sport was to be legislated out of existence by the county council. Six miles from Red Deer there is a little road that runs up over the side of a ridge, on the south slope of which deer have bedded in a saskatoon tangle, probably for hundreds of years. One early morning or dusk in the distant past, some road hunter bagged a deer either sneaking into bed or out to feed, and the word got out.

At 3:30 p.m. I eased my vehicle into the parade, and away we went up over the ridge, U-turn at the end, back up over the ridge, U-turn, back—and so on. When the woods, in a manner of speaking, are full of hunters, it is sometimes wise to sit beside a good trail, so I eased

129

her out of the line and parked in the approach to a farmer's field.

Bang! Bang! from behind. I dismount and go back to locate the lucky hunter. A car is parked in the middle of the road, motor running. A youth emerges from the fringe beside the road with a headless ruffed grouse, the result of the good one of two shots with a deer rifle.

"Oh, Jeez! Are these in season, Mister?"

"What are those?"

Back on my "stand" I spot a nice spike Landrover going by and watch it through the glasses. It heels over badly on the U-turn. "No cripple for me," I think, and pass up the shot. Then I hear a twig snap. The rest of the world seems soundless. I turn my eyes without turning my head and catch the flash of a Lincoln Continental with a magnificent four-point hood ornament going by full tilt. Buck fever set in, and while I debated whether to try for a carburetor or a gas-tank shot, this magnificent trophy came to the opening at the end of the trail, and, instead of making a U-turn, simply turned left and out of my life forever.

For the remaining quarter hour until shooting light was gone, I sat and cursed my nerves and clumsiness. In that time nothing of consequence went by my stand save a couple of young of the year: half-grown Japanese pick-ups. As I drove home, I mused that anyone who has not tried road hunting does not know what he is missing. Now, courtesy of the County of Red Deer, he will never have the chance to find out.

8. Grousing in Paradise

The Drums of Spring

There are a few things for which I will rise at 4 a.m. Not for ordinary fishing, although I have been known to do so to catch the tide for albacore or salmon; not generally for hunting, however, I am willing to do so anytime just to hear the Canada geese come ker-honking over the pits.

Anyone who has never heard another of nature's great sounds, the drumming of the ruffed grouse, is living in poverty; most only think they have heard, but they really haven't unless they have arrived in the grouse country to the east of Red Deer at 4:30 a.m. of a windless May morning. That is an opportunity to hear a virtuoso solo in nature's symphony for which I will gladly rise at the ungodly hours. They merely snooze who march to a different drummer.

I never really seem to hear the distant ones at first; I feel the vibration at the back of my neck, then I hear. The close ones seem to be within my own rib cage, like a pounding heart.

131

"Okay," Dave Neave decreed.

"Seven," I said.

"No, nine."

There was no argument. Dave Neave, local wildlife biologist, has been listening to ruffies drum for several more years than I have. Nine it was, an exceptional number of drum rolls for any stop on a drumming count, but glorious for the first stop on the transect.

The idea is to stop every mile on the predetermined transect; you count pheasant crows and grouse drum rolls for the first two minutes and only drums for an additional two minutes. The average number of pheasant calls and drum rolls per stop can, when a complicated formula is employed, produce a reasonably accurate estimate of density of breeding birds in the area.

Trying to pick out the distant drum rolls is like trying to appreciate only the tympani while listening to a symphony orchestra a mile away. Frogs croak, ducks splash and quack, wings whistle, redwing blackbirds swing on their rusty gates, deer snort, and at least two sections of coyote wail at each other from opposite horizons. But often enough comes the raucous solo of a cock pheasant bent on love, and many, many times come the thump... whump... whump... whump... whumpwhumpwhumpwhumpwhump indicating a male ruffed grouse has paused in strutting his log, braced his tail, fanned his ruff, stretched his neck, and walloped the air, his wings producing the thumps by breaking the sound barrier umpteen times in two or three seconds.

Just before one stop, Dave warns me there is a drumming log right beside the road. Sure enough, the first thump comes from within my chest, I look, and not 30 feet away the old cock is a brown flower on his log, so quickly do his wings beat and blur the light of a rising red sun behind him. As often as I have heard the drums of spring, never before have I seen the drummer in action. For this I would have risen even earlier and oftener.

We end the pheasant and grouse transect with 1.5 pheasant crows per stop, good for this area, and 5.7 grouse drums per stop, phenomenal for any area in any year. Even statistics exhilarate me on this May morning, for they mean to layman and scientist alike that the grouse population did not crash last winter, that there are high populations of breeding ruffed grouse in my favorite covers this spring, and that, given good hatching and brooding conditions late this month and early in June, huge populations of ruffies will buzz me crosseyed come October.

So then, to give the ears a rest, we go looking and Dave takes the opportunity to count waterfowl. You name them, they are there, even ringnecked and ruddy ducks and canvasbacks. The colors of the mallard and pintail drakes make a man want to cry. The mallard drakes are starting to hang around with the other guys down at the pothole, indicating their hens are already home brooding.

The deer display their characteristics: a whitetail crosses the road flat out and under the lower strand; two mulies graze peacefully on the new green in a stubble field, even when we get out of the truck. It is a pleasure to see them after the winter they have endured.

On this May morning everything seems to endure in spite of the news of violent peace protests that come over the radio as we head home. To discover the world is still very much alive, I will get up any day at 4:30.

Grouse Banquet

The upland game season is now open in all parts of the province, civilized and uncivilized. For the first time in many years, a little civilization is being brought to the whole procedure just by the fact that the opening comes immediately prior to the long Thanksgiving weekend, making an army of eager upland hunters thankful for the lengthy early opportunity to enjoy their sport that this weekend offers.

No doubt the majority of hunters in the area will, as usual, be vainly beating the boondocks for the exotic pheasant, while the happy minority will be going to known coverts to enjoy abundant sport with the ruffed grouse. This year, like last and the year before, the ruffed grouse is the best upland game hunting prospect in central Alberta, and the majority of hunters do not seem to know or care.

According to Dave Neave, local wildlife biologist, the ruffie is approaching the top of its population cycle and should provide excellent hunting in this area for the next couple of years until the arrival of the sudden, mysterious population crash. So dramatic has been the rise in ruffed grouse populations in this area in the past couple of years, that some veteran hunters are claiming these ruffed grouse are a new species establishing itself, especially in west-central Alberta. It seems as if, during the down years of the ruffies' 10- or 12-year cycle many of our hunters forget there is such a bird and in the plentiful years do not hunt them hard.

Dave Neave thinks there is another factor: Alberta hunters have just had it too good for too many years with the imported Hungarian partridge and the pheasant to bother about hunting ruffed grouse. Certainly the hunting of ruffed grouse out here has never attained the popularity it has in eastern Canada and the United States, where the ruffie has a deserved reputation as the king of the game birds. Out here, in fact, the ruffie has a very poor reputation as a sporting target; hunters complain that it is almost impossible to get one to fly. In this regard, the ruffed grouse is the victim of a vicious circle. He is hunted so seldom that his naturally trusting nature completely dominates his personality, and so he sits tight the few times men come poking into his thicket.

Now that the pheasants and huns have fallen on evil days for a few years, more and more hunters are turning to the ruffed grouse, and they are finding that a very little hunting turns these gentle Dr. Jekyls into the explosive Mr. Hydes of the game bird world. Hunt the same cover four or five times in the same season, and you will find that "your" birds have mastered tricks pheasants are too gentlemanly even to consider, not the least of which is bursting up with a great clatter behind you, then silently swooshing away in, around, among, and behind every bit of impenetrable brush between you and the correction line.

Dave Neave wrote his master's thesis on ruffed grouse, and he loves to hunt them. The combination of scientific and sporting interest seems to drive Dave on to encourage more hunting of a great game bird and at the same time to strive to insure a more constant supply. Actually, the two objects do not really contradict each other. Dave believes the periodic crashes of ruffed grouse population come when the population reaches its peak and result from the stresses, strains, and diseases brought on by overcrowding, and that the way to prevent the crash may be to prevent the population from reaching its peak.

An experiment is being tried this fall in an attempt to test Dave's theory. Six areas of good grouse cover have been chosen, three in the Delburne area and three in the Pine Lake area, over which grouse population trends are being determined. Two of the areas will not be hunted at all owing to difficulty of access, and the effect of heavy hunting will be measured in two other areas. "It is hoped," Dave says, "that the hunting in these other two areas will be severe enough to keep the ruffed grouse population below the peak required before a crash."

To assist his experiment in various ways, Dave is collecting the data from grouse wings from hunters in this general area. Science is wonderful. Now you can aid it and yourself and perhaps even the birds by going out and having some top sport.

Birthday Birds

On the afternoon of my late November birthday, this windbroke old columnist snuck off, in defiance of medical science, for my first ruffed rouse hunt of the now-departed hunting season. A gunsmith had finished work on my secret grouse weapon after last season's close, and it had lounged around unshot ever since. It is modelled after a custom-made grouse gun owned by a friend who never misses a grouse with it, even if he has to defoliate a swamp spruce first to get at the hurtling bird.

Like my friend's, my gun is an ancient 12-gauge Ithaca double. But to get mine like his, between four and five inches were sawed off the barrels, and then all vestige of choke was honed out to produce two cylinder barrels. This gun, loaded with low-brass shells containing 1⅛ ounces of #9 shot, is designed to plaster the whole of the proverbial broad side of a barn door at 30 paces.

All fall I have been pining to see if it would at least produce hits on one out of five flying ruffed grouse. On my birthday, two ruffies obliged by leaving their launch pads with thundering roars before I saw them. On the first, my shot killed a diamond willow thicket and, I was sure, the grouse. My companion, a kind man—and it *was* my birthday—says he heard the bird drop and flutter near him after the shot, but hunt though we did, no evidence was found. Only a possible.

On the next there was no doubt. The bird exploded from a thicket alongside a little wooded trail, to my left out over a ploughed field, a nice screen of brush between us. I swear that new gun had not even left the port arms position, so casual was the aiming, but it made a clean kill on my first grouse of the season. Such an appetizer, taken at no expense to my health, whetted my appetite for what I have been missing all fall and drove me forth on the last day of the season for a go at the fascinating sport of hunting upland game in fresh snow.

There had been fresh snow the day before and a spanking southwesterly breeze was sifting a fine skiff of snow over the

135

landscape, erasing all but the freshest tracks. In the last vestige of a sodbuster's dream of paradise we found a hunter's heaven of tracks: an ancient garden patch covering about an acre of ground on top of a knoll surrounded by a grainfield. The patch is distinguished by many exotic trees, many fruit-bearing, surrounded by about six parallel and intersecting rows of dense caragana.

Earlier that morning, perhaps even while we were there, as we later came to believe, every upland game bird from there to the correction line had gathered in convention in that sheltered paradise. So around and around we went, following those tracks through the maze, until my companion and I bumped into each other coming or going a couple of times and decided to give up. He claims pheasants were there, running us ragged, and that he saw where one had crossed his own tracks. We shall return next year, with his new dog.

In the afternoon, to finish a season that never got started, I went west of the city to a jungle of spruce, aspen, and diamond willow on the edge of an endless red willow swamp. By then the wind was gone and the sun was out, but, in all the likeliest places, all was silence and mystery: millions of grouse tracks and no grouse.

Tracks sometimes tell things even to over-civilized people. I gradually gathered that all grouse roads led to an isolated patch of willow and spruce on the sunny edge. A squirrel sputtered as I entered this patch and, when I got to the middle, he paused in his cone-munching to give me a dirty look. Bending very low to get into a willow tangle, I saw one of the brick-red brand of ruffies take two steps into the air and head for the dense spruce to the north. The new gun points fast. The first barrel got her and started another into flight to my right, which the second barrel got just as she entered a small clearing. Then all grousedom—well, six anyway—broke loose, and in a situation like that a double-gunner can only grin at them.

Besides, why push my luck? Three for the first four shots with my new gun, and a double on flying grouse on the last day of a short season. There will be time enough to ruin that record next season.

How to Hit Them

Call the birds what you will—bush partridge, birch partridge—but call the hunting for ruffed grouse this fall superb. Hunter success reports are fantastic, especially from the area north and west of Eckville all the way to Alder Flats. But as more and more converted pheasant hunters take to busting brush, two deep philosophical questions arise: how do you make a ruffed grouse fly and how do you manage to hit one with a shotgun once he does fly?

There are some obvious answers to the first question. Stubbornly roosting birds become a dream of the past once they have been hunted with any frequency, as any nervous down-easter will tell you. A good bird dog will not fail to get the grouse up in the air and generally close enough to you that you will have time to get off one shot.

Also, I fear that the lean-years habit of ground-sluicing ruffies dies hard, even in this year of abundant birds. I find that they will fly if you really give them a chance. When hunting without a dog, progress noisily through the woods and stop frequently for a minute or so; this often makes the birds so nervous that they fly away. Infallible ploys are to get engrossed in lighting a pipe or relieving one's self. Some of the most spectacular shots in outdoor sport have been made on grouse that have flown during such operations.

I believe the answer to the second question lies in an experience I had on the opening weekend of this still-young season. Twice I snapped off a shot at a grouse hurtling through the brush and had already started my string of curses when each bird crumpled and fell stone dead. No one else had fired, yet I, the world's leading expert at missing upland game, knew I shot at least two feet behind each bird. The answer is found in my new old gun, a new kind of shell, for me, and simple ballistics.

My introduction to ruffed grouse was quite recent, but I have had the opportunity to hunt them with a friend who has been shooting them ever since he was knee-high to a fire hydrant. I swear he can shoot in front of him and crumple a grouse rising behind him. His gun, an ancient 12-gauge Ithaca double, was custom-made for down-east grouse and had been in the family for years. So I located a double 12 Ithaca of the same vintage with the usual full and modified 30-inch barrels we see in this country and took it to a gunsmith, along with the friend's gun.

What I found is that the barrels on the friend's gun are bored cylinder, that is, they have no choke constriction whatever, and that mine would be the same with four inches sawed off. The result is a short, well-balanced gun that points fast: requisites for grouse shooting in the brush. Jack O'Connor, gun editor of Outdoor Life, in The Shotgun Book speaks of another requisite: "Some types of shooting demand the widest possible spread...shooting...grouse in the brush is one of them." My gun has more spread than a peanut butter factory.

Most of us are mediocre shots with a shotgun, and for some perverse reason, most of us handicap ourselves further by using full-choke guns. To understand the nature of the handicap, the fact is that most shots at flying ruffed grouse are within 20 yards, if a shot is to be taken at all. Ballistics tell the rest. At 20 yards the spread from the cylinder barrel is 32 inches and that from a full choke only 16 inches, so the chance of a hit with the cylinder barrel is twice as great as with the barrel most hunters use. And should a hit be made at 20 yards with the full choke, the result is generally grouseburger garnished with lead.

In my gun I use low-brass skeet loads with 1⅛ ounces of #9 shot. As a rule there are about 585 pellets in an ounce of #9 shot and only 225 in an ounce of #6, the most common shot size used in Alberta. One pellet will bring down a grouse and, in the brush, one pellet from a load of nines has twice the chance of one from a load of sixes to get through. Theoretically then, the cylinder barrels and the #9 shot together have made me four times as good a shot at flying grouse as I was formerly. Actually, they have made me an infinitely better grouse shot, as I used to be a dead loss and am now making enough shots to believe that ruffed grouse hunting is the greatest upland shooting sport.

The options are many. You can buy a reliable old gun as I did and have the barrel cut behind the choke or the choke reamed out, or you can have the barrel of an automatic or pump cut off and a good variable choke installed. An extra cylinder barrel can be purchased inexpensively for many of the common pumps and automatics.

The shells are available from your favorite supplier, but they will likely have to be specially ordered. Thus armed you are a new man, and the ruffed grouse—the king of the game birds—are abounding in the bush this fall, waiting for you.

9. Pheasants
and Other Phoul

Philthy Pheasants

It happens occasionally that some well-meaning but completely mistaken person refers to me as a professional hunter or fisherman, implying I possess the unspeakable aptitude of one who plays for pay. Such a charge infuriates me so that whenever it is made I feel like screaming that I will stick my ineptitude up against that of any outdoorsman anywhere any day.

As an outdoors columnist, however, I could not make such a confession, so I generally smile sweetly, say nothing, and think of those philthy pheasants. They know. I have not so much as ruffled the tail feather of a pheasant since I started writing this column. I am now well into my second season of being shut out. They are slowly driving me nuts.

Do not pat me on the head and tell me pheasants have been

scarce the past few seasons and lots of people are not getting any. They are scarce for other people. The pheasants fight for the privilege to jump up in front of my gun. It's how they get their jollies.

It all started one day two seasons ago when I missed 14 pheasants in a row, by actual count. After about the fourth miss I just knew I was going to hit nothing but fresh air as each bird got up. Since then these enterprising birds have found new and better ways to torment me. Two Saturdays ago down at Brooks, while I was driving along the road, a high wind was blowing and the roosters were flying across in front of us, on near-collision course toward us, or even alongside us, looking curiously in the windows. But they were nowhere to be found once we got out of the car, even for Susie, a dog who can smell pheasants from farther away than a perfectly aged soupbone. I reject out of hand the suggestion of a friend that I buy a convertible and start riding shotgun.

Late in the afternoon last Saturday, Susie and I were mulling over a magnificent tule patch when a nervous cock got up a long way out. I gave him both barrels anyway to try to change my luck. He laughed and flew to a hen over the hill. The shots roused three roosters, all in good range, all of whom were most disappointed that I had no shells in my gun to add a two-barrel salute to their departure.

Sunday my father and I went on an errand which took us about a mile out of Brooks and, as luck would have it, two cock pheasants paraded on the road. One went into the ditch on the left and one on the right. So I decided to play the game, drove past, stopped, and we each got out to see if we would have got them had it not been the Sabbath. Those roosters did not run back away from us but forward toward us, one flushed from the feet of each of us and straight away. Up went the imaginary guns. The Governor says he got his, but I know I missed mine.

The next day the same sort of thing happened with real guns and live ammunition, at least in my gun. I spotted three hens by the side of a road that cuts through the biggest tule patch in the country. They flew as we went by and stopped, but we went back to see if there were roosters in the bullrushes. There were. Susie rooted four out right at my feet, and all few straight away without a casualty from my two shots. Father's gun said not a word, notwithstanding that my father knows I never miss when someone else shoots the same time I do. Has he not heard me say "I got him" umpteen times when we have both shot? Father has become a hippie and opted for non-violence, or something, since he retired. At any rate, he had no shells in his gun and as those roosters got up was remarking what a fine day it was for growing tobacco.

Later in the day Susie busted another one straight away from me off a railroad track. Once again I missed and proved the truth of my father's saying: "You flock-shoot pheasants—even when there is only one of them." My own dad!

Yes, I have tried everything, almost. I have tried shooting when they are close and waiting till they get far out. No, I have little trouble with ducks and, unaccountably, less with Hungarian partridge. I have tried every gauge except 8, and every barrel choke known to man, but no choke or gauge can compensate for the way I choke when a male pheasant in full cry rises before me.

Perhaps the hippie colleague in my office has diagnosed it correctly when he says, "It's your hangup man. Those birds got you psyched." Does anyone know a good, unbiased psychiatrist, one who does not hunt pheasants? There is not room on one couch for both of us.

Tiptoe through the Tules

Late November in what used to be pheasant country. A time when every man and his dog should tiptoe through the tules: as many dogs and as many men as possible, if those tules are vast enough to look like a sea of brown bullrushes. A spanking chinook blowing, the late afternoon sky clouding in the north, the line of human heads advancing, the unseen dogs plunging and crashing ahead, marked only by the waving rushes and the occasional explosion of fluff.

Out in the tules a man has plenty of time to think if the fates so have his number that he knows no male pheasant is going to bust out in front of his gun. If that man has so recently recovered from pneumonia that his wind gives out before his legs and he has to go down to the other end and block, he has even more time to think random thoughts, perhaps even to think a column.

So you think how the tules, those huge patches of bullrushes, especially when surrounded by grainfields, are the perfect winter cover for pheasants in this northern extremity of their range, providing shelter from the icy blasts, the drifting snow, and any human or animal not willing to tiptoe in and play their game. But count how many of the great, famous tules have gone—drained, burned, and under the plow—since I went away to the big cities 14 years ago. When the tules are all gone, where will all the pheasants go?

The essential is ice. There must be ice before a man can get in there with all those birds and compete on an equal footing. A couple of us saw a venerable old roue of a rooster hop from the side of the road onto a big patch of ice in the tules. He went rump over spurs and bent his magnificent tail. Twice more he flopped, before strutting into the rushes injured dignity and all, far more concerned for image than safety.

Encouraging numbers of birds jump from this tule patch from time to time, particularly when beaters and dogs approach blockers, but a very large proportion of the birds is hens. Just south of this sea of bullrushes is the area where the second hen season in a row is being completed. I do not understand the figures, but officials in the Fish and Wildlife Division are saying their experiments are beginning to demonstrate that shooting hens has no effect on the pheasant crop produced in the wild. My prediction is that we will have a general hen pheasant season in the province within two years. Then what will happen to bedevil me in my vendetta with the pheasants? Will even the hens shun me and only meadowlarks flush within range?

Many strange pheasants are around and about, all banded, some released as a control and check on the hen pheasant experiment, others released to see if they will leave their genetic mark on the wild-bred population of Chinese ringnecks. There are Mongolians, popularly known as red rumps, examples of which have been taken this year weighing more than four pounds. There are various hybrids and mutants, one type of which is being called the green pheasant by those who have seen it, because of its magnificent green sheen.

One form of mutant, the so-called black hen, is not pleasing many sportsmen. This hen is larger and much darker than ordinary hens, some forms being pitch black. I now know of three that were shot by sportsmen who mistook them for roosters. This is an experiment become a trap, because a hen is a hen as far as wildlife officers are concerned. Yet the Fish and Wildlife Division made no effort whatever to warn Alberta hunters of the presence of these dark hens and of the dangers of mistaking them for cocks.

At any rate, about half the cocks shot by our party of six wear bands betraying their hatchery origins. Are there very few wild cocks, are they smarter, or does anybody care?

The yell from the beaters alerts me a pheasant is headed my way. My luck holds. She sets her wings and lands in the bullrushes not five feet in front of me. I am certain I hear her cluck contentedly.

Broken String

As if I were not already tense enough about the coming day's attempt to better my record, my dear old dad had to make his remark. Mac Johnston, the Governor, and I were sipping some proof against anticipated chills and mulling over a fine piece of dog work over three years ago by dad's now-departed dog Susie, which resulted in a cock pheasant falling to my gun. "That was the last pheasant you ever shot, wasn't it?" remarked the Guv. "Thirty nine-straight misses since then, isn't it?"

The realization that the old scorekeeper was right stabbed me to the bone with the task I would have the next day keeping the string intact and successfully miss my 40th straight cock pheasant. The cards are always stacked in favor of the birds in the late season when the surviving roosters are wild and wily, thereby giving me an edge in the struggle to maintain my record. My worry was that I had just been shooting too well this season, even unto getting my first limit of ruffed grouse the previous Saturday. If a man allowed lapses like that to become a habit, he just might accidentally hit one of those cock pheasants. Face it, I thought, you are not up to it; somehow you are deficient in that absolute confidence to miss which marked the shots taken at those previous 39.

Friday morning was good and bad. Plum was having his first bash at pheasants and being led merrily on scenic tours of far townships. When he did pin one down, nobody believed him or we would see a rooster purring on a farmer's doorstep—good things which meant that the birds were as tough as ever, so tough in fact that I did not fire a shot. Which is bad: shooting is essential to missing.

After lunch we were hunting out some small tule patches, places where a man takes a big risk of getting a good shot at a rooster. Plum hove up beside me on the downwind side of a tangle of sweet clover growing on the edges of the tules and slammed on point so hard he resembled a concertina at half mast. He quivered like a banjo string, you could have knocked his eyes off with a stick, and other trite expressions from pointing dog literature.

"What's he doing?" asked his owner.

"Pointing," I observed, then crooned "Whoa...whoa," to the dog, like it says in the best books on the subject. I took two steps, the pheasant screamed the usual obscenities and headed west. Secure in the knowledge that good old Mac was about to shoot also, I touched off the first barrel. The bird folded and Plum nabbed him.

"Nice shot," Mac said.

I was enraged. "You got him! You got him!" I screamed.

143

Mac insisted he had missed, that the bird took at least six wingbeats after he shot and folded when I shot. Then the Guv had to put in his two bits worth and agree with Mac, and I had to give in knowing, as I did, that dad was objective and cherished every one of those previous 39 misses almost as much as I did myself. So, as they say in the sporting world, I hit that 40th bird on a lousy judgment call. Thus, in a trice, are records broken, strings snapped.

Actually an incident that next morning revealed the extent of the loss of all my "moves". Mac and I, with the dog, were driving a ditch toward dad, blocking the end. There was a little slough where the ditchbank had broken near the end, and the Guv said he was sure he had seen something sneak out of the ditch and then heard claws on the ice. So I swung around to the end of the slough and was minding my business near a tiny patch of bullrushes when Plum, hotter than a pistol, swung around and ran over that patch, remembered something, and started to come back. The rooster wiped my nose and headed for Tilley.

Now I know I was not on that bird. So much do I know it that I was already planning how I would miss my second shot. But the first one folded him, and Plum wagged his way over the prairie to retrieve. Nobody else had shot or was even close enough to shoot; nobody but me to blame. Thus do champions fade away.

Actually, a new string may be starting. Dad missed one rooster out the end of a ditch when a small piece of paper interfered with the action of his gun just enough to prevent it from cocking. Then, in the late afternoon of the second day, the Guv announced he was tired and would stay in the car while Mac and I went to drive a ditch, but promised to get out, walk 10 feet, and block the end as soon as we came in sight.

A quarter mile from the end, we heard a cackle and a rooster flew out and by the car. No shot. A hundred yards or so and another one cackled at the car as he flew out the end. Again, no shot.

He had been sleeping like a babe in that car, but I suspect that last cock sounded off just enough to wake him, as the Guv was sitting up and ready to take nourishment when we arrived.

I have run my string. From record setter to statistician: now I am counting. Great gaudy roosters, how I am counting!

The Sick Parade

Over the years my annual safari into the pheasant lands of the deep south have been many things, but seldom pheasant hunting trips. This year's was a highly-organized sick parade.

Four days before departure I came up with one of those very localized infections in one of those locations where it is nothing but decisions, like whether it is less painful to stand or sit. For the past three weeks I have been battling with the latest affliction of my hypochondriac Brittany pup, Quince. This time it is coccidiosis, a well-know poultry disease. I had poured enough "gripper" into that pup that he should have squeaked when he walked and solidified on point. But he didn't, up to the time we left anyway.

We were going down to hunt with my father, as usual. But this year the Governor had not picked up his musket since having been separated from his gall bladder in late September. Mac Johnston was relatively clear of eye, which worried me somewhat, as did the fact that Mac's contrary Brittany, Plum, seemed to be in a good humour. Young Iain suffered a bad case of the "when I grow ups," brought on by fatigue from sleepless anticipation of his first major expedition. All in all, it was a ragtag platoon to throw up against the battalions of late season pheasants alleged to be gnashing their beaks in the coverts around Brooks.

It is a fact generally accepted by game managers that 90 per cent of the pheasants bagged are taken in the first two weekends of the season and the rest are bagged by about 10 per cent of the hunters throughout the entire remainder of the season. Mac and I are by no means in that elite 10 per cent, but we enjoy hunting more than we do shooting pheasants, and we wanted to see what our dogs would do with the cagey, late-season birds.

Up the first ditch Quince got on a bird, pointed, then looked guiltier and guiltier as he realized the bird had slipped away. We short-cutted across some oat stubble, he pointed again, I told him to go on, he did, and away went a rooster as big as a turkey cackling gleefully. He was in range, but I let him go. Quince watched me as I looked guiltier and guiltier.

Just after noon Mac shot a cock and Quince made a spectacular long retrieve on a runner. The Guv had found he was fit to shoe horses, and late in the day he got a bird over an excellent point by Plum. I still had nothing and was getting ready to go soak my localized infection when we saw a rooster scale into a swale surrounded by barley stubble. Plum and Mac went around the one side and Quince and I around the other; we barely got started when that rooster flew wild.

Quince started beating that stump of a tail, then wiggling his hips on the stubble between the swale and a ditch. He went on point several times but was learning to relocate moving birds and moved up quickly each time. Unaccountably that rooster decided things were too hot, even before he reached the ditch, and flushed with a great clatter. It was a long shot and the light was bad, but I downed the rooster just like I knew what I was doing.

The next day was a disaster. Quince had thrown off his affliction, and both dogs were hunting well. We discovered that the trouble with the beautiful cover on government land near Millicent is that it is hunted so much that the birds clear out until the season is over. We started to find birds on other, more remote land. Twice Quince pointed roosters perfectly. I stepped in to flush and missed them going straight away. Once the second barrel refused to fire. Once I refused an excellent crossing shot because I knew a horse and rider were in the near vicinity. Even Mac missed a couple of fine shots.

Then the Guv flushed a couple of roosters out of stubble as he was crossing the field to meet me. Up to that time he had said he did not know whether the second barrel worked on his new Beretta Silver Snipe, as he had never used it. This time both his barrels worked, but not on the birds, and I missed an excellent but hurried first shot, really got my head down for the second, and nearly got a hernia pulling on a trigger that would not fire. I figured out why that second barrel would not fire and fixed it just as a covey of huns buzzed up. I carefully picked two birds and missed the first one twice. By that time we just knew the birds had us on the run.

Quince was so disgusted he got on a live one and decided to catch him by his own efforts. In the process he nearly trampled to death two other very startled roosters. He came back grinning just like the fool his master felt, and the whole body of boneheads called it a day.

The next day came up glare ice, fog, and drizzle. To most pheasant hunters this means futility in solving the mystery of where the birds are. We did find three or four hens that we declined to shoot. We also got soaked hunting a tule patch so thick you couldn't see your hand in front of your face. In there Mac scratched down a couple of long shots, and we could not find the birds, the first we lost since we got the dogs. This so discouraged us that we went off and hunted cover we knew contained no birds on such a day.

But the trip was a success. Three days of exhausting misery restored everyone's health and made the Guv decide he will not again consider quitting hunting until he is 80. It also restored the faith that will bring me back next year: that after 20 years of hunting pheasants, as a man and as a boy, I still know absolutely nothing about it.

Going to the Dogs

This year my annual late-season foray into the southlands went to the dogs. Oh, we went to Brooks all right, Mac Johnston, his son Iain, and me, just as we have for the past two or three years, about the middle of November.

The roosters were just as hard, if not harder, to come by as they have been in late season in past years, which is really why we go then: for hunting where the competition with game is keen and non-existent with other hunters. This year's story is really the workmanlike performance of Plum, Mac Johnston's agressive Brittany and my Quince, Plum's son out of Ron Vanson's Toni.

Things did not look too good right at the start. I caught Quince bumping a hen pheasant. He got hot on the bank of a draw where there wasn't enough vegetation to cover a mealy-bug. Just as I saw the hen crouched about 10 feet from me, Quince broke a quick point, scooped the bird into the air himself, and then ran her to the correction line. I went by the book, stood right where I was, fanned the pup's fanny when he came back, set him up on point, and for five minutes told him what a marvel of perfection he was as I tried to knee him forward into that hen's scent. He would not budge.

Later Plum bayed like a blue tick hound on a hot scent. While Mac writhed, I found the dog solidly on point and obviously cursing the wise old rooster that had simply walked away from him. About two minutes later I writhed as my own dog roared from further down the ditch at a big rooster who flew out from under his point and safely away.

Iain earned his supper spotting three roosters sunning themselves high on a poplar deadfall beside an old stock pond. We surrounded nothing, as so often happens with pheasants, and Quince just disappeared. Mac found the dog in a strange posture and when he moved up ahead of the dog was astonished to flush a huge rooster that provided an easy shot. A wonderful experience for my old buddy, who also did not recognize the first point Plum ever made on a rooster and which I shot three long years ago.

Then Mac and I moved up a ditch, Plum working in close and Quince making a wide cast and coming back toward us, upwind, along the edge of the ditch. Suddenly Quince pointed and Plum, bless his black old soul, froze on point himself, honouring his pup's point like a southern gentleman pointer or the more aristocratic English setter. It was a picture I kick myself for not taking, especially as I carried an excellent camera. Instead, I stepped ahead of Quince, flushed a young rooster, took my first shot of the day, and dropped him.

Mac and I are pretty now-and-again about blocking ditches, but after the first day, when umpteen roosters ran out the other end on us, we decided to block the first ditch we got permission to hunt early next morning. Mac let me out and drove to the other end. Better we should have stayed in bed or at least employed our usual slipshod practices for, with Mac on deck, we would have had roosters galore right off. No sooner had I started up the canal bank when my contemplation of my aches and pains was broken by the deep silence. Quince's bell had stopped ringing! There he was, on the other side, in heavy weed at the edge of some wheat stubble, rock on point. I arrived there about two minutes later, blowing like a beached whale.

When I stepped ahead of the dog, a rooster fanned me as he jumped and went back over my left shoulder, gaining altitude and going downwind like a windmill. My first shot was just a howl of surprise and, as I lined up for my second and last shot on a lost cause, another rooster cackled and went straight away behind my back. Instead of turning and taking the easy shot, I just let go at the wide world. "Sorry, old Quince," I muttered as I stood in place and reloaded.

Right then Quince was about to give me the reward for being steady as he was to wing and shot. He just did a 10-foot circle down and then upwind, and locked on point again. "They were there, but they're gone," I told him. He insisted, so I stepped ahead of him and out went another rooster three feet over the stubble and curving to the left. I have missed so many shots exactly like that on ruffed grouse that I must have been due. Quince delivered the huge late-season rooster to me, as he did another about 500 yards down the canal.

But faithful readers ask, what's this? How can a man who once chalked up a record of 39 straight misses on pheasants and was honest enough to report it suddenly report he has hit three out of five? Simple. I was finally driven to such desperation that I took my own advice and started shooting a double 12-gauge with two cylinder barrels, no choke at all. Obviously the wide, even pattern of this gun compensates for the mediocrity of my skills on wing-shooting pheasants, especially when shooting quickly at close birds, just as it does when I shoot ruffed grouse. Good thing, too. I don't know what those dogs would do next to get me a few pheasants.

A Limit of Misses by 4 p.m.

Most of the handful of hunters that braved the opening of pheasant season near Brooks last weekend were wearing wide grins and noting that the death knell of the pheasant in Alberta may have been sounded prematurely, at least for this area. Each opening weekend for the past few years, I have mounted a safari, the purpose of which always turns out to be to further educate the philthy-minded pheasants of this area. I was raised here and have been a pheasant phanatic for many years, but never have I obtained the nirvana often heard of "getting my limit by 10 o'clock". Somehow to a person who hunts pheasants that nirvana, like most accounts of paradise, sounds dull.

This year my expedition scored a first, a new nirvana for dedicated pheasant hunters: we had missed a limit of absolute cinch shots by 4 p.m. on opening day. My companions were the Uncle Ben of Red Deer recreational vehicle fame, his eldest boy Rob, my father the Guv, and Quince, my four-year-old Brittany. Rob was shooting a single-shot .410, and in the morning the perverse pheasants were giving him most of the action. Just not to let Rob get all the credit, I must say that I personally missed four of the finest shots I have had in at least 20 years of dedicated pheasant missing.

In the afternoon I outfitted Rob with one of my 12-gauge doubles, and after that the pheasants were much more wary of his part of the boondocks. It was in the afternoon, too, that old Quince pinned a rooster at his siesta on the south slope of a ditchbank. As it happened, this old boy, surrounded by our entire outfit, shrieked his outrage and headed straight at me. I dropped to my knees, touched off the first barrel and somehow, perhaps the jar of the drop to my knees, my usual grooved swing was so unhinged that I hit the bird. It turned out to be about the fifth pheasant I can ever remember losing when hunting with a dog.

Actually, after the earlier display of shooting, I suspect Quince did not really believe a bird had been grassed. My companions spend a goodly amount of time hunting for the bird, grumbling all the while about the trouble caused by someone who would actually hit one. The lost bird just typified for me the kind of luck we were having on opening day.

It appears that most Alberta hunters were sufficiently disappointed by the disaster of a pheasant season last year that they just did not turn out this year for the annual extravaganza. The handwriting on the wall was writ in the neon "vacancy" signs of Brooks' finest motels on Thursday and Friday evenings. Vacancies are just unheard of

149

down here on the eve of a new pheasant season.

The absence of hunters surprised me, as about 10 days before the season the rumor was rampant that 7,000 birds were being released in this area. Chief Provincial Wildlife Biologist, Dave Neave, soon laid that one to rest when he told me that the total number of pheasants the Fish and Wildlife Division has is 7,000, that 3,500 must be held for breeding stock, and of the 4,000 available for stocking, very few would be released in the Brooks area, which had been less hard hit by last year's decline than more southerly regions. The official word notwithstanding, a Brooks gas pump jockey knowingly told me I was seeing so many more birds this year than last because "they" let more go this year.

The second afternoon of the season I hunted virtually alone, as the Guv had been cross-checked by his new Lab pup and had a bum knee. So the Guv mostly drove Old Jeep while I walked and watched Quince hoover the ditches. Quince was in top form and, in spite of brisk winds, showed me more pheasants than I have seen in many a long day of pheasant hunting. The pup also had three perfect points on cocks. Only once did I foul up and not get the bird for him, and that was the one that flew straight away, the safest place in the universe when I am doing the shooting.

One of the cocks came straight up at me out of a tangle of tumbleweed and corkscrewed up out over a full stock pond, where he accidentally ran into my shot charge and dropped into the middle of the very deep and very stagnant water. Quince hates to retrieve almost as much as he hates to swim with anyone other than my kids. We had a very serious discussion, and the dog seemed suddenly to make up his mind and quickly executed a water retrieve that made up in result what it lacked in style.

All that second day success drew me a trip to the people who clean birds, and they assured me that lots of pheasants were being brought in and the hunters were happy. On the Sabbath I socialized a little and confirmed that the hunters were pleased both with the number of birds they were seeing and with the absence of other hunters, particularly non-residents, who are barred this year for the first week of the season.

Back to opening day. Uncle Ben missed our limit or 12th bird at 4 p.m., and we withdrew to celebrate in triumphant disarray. The brightest thing I did all day was opt out of the evening duck shoot Ben had laid on. He and his boys and brother-in-law spent till midnight unsticking the truck they borrowed to pull out the jeep they had sunk to the gunwales in an innocent patch of alkalai. Then they spent most of the next day jerking the jeep to shore. I've always said opening days were for the birds.

New String

Things started as usual for the hunting version of the keystone cops I annually assemble for opening day of the pheasant season. First off, my Brittany, Quince, vanished into the grass that seems taller than ever this year. Silence. Instead of going to find him, I blew the whistle; he came, but not before he ran to me right over and flushed the cock he had been pointing.

To get even, Old Quince roared off out of range and joyfully scooped another cock into the air. Then the dog went solidly on point in the midst of willow thicker than the hair on his own back. In I plunged, but not before suggesting to the Guv that he mosey out to where had had a clear view of the nether side of the thicket whence, most assuredly, a male pheasant would soon emerge. Out went the bird, cursing and cackling. So clear a view did the Guv have that he did nothing but admire that bird clean out of sight. That was one free for each of us, and in the meantime the other members of our party were missing pheasants hither and yon, as could be understood by the shots followed by loud protestations of "Oh fudge," etc.

So we regrouped and went over the same ground. Quince went on point for me, out went the cock, and I got him! Nothing really. A pheasant is supposed to be an easy target, but for me to get the first pheasant offered is an event: through the latter part of the 1967 season, through the 1968 and 1969 seasons, I missed 39 straight pheasants by count meticulously audited by the Guv. Pheasants had me psyched. Every time a bird got up, I knew I was going to miss. It was terrible. Here I had a fine pheasant dog coming along, and he had a boss who could hit nary a pheasant. My head was candled by sympathizers, both professional and amateur. I tried shotguns with so little choke that you had to be careful of taking too wide a stance for fear of clipping your toenails. Things got a little better last year, but still, on my last hunt of the season, three of us missed a limit of birds.

The pup was supposed to reach his prime this season, and he was already too good a dog for the lousy shot I was two seasons ago! In desperation I turned to skeet. Maybe it was working. On opening day my party picked up a few more birds, and I got two more without a miss. The next day I hit a limit, again without a miss, and the pressure was beginning to mount. Quince saved me after I touched one off at number six, a shot I would formerly have considered impossible for me, though the bird was in range. I had turned away and was contemplating the end of the string when old Quince hove up behind, bearing a beautiful cock bird. Shortly after that, the dog picked up and delivered a young cock that held too well to the dog's point.

The wind became a factor for all Alberta pheasant hunters throughout the opening days of the season, and we did not truly know how good or bad the 1975 season was until the hunters got a few complete calm days. Pheasants are notoriously nervous, prone to run, and reluctant to fly when the winds are blowing. The winds appear to have blown throughout the prime Alberta pheasant areas, and the reports I have are that the birds are in fair numbers in the Eastern Irrigation District, the Taber area, and scarce in the Lethbridge and Claresholm areas.

Friday a regular in my group of pheasant fanatics, Mac Johnston of Red Deer, turned up. So did the wind turn up to "whar's the barn" intensity, all day long instead of just in the afternoon. All day we managed one pheasant on which we were both credited with a hit. That evening was calm briefly, and we each got a cock. My eighth straight was over a point of my own dog that I will remember long after Quince himself is a memory. He first winded that bird half a mile from where he finally pinned him, in the last clump of willow in the corner of the stubble just where miles of prairie start. The dog had almost passed the bird, and bent his body into a U coming back to point. The shot was the simple straight away that I had missed by the dozen in the bad old days.

The next morning it was quiet briefly, and Mac Johnston ran his string to three straight then unaccountably stood numb and allowed another to fly gleefully away from him. Quince went on a long run and eventually presented me with a big male pheasant with a broken wing that someone had lost the day before. As the wind was approaching the gale intensity it reached on Saturday, Quince pinned a big cock just at the end of the ditch. I refused a good shot because a farmhouse was close and I believed our car to be on the other side of the bush—not because I was afraid to put my record on the line, with the bird twisting and skewing in the wind.

On the last run of the day, before the winds blew us homeward, Quince took off baying after a fleeing wraith. I have burned him out on rabbits, but training a dog off tumbleweeds is ridiculous. Just before we were to get in the car for the long trip home, the dog rolled luxuriously in the most fragrant cowflop from here to the correction line.

Sunday at the Red Deer Gun Club I had the worst two rounds of skeet I have ever shot. All of which must prove that middle-aged dogs and men feel most comfortable with the old tricks.

10. Duck!

Duck Days

"Ducks won't fly in the fog," Mac Johnston announced. The Governor and I nodded wisely at this conventional wisdom.

From his cage in the back, Old Plum, Mac's Brittany, moaned, whether in anticipation of the dreary day we were about to have staring eyeball-to-eyeball with the socked-in ducks or just at the whole concept of duck hunting in general, is not known. Plum is a fiendish grouse and pheasant aficionado, to whom ducks are simply critters that tumble from the sky without being hunted and then hold well for a point, most being dead on arrival.

Down beside Sylvan Lake it was still unaccountably foggy when you consider that a north wind was blowing that would etch glass. An unpromising duck day was getting better and better as that wind blew conventional wisdom and huge flights of ducks hither and yon wherever we looked, and the fog be damned.

Plum was leashed for the mile walk through those grousey

153

woods in order to assure ourselves of his doubtful services on the ducks. Once he hopefully turned right angles to the trail, and snapped on to one of his rare points and certainly his finest point, at a rabbit. At the start we were wishing fervently for our Stanfields' Red Labels, but after lugging decoys, lunch, guns, etc., through those sheltered woods, we were glad to have been more lightly armoured by the time we reached the point.

While we set out the decoys on the windward side, the wind gusted up a bit and blew in still more fog. Still, it was practically bluebird weather as far as ducks go. And go this year's legion of mallards did, formation after formation of them, swooshing downwind fit to pop a gunner's discs as he swung with them. The decoys were a little light and bobbed treacherously in the chop like the false flotsam they were. The ducks were not decoying well, and the shooting was positively mediocre. Chained as we are to two canine upland game hunting specialists, Mac and I have not hunted ducks much in the past couple of years. Things like angles and shot drift in the wind are merely bad jokes to us in our annual free-style mallard harvest.

Despite eight casualties, about noon it became obvious that the fat mallards had no intention of giving up the laughs they got every time they buzzed our decoys. It also became obvious they would get few more laughs and we would get even fewer ducks unless we got more ammunition. Powder-monkey Mac, owner of the car parked a mile away, got elected for the run to Sylvan Lake for more powder and shot. While he was gone, the weather got better and better: the wind edged around a little more from the north, and it started to snow. I began to groove my swing, centred a couple of drakes, and blissfully waded over the top of my hip boots while retrieving one of them. The adage is that no man is so unhappy as a wet fisherman, unless it is a dry hunter. Besides, the true insulating qualities of pure wool logger's pants cannot be appreciated unless they are soaking wet.

With my boots immersed in eight inches of ice water so there was no danger of the gallon or so of water in each of them warming up in the slightest, facing an icy sleet now being driven by a gale, I sighed in satisfaction that at last it was a perfect duck day. Suddenly, three mallards started their descent into our decoys. It took the only two shots I had left to harvest the drake. "Why didn't you get all three?" someone shouted.

Baby Huey—so called in these columns before to protect the guilty—Grand Marshall of the Marshlands, had arrived with his army. Out streamed a fleet of a thousand decoys, just downwind of ours, and the first duck to drift over was given a 21-gun salute as impressive as it was harmless. Does a man good to see shooting just as bad as his own accomplished with a flair by five practitioners.

About the time Mac and Plum came back after having had to go all the way to Red Deer to get the 16-gauge shells the Guv and I use, the army had found the range. Huey waded half way to the Sylvan Lake wharf half a dozen times, as he demonstrated retrieving to the bemused 10-month golden retriever he fondly calls Ginnie.

Huey called her a few other things, and not really fondly at all, when that ungrateful blond wench, ice water to her shapely withers, began cavorting amorously in the reeds with our Plum. Actually, it was the first time old Plum's teeth had stopped clacking like the percussion section of a Mexican street orchestra. Even he began to think there was something in this duck hunting after all.

Ill Wind and Ducks

Number me among the nobodies who were blown some good by Saturday's ill wind. Ill wind! It was the premiere of winter 1966, which blew in on a 60 miles per hour wind about 4 p.m. as I stood with a father, a friend, and an exotic mixture of black Lab and Weimaraner named Suzy on a point jutting into a southeastern Alberta lake. Before the wind came we watched flocks of mallards go by over the water, far out of range.

The north wind fixed everything. For one thing, the ducks were coming from the south, which meant that the gale need not be faced. Parkas that had been soaked by the rain all day soon froze, so we stood facing south, listening to the sound, like hail on a bucket, of snow pellets hitting frozen parka hood, and watching for the flocks of ducks appearing like fine black lace against the glowering sky.

As they came, the ducks would hang over the edge of that cliff of wind, bobbing and weaving, zigging and zagging, spilling air from their wings to let themselves down. Their path would often be low over our point, and the guns would speak to the howl of wind and the rustle of rushes. Shouts of surprise would get lost in the wind as the hunters discovered that the ducks were really moving north and the shot was blowing south. Finally, a lead of about 20 feet was fixed on, and a few ducks started to fall. Then Suzy, clad in armour of ice, went gleefully to work, picking her way out onto the ice, plowing through the whitecaps, searching the rushes, delivering each duck with much pride. It was the kind of hunt that warms the heart of every duck hunter, and it came with that sad event, the arrival of winter. It came late last Saturday, but early enough to save a black day.

Something has decimated the once great pheasant population of the Eastern Irrigation District to the point where the normally amiable residents speak bitterly of the release near Strathmore, just before the season opened, of nearly 1,000 pheasants from the hatchery at Brooks for the benefit, mostly, of Calgary hunters. Rumours of a hen pheasant season near Scandia this year have annoyed many locals who argue that hens should never be killed, especially in a year when the population could stand some building up.

At any rate, our party scoured the willows, slogged through the tules, and walked the ditches all last Saturday in the EID, and saw five hens and two cocks in range and three cocks that ran and flushed a mile away. To make matters worse, it was cold and rained all day, conditions neither conducive to getting the pheasants flying nor to Suzy's being able to scent the birds holding tight.

It was a day for ducks, and at 3 p.m., after getting dry britches all around, we decided to hunt them at the point already described. It was early yet, so my friend and I decided to take one more crack at pheasants. We hadn't yet encountered either of those cocks that flushed in range, so we took Suzy to hunt the tules that go all the way up one side of the lake. Leaping and weaving back and forth in front of us, Suzy immediately flushed a hen, then about halfway down the lake, got as excited as only running roosters can make her. About then we met another hunter, a stranger who asked the usual question. Suzy continued to study the puzzle of the vanishing rooster as we told the stranger how paltry our luck had been and regaled him with bloodthirsty promises of how fast the first rooster to show himself to us would join his ancestors.

Sixty-seven seconds later a huge old rooster who had overheard everything nearly tipped me over as he burst from the tangle at my feet. He headed straight away over a mud flat, and made such a liar of me that I bet neither of my shots so much as showed up on his radar. My companion, courteous to a fault and having misplaced confidence in my marksmanship, missed a late crossing shot. Another rooster, having heard three shots and having calculated one empty gun, exploded from under my left fallen arch and flirted his tail as he cruised east over the tules. My gun was empty and my companion did not fire as the rooster was directly between him and the stranger, who missed as the bird went by him. There is some justice in the world, for I would have retired had the stranger hit.

My father, the humourist, had heard the thunder of guns followed by curses, and his inquiry about excuses hurt not half so much as the pain on Suzy's face. But then the wind, the winter, and the ducks came, and Suzy started speaking to us again.

Return to Pneumonia Point

One year after my defeat and retreat, I returned to Pneumonia Point. Last fall I was setting out decoys off a point in a likely slough when I stepped into a hole and foundered to the withers in very cold and fertile water indeed.

My companions, one of whom I shall call the Vulgar Boatman, the other learned in medicine, would not paddle me back to the mainland in the canoe, so I stayed soaked all afternoon and incubated what turned out to be pneumonia. Local humourists named the location Pneumonia Point, completely ignoring the fact I also seemed to have incubated the seven-year itch. Paddling back in the clammy dark, between sneezes, I vowed a solemn vow: I would return.

So about a week ago the boss looked up to find the lower ranks had defected to Pneumonia Point and, hopefully, ducks. The assault force was formidable. There was the Vulgar Boatman again who, a week after events here related, was to rise from where we sat watching a small boy catch fresh-water shrimp, fire one barrel, run like hell, and yell "Duck!" just as a falling gadwall took the ash off my cheroot. In addition we had Cousin Weakeyes, Baby Huey, and myself, windbroke as always, but recovered from all the pneumonia and one year of the itch.

We go by land this time, not by sea, in a beautiful peagreen jeep which has probably been salvaged after abandonment during the retreat from that famous Pacific isle during the war to which general what's-his-name vowed that he, too, would return. The jeep's transfer case tells the story, howling uphill and humming downhill.

Cousin Weakeyes and Baby Huey own genuine doggy-type retrievers of great ability, or so the owners say at coffee hours and other events where only the truth is told. The Vulgar Boatman and I generally rely on small boys in two pair of pants, long poles, and canoes to retrieve for us. Apparently, the canines are not to be subjected to our bad influence: dogs are left home and the canoe rides on top.

Baby Huey, a fine broth of a lad, proves he can carry one end of a canoe, two bags of decoys, his gun, and then one string of ducks. He can't be all bad, though; he shoots a double gun. Offers a dollar, Huey does, on the first duck. Pessimist in all other things though, our Huey, especially whether or not the ducks will arrive.

Right smart like I "take" Consumption Hill. From high and dry I can see and hear just fine. Just after the decoys are out, two or three ducks are downed. Huey is astonished, for all he gets is sunburn, on the roof of his mouth. Nobody gets a dollar. Cousin Weakeyes and Huey coo away, trying to coax me down into the water, mud, and reeds with them. I'm OK, thank you. Huey makes another pitch, and the Vulgar Boatman gives him hell for spoiling the harmony on the duck calls of the maestros in the woodwind section. "Action's all over, anyway," moans Huey, for the umpty-eleventh time.

One scotch duck call dangles in the drink. "Squee! Squee!" it cries. A cruising marsh hawk looks for the rabbit in distress. All the planning pays off. When the sun sets, the ducks come.

"Heads up, here they come!"

"Where? Where?"

"South! Aww! They're gone!"

"Geez! Name the direction!"

"Going to or coming from?"

Weakeyes swears by quantity: he always shoots his automatic three times, followed generally by Huey with his two big booms and one "I got him!" Love that kid. That's just how I get my pheasants.

Or maybe he has to shoot alone: Whump! Whump! "Heiferdust! Can't you guys re-load faster than that? Scammell, get down here!" Not a chance.

But there's ducks down anyway, probably died laughing, and the Boatman launches in the last light to pick up ducks and decoys. I see him lose the paddle and marvel at the skill with which he flails the water with his hand to get to it again.

On the duck hunter's calendar this is the year of the shoveller, as the canoe is loaded with these teal-like ducks with sinus trouble. "It's okay," says Weakeyes. He has a friend who needs bushels of spoonies for Spoonbill Gai Kue and other exotic recipes. There are also scaup, widgeons, even a few mallards. I have one huge canvasback in the pot. Roasted and stuffed with sauerkraut, I will not trade it for all the teal in China.

What is more, so far not a sneeze, sniffle, rattle, or hack. But I do seem to have this trouble stopping giggles.

A Night at the Opera

Perceptive readers have noted that sometime between the end of good fishing and the start of good, festive socializing, I must do something to reinstate my hunting licence. This year it was a weekend trip to visit friends in Edmonton, with one evening spent at the opera. I dutifully removed from Old Jeep all impedimenta of the sporting life and refurbished it for the transport of one wife, two small children, and the incredible trappings thereof. After all, I am a man of intense concentration: when I hunt, I hunt; when I opera, I operate.

The trouble is that I am mere chaff before the wilful winds of fate. In 1967, for example, I took Herself to Expo and was positively mortified by all the prospects for good fishing I found right on the Expo site. Last weekend we were staying with old friends, Chief Provincial Wildlife Biologist Dave Neave and his wife, Nancy, and I felt the first puff of a fateful wind as soon as I broached their threshold in Edmonton. "Where's the dog?" Dave asked in an astonished and aggrieved fashion. Now, Old Quince, not being an opera buff, was at that very moment back in Red Deer languishing in his two-room split-level kennel.

As it turned out, Dave and I had not had time to communicate, and somehow the subject of hunting had not come up between the ladies in their planning of the weekend. Nevertheless, a trip had been laid on to commence at 5 a.m. to demonstrate to me the tremendous hunting pressure and other problems faced by the urban-based hunter. The immediate problem for this newly urban-based hunter was simply one of outfitting. Boots from here, a union suit from there, even borrowing a shotgun from Fish and Wildlife Division Director Gordon Kerr, and I was set.

I am one of the sane among us who knows that pre-dawn is not the best time of the day, that rising early is really essential only to deer hunting and Pacific salmon fishing, but everyone but me and the ducks knows you must get up early to go duck hunting. Such bitter thoughts were kept down by a twinge of enthusiasm and wonder that this was to be my first duck hunt of this waning season.

At the appointed hour, we met Brent Markham, habitat wildlife biologist with the Alberta government, and Bob Urquhardt, a draftsman. While my companions debated the relative merits of this swamp, whether the moon was in the right phase for that spot, or whether there would be hordes of hunters somewhere else, I just drove through the gloom.

Eventually we arrived at DeMay Lake, a shallow, periodic lake with fences criss-crossing it far out in the water. The rising sun glinted nicely off the exotic dome of the church at Round Hill. Out went a fleet of about 30 decoys, and I shook hands with Gordon Kerr's shotgun, a venerable Model 12 Winchester, and grinned at the fun that gun was going to have with me. The plain fact is that I have never so much as fired a pump gun, having been weaned on double-barrels with tang safeties. In fact, as I recall it, I have fired only one rifle with the same cross-bolt safety at the front of the trigger-guard as that sported by the model 12.

For the first duck I was ready. I shot, nothing happened, and then the mallard crashed stone dead in the middle of the lake. One piece of equipment I had been wise enough not to accept was chest waders, so Dave waded half-way to Round Hill for that one. Some day I will do a scientific treatise on my observations that day of the best way for a man to negotiate a barbed wire fence while both man and fence are awash to the withers in water.

Then my troubles started. I tore the ligaments in my trigger finger and developed a hernia pulling up on decoying ducks and on a safe trigger. Next I wore a hole right through the thumb of a new deerskin shooting glove "thumbing" for the absent safety on the tang of that model 12.

Eventually I was getting the first shot off and even knocked over a mallard or two. The alleged second shot then became the laugh riot of the swamplands. If you have ever seen a trombone man trying to pump a double-barrel, you know the embarrassment of a double-trigger, double-barrel man leaning into the expected second shot while trigger-finger waves around under his chin looking for a second trigger that just isn't there. Finally, I mastered pumping that old corn-sheller, but not before I pumped it with the trigger held down once and did in a mallard coming in at 11 o'clock rather than the one I had in mind at 5 o'clock.

It was bluebird weather, but M'Lord Mallard was keeping banking hours. When we got smart and built blinds and got our decoys out on the lee of a spanking breeze that came up about noon, we got good action from ducks decoying well to Brent's fine calling. They were still filtering in about 2:30 when we had to leave. The only example of hunting pressure I had been shown was a venerable native farmer's assistant who spent some time doing a stalk on our decoys.

We had some excellent mallards and good laughs in shirt-sleeve weather, and I even parted with that model 12 reluctantly, having eventually touched off a shot or two the results of which showed me why thousands of shotgunners worship their shiny model 12's. What is more, I remained bolt-upright and staring awake that evening through four acts of *Carmen*.

11. To the Dogs

Kindergarten

With upland game season opening next Friday and the whole country a-boom with ruffed grouse, the full tragedy has just struck me: the only grouse I will get this season will have to expire of its own hilarity. What will keep me from getting the birds is my acquisition of what purports to be a bird dog, and Mac Johnston, with whom I customarily hunt grouse, having what I know is a bird dog, alas, in his second season.

Let me explain. Mac's Brittany spaniel, Plum, last season gleefully flushed every ruffed grouse from here to the correction line for us, most within range, and retrieved every one of the over 50 ruffies that unfortunately collided with a pellet or two as they zigged when they should have zagged. This year Plum has been to college, learning to be staunch and pointing rather than flushing his birds. But the roughnecked grouse, as *The Rocky Mountain House Mountaineer* once called him, is no gentleman, and goes off on tippy-toes as soon as Plum goes on point; Plum forges ahead and bumps or flushes the bird, the sin without absolution for a dog with a college degree in being staunch on point.

The book says you should not shoot until the dog who knows how to do it right does it right, so I fear Mac may permit no shooting over Plum this season unless we find some ruffed grouse willing to co-operate in in furthering the career of a bird dog educated beyond reason.

Before Plum went to college, he went calling on Ron Vanson's Brittany bitch, Toni, and I now own Quince, one of the seven fruits of that union, now four months of age. Just a baby, I know, but I have hopes for precocity. It is obvious Quince is capable of learning anything, particularly many things he ought not, but the question in any hunting dog owner's mind is whether or not the pup will hunt, the one thing that cannot be taught. Desire to hunt, they say, is either there or not.

For many days now, it has been bush and more bush for Quince and me, for I believe if he has the desire it will be there now, and the pup will show it by taking so much pleasure in chasing birds that he will associate the sound of a shot in the air with that pleasure. I shall shoot at no bird over Quince this fall until I am sure his delicate ears and sensitive nervous system will not be so offended by the sound that I will not have to add the services of a canine psychiatrist to those of the vet.

So far the high point came on a picnic last Saturday when Quince's ears were not at all offended by the piercing shrieks of her what lives with me and who Quince adores; he ran to the rescue and completely routed the marauding whisky jacks. Alas, I do not carry even a cap pistol on picnics. On the next day, the Sabbath, I went out to give Quince a real opportunity to make his decision for birds. First it was a ruffed grouse twittering like a demented canary in a strip of brush along a road allowance. Quince heard not a twitter, saw and smelled nothing. In I went, busting brush, and herded that grouse back and forth. Quince sat on the road, cocking his head and wondering about my sanity.

Next, a covey of at least 30 Hungarian partridge, snuggled into a stubble field. We walked right into their midst before they exploded. Quince did not even lift his head or chase so much as the ghost of his long lost tail. Finally, the kind of grouse Quince should and would find, came. The ruffie sat and posed, turning that profile for a better three-quarter shot as I finished a roll of film. Quince studiously ignored the bird, so I threw the pup at the grouse, which merely sidestepped, and Quince gambolled back for more play.

Later, Quince stiffened as though on point. Hope rose. There in the bush, before the dog's nose, its matted tans blending with the litter on the forest floor, was a cow pie. Quince pounced and munched. Good memory for scents, my Quince, for back at the car, the pup noticed, barked, growled, and made as if to attack the cattle grazing in the field across the road. This is verboten, the dog knows it, and he got whacked. So he retired under the car, from which sanctuary he continued to bark at the cattle. When he finally came out I could not punish him for doing what I had been coaxing him to do for 10 minutes.

After umpteen outings, I have fired not a shot in anger nor in the air, and if this continues, it is a no-grouse year. Get a bird dog and take up golf, say I, and Mac Johnston may add "amen". Perhaps I can get Herself to come out and shriek every time we spot a grouse. The shriek will be easy; it's getting her out there that will be hard. Maybe Quince, if properly motivated, will rise to the rescue and rout the ruffian grouse.

It's either that or trade him in on a poodle. Compared to that fate, even Herself would probably prefer shrieking at grouse. Me? Next time, see, I catch the grouse, then I throw it ever so gently at the dog.

The Graduate

Some of my expeditions are strange interludes, and last Saturday was invested in a strange graduation. It was an honour to be invited by the graduate's family and a pleasure to be chauffeured the 150 miles to the campus.

Actually the campus was a township tract 30 miles southeast of Coronation. But neither the hard facts of the threatening clouds nor the bitter wind could staunch the flow of our pride as we watched Professor Ivan Hosler of Red Deer put the student through his paces on a stubble field.

The graduate quartered the field like orange and white lightning in response to the whistle and arm signals of the Professor. The sharptail grouse were all away keeping their drumsticks dry in the bottoms of various ravines. Occasionally, as the graduate coursed the field, he would do that wonderful thing: pause, flash point, and then run some blackbird or sparrow clean to the correction line. "Just a baby now, but he's going to be a great gun dog," was Ivan Hosler's verdict.

The kids wonder about the "baby" delivered to Ivan six weeks before. "Is he bigger?" Probably not, but the work that is play to a hunting dog has made him lean and hard. Young Iain takes the leash and the pup runs a furrow in the stubble with his young friend's nose for a plow. Even I am amazed. Was it only yesterday our student was knee-high to my hush puppies and sprinkling all over them?

The baby, the graduate, is a Brittany spaniel answering to his enemies and those who love him the most as Plum or, particularly for the kids, as Plummy. To the owner of the kennel where the pup was born, who could not bring himself to write "Plum" in the application for registration, he is "Sunawagold's Ripper".

The opinion of Ivan Hosler on Plum's future is not to be taken lightly. For many years Ivan has been running his camp, his academy for higher learning for pointing dogs of many breeds and degrees of nobility, and is regarded in many parts of North America as a superb trainer. For six weeks Ivan has been in charge of Plum's elementary education, along with the high school and college educations of some two dozen other pointers, some of whose relatives, personal credentials, and attainments must have awed the eight-month-old pup.

It turns out nothing cows Plum but horses, especially the dog-wise horse Ivan rides behind the dogs. In fact, back in the farmhouse Ivan tells us about Plum slipping his collar one day, quartering through the screen door, and landing in one great affectionate lump on the chest of the sleeping Professor.

I regret that I must not reveal the name of the owner of such a prodigy. The head of the family is a good friend and has let it so publicly be known what he thinks of sending kids to camp that now he dare not let it be known that he sends his dog to one. To his credit, my friend recognized Plum's early promise and realized a few sacrifices would have to be made to ensure his potential was realized. Was that not a refined and noble spirit Plum was demonstrating the day he was found by my friend's wife on top of the stereo, lapping up the water after having overturned and eaten the tulips? What about the day he drank the unguarded glass of sherry of that same lady of the self-same house? Did that not promise, if anything did, an exacting, discriminating and full-choke nose?

On this graduation day we have the first realization of all that promise, for Plum, while still so young, demonstrates the *sine qua non*, that without which you have a doormat, not a gun dog: bird sense and a tremendous desire to hunt.

So Plum will be invited along this fall, and will no doubt cause his human companions to laugh, cry, curse, and marvel from time to time. But he will always be hunting and preparing himself for his high school and college courses in such things as being staunch on point and steady to wing and shot. He may even become educated beyond his instinct and breeding and take to retrieving.

Ivan Hosler doesn't say so but makes it clear that he enjoyed the variety and clowning of this Brittany spaniel in his usual diet of English and Irish setters. He even reminisces a bit about a champion Brittany he handled once in a field trial. "Cross that one with a milk pail," Ivan said, "and the worst you would get would be a good gun dog."

That straightened us up. But no, our Plum's parents have honourable and un-pail-like names on that fancy paper, the one that calls him Ripper.

Addicted Canine

Really, I just do not know what is to be done with Quince, my Brittany spaniel pup. I suppose I could say that at 16 months he is approaching what in humans is called the teens and be satisfied that that explained everything.

But did I not provide him with the finest custom-built kennel money could buy, without so much as a penny of NHA financing? Has he not been immunized against the serious canine afflications and been afflicted with all the rest, until I have become Canada's leading advocate of the extension of medicare and Blue Cross to dogs? Have I ever complained that his appetite waxes the sicker he gets?

I have denied him nothing, not even a first-class education. Quince has just returned from two months at Ivan Hosler's eastern Alberta bird camp, where he was offered the kind of training formerly available only to the canine charges of southern "kernels", the owners of quail plantations. The idea of it all is that Quince should become that most noble of beasts, a first-class grouse shooting dog, through association with the sharptails abounding in the east country this year.

So how are we rewarded by that ungrateful pup, me the bankrupt owner and kindly Professor Ivan Hosler who has such high hopes for all his pupils? Quince shows the decided uppity tendencies of a dog that prefers pheasant.

The pup's perversion was revealed to me on the Sunday before grouse and Hungarian partridge season opened in this zone, when I took him to a place I know just five minutes from the house, hoping to find the flock of huns that calls the place home. Not five minutes into the cover, he snuffed himself near inside out and stomped up in front of as fine a pair of cock pheasants as I have seen in the area. I flushed the scrubby beasts out of there almost without wishing the season was open. From then on he was like the farm boy that has seen "gay paree". Five minutes later he slammed on point in lamentable style, his head under some bent over marsh grass and his stump of a tail revolving so ferociously that he was in danger of taking off backwards. I walked over and booted a hen pheasant out of there, then had to snap the leash on the pup and drag him out of that cover and the bad influence of its habit-forming pheasant fumes.

The next day when we went after grouse I learned how far the affliction had gone. Quince was sashaying down a wooded trail when he turned 90 degrees and stood relaxed, as though lost in thought. It was early in the day and we were watching him closely, so I ordered him to "whoa" and walked up there and ahead of him. Much to my surprise there was a ruffed grouse there which turned out to be my first of the season. That first point disturbed me, it was so casual. The dog was not intense on point. He did not quiver like a banjo string, and you certainly could not have knocked his eyes off with a stick. His relaxed attitude seemed to be saying, "Here, boss, is another of those boring grouse."

I would have been inclined to say he did not point another all day, but that would be untrue. He pointed three others in the same casual manner. I did not believe him, did not see the birds because the leaves were still up, just walked by and then got the fits when the thundering birds took my hat off. It is natural, I suppose, that Quince should then assume I had gotten over my incredible grouse fixation and perversely spend the rest of the day getting very interested in them and busting them out all over without so much as a pause in the headlong rush. Actually I should not have been surprised since, even as a pup, Quince gave warning of the twisted dog he would become.

I have recounted previously in this column how I was obliged to throw the pup at the first ruffed grouse he ever saw. But I was out with him on a warm day last February when he made his decision to be a bird dog. His head went up into the wind when we were a quarter mile away from a half-acre poplar and willow bluff. Quince porpoised that quarter mile through deep snow, then proceeded like famine, plague, and pestilence through that bluff, hoovering it like a mad housewife. For five minutes it exploded pheasant. A couple of fine roosters nearly buzzed me off my snowshoes in their haste to get away from the whirlwind in their midst. Then the pup dragged himself back to me wearing his tongue like a pink scarf. His eyes were glazed, the pupils like pin points. Sadly, I leashed the addict and led him out of there.

Somehow I do not think the cure, cold turkey—that is, cold pheasant—withdrawal is the answer. I will just have to compromise, go halfway with the dog. I will make the sacrifice and be more casual in my dementia, grouse, and watch Quince closely for those casual points. Then I will have to indulge him a little in his delight and take him south for pheasants a time or two.

Come to think of it, I had better do it quickly, before the ingrate decides that something more exotic, like the Iranian peahen, is the thing to hunt this season.

Pointed Lesson

With any luck at all this year, I would have missed all the opening days of all the hunting seasons that interest me. I have missed duck season opening every year since they decided to open Supreme Court in Red Deer on the same date. That leaves the opening day of pheasant season and the earlier opening day of upland game other than pheasants, to torment me.

This year my abominable memory came to my aid, and something less important but more pressing than hunting was scheduled for the opening day on Hungarian partridge, ruffed grouse, and that ilk. Only pheasant opening was left, and I should have been a cinch to miss that; the authorities this year scheduled pheasant to open on the first working day after the Thanksgiving weekend.

But the weather and my own taste for torture did me in. All day last Saturday I busted brush in the rain for ruffed grouse. Quince, my Brittany, had two perfect points, and I had one grouse. All day Sunday I snarled about why there is never such a perfect fall day on a day when it is lawful to hunt. Thanksgiving came up so lousy that I worked and only went out in the wind long enough for Quince to false-point a covey of Hungarian partridge and then bump them wild by being too careful when relocating the covey. So by Monday night when I should have had enough hunting for, say, four days, I hadn't even started.

Tuesday morning, opening day of pheasant season, came up with a skiff of snow and a wind that would shave a wire brush, the kind of morning that cries out to every man who has a drop of hunting blood: "Go hunting!" Usually all men, including me, reply, "But I have to go to work," and do so. Instead, I resolved to go hunting and rapped on my bedroom window. Old Quince, my Brittany pup, out there in his house, stirs not at all. But he stirs up a storm when I come out of the house and the north wind carries him the scents of my old hunting jacket and the 40 years of oil and gunpowder on my old Ithaca double.

We choose, for its abundance of pheasants, a railroad embankment not far from the city. About halfway down Quince locks up so tight on point that he creaks when he shivers. His concentration and revolving tail bespeak no doubt, but nothing flushes when I step in front of him.

It must be huns, I think, as only the large scent-cloud left by departed covey birds seems to cause my dog to false-point. Two minutes later I am right. The pup points well, but the birds, always skittish in the wind, flush wild. The first barrel goes where I think they are thickest, and the usual happens: absolutely nothing. Three of them tower, turn, and careen downwind back toward me, high. For once I don't hurry. I turn, swing under one of the birds, and drop him cleanly.

On the way home for a hot lunch, I am warmed by that one shot. Perhaps I should hang it up for the season? Well, for the day anyway. But I remember the surest spot in Alberta for pheasants, and it is about 2 p.m. when the proprietors thereof, very fine people, give me permission to have a go at it.

Right off Quince points at the edge of a tule patch, a perfect place for a pheasant on a blustery day. As I step ahead of the dog, I see the porcupine. I manage to call the dog off and inform him he is the misbegotten progeny of ancestors of doubtful origin and legitimacy. This is the first time the pup has shown any interest in porcupines. I wonder whether I should have walloped him for his own good. But how can you wallop a dog when he leaves the critter alone when you tell him to? Especially when you are an old softie like me.

Half an hour later, judging by the tracks in the snow, we are working our way into pheasant heaven, a long hedgerow between two barley fields. It is so thick that I can locate the dog only from the sound of his bell. Suddenly he is out on my edge, shuffling toward me on three feet while he paws at his nose and huffs and snuffs like a punch-drunk club fighter. Old Quince has lost a bout with a porcupine. Reporting the quill count would be too painful. Suffice it to say that somewhere west of here there is a porcupine whose completely nude tail makes the beast resemble a giant muskrat.

On the way back to the car and the run to the vet, I make a slight detour to that first porcupine with Quince on the leash, the idea being that, much as it will hurt us both, I will teach Quince once and for all that you can point porcupines if you wish, but you never, ever, break point and attack one. But as far as Quince was concerned, that old porky was just a figment of my imagination. This pup can stand on point 40 feet away, drinking in great draughts of the scent of one ruffed grouse, but three feet downwind of that bristling porky, old Quince turned away and grinned at me through those quills like he does when he cops a lick of somebody's popsicle.

Quince plain ignored that porcupine, which may mean he has learned a lesson. I doubt if I can say as much for myself and opening days.

12. Imaginary White-Tails

Theoretical White-Tails

Theoretically, I am a deer hunter. Or, I am a hunter of theoretical deer. At least I was until the recent opening day of the white-tail season in the parkland east of the city when I went deer hunting for the first time.

For me the whole process had to be based on pure theory, as there was no deer hunting done in my family and the deer hunters I know are a strong, silent lot. The result is that I have read everything available to me on the subject of deer hunting and became so entranced, particularly by the game qualities of the white-tail, that I decided to invade the prime white-tail cover just east of Red Deer.

Before the opening of the season, I located three areas that appeared to be full of deer and then got down to the more difficult task of trying to find a crossing of frequently used deer trails and a stand from which I could watch the crossing early in the morning when, theoretically, the white-tails would be wending their way to their daytime beds after a night of feeding and generally earning their living. It was not until the Sunday evening before the Monday season opening that I found a stand on a ridge overlooking what appeared to me to be a heavily used trail between an obvious feeding area and the high ridge where I suspected the big bucks bedded.

My final choice was based on hunch as much as theory. It was snowing that Sunday evening, and I was also out for a walk with my father and my son, who was directing the operation from his seat in the backpack. The only sign was a fresh deer trail coming out of a thicket into which the "hot" trail led. That, I thought, was a good omen, and that would be my stand next morning.

The first time I wondered about deer hunting was when the alarm went at 5 a.m. on opening day morning. The next was when I left my car and discovered that the wind had completely reversed from the evening before and I would have to approach my chosen stand from exactly the opposite direction. Stumbling and lurching a mile through dark and foggy woods is novel enough experience for most of us, let alone down an unfamiliar trail. Finally I arrived where I thought I should be, set a camp stool up against a substantial aspen, sat down, arranged self and rifle as comfortably as possible, and concentrated on not moving a muscle while said muscles froze as gradually and painfully as it was getting light.

Then you really wonder why. But white-tails are uncanny and fascinate me, and there is nothing whatever the matter with hunting them, except for the difficulty. Venison is delicious, and those kindly persons who used to supply me having left town, I am obliged to bring home the bacon myself, a motive that is satisfying and justifies much hunting.

Briefly I consider the hated pleasures of road hunting and reject it out of hand as not being the same at all. As the sky grows lighter, so does my unease. Finally day and truth dawn at the same time: I am about 50 yards from where I should be, and my view of the crossing is obstructed by the crest of the ridge.

Do I move? The books say no. A good thing, too, because the world is waking. Some big birds fly low overhead, and I do not move to see them. Then comes a soft "swish, swish", and I know something is moving upwind along the trail through the willow. A magpie swoops from the east, lands on a tree just about where I heard the last "swish", and gives two minutes of hell to whatever stands below the tree. Then some more "swish, swish", a twig snaps, and the magpie moves on.

You convince yourself it is too late for anything else to be moving rather than admit that you cannot stand the freezing immobility any longer. In any event I went to the trail, and there in the night's fresh snow were the big tracks of one big deer having come from the feeding area down the ridge toward the higher ridge. Further down the trail, below the magpie's tree, freshly-minted and still steaming faintly, was evidence of the deer's complete ignorance of my presence as it stopped in a place where I could not possibly see it. It was triumph enough for a theoretical deer hunter gone actual for the first time—to have picked out a live trail and been within 50 yards of a deer coming down it.

So I moved off and confirmed in the new snow the movement of deer from all sorts of feeding areas back and forth to and from the high ridge. So fascinated did I become that I found I had to hurry back a long way to the car and home to work. I short-cut the last 200 yards to the car across a small clearing bountiful with browse. There had been a deer convention there the previous night. Not a hundred feet from my car, screened from it by heavy brush, were two snow-filled beds where deer had rested during their browsing. Perhaps they had lifted their heads and tested the wind when the sound came to them of my pathetic efforts to close my car door quietly.

My personal credo is for a white-tail only and a buck only, but the question remains unanswered: which weapon of the two I carry I shall choose when the time comes, rifle or camera? I do know that, given my theoretical and the white-tails' practical approach, I have many years of pleasurable hunting ahead before I ever have to make the decision other than in theory.

No Bucks

From time to time, through my labourious following of various outdoor sports, I have heard various members of the non-partici-pating great unwashed slander many fine people by saying "You have to be crazy" to hunt ducks or fish, or one thing or another. Now, after only one season and one week of hunting deer, I assert without any fear of contradiction whatever that not only do you have to be crazy to hunt deer, but you are a truly great sportsman if you do, for you hunt a quarry that does not exist.

The fact that there is no such thing as a buck looms extra-large in a year when there is no season on does in this area. Does do exist, by the hundreds, so just don't get me started. Actually deer hunting had a tough row to hoe with me to start with because I firmly believe you are crazy to do anything for enjoyment that involves rolling out of the sack before 8 a.m.

Last year the weather during the season was fairly decent, and I managed to make myself comfortable enough on those deer stands on which I sat that I fell asleep. This year I was still of the belief that sitting on a stand beside a likely trail was the most plausible way for a novice like me to get a deer. I had a likely spot all picked out for the unholy hours of opening morning this year. Fortunately, I went out to scout the area the Saturday before opening, and I worked up such a lather that I contracted a dose of the plague so severe that I knew by noon Sunday I would not be able to answer the bell on Monday. From what I can gather, the weather was so lousy on opening morning that most of those who did answer the bell wished they had had the plague instead.

Saturday morning a fit of coughing awoke me a 6 a.m., and deer fever took over. Faster than a hiccup, I was out in a likely cover, seated on a frozen log and resting my back against a great spruce trunk. My determined scanning of two intersecting trails without moving anything but eyeballs lasted until I tore ligaments in both eyeballs and realized that I was freezing to death. Besides, I am too much a fisherman to have any patience.

So I burned out forever on trail watching, you might say, and decided I would become a great still hunter instead. I picked out a likely-looking ridge and started pussyfooting down the magnificent game trail running along just below its top. It seems to me that I take naturally to this slow-moving bit, as I was hard-pressed to cover a little better than a mile from 2 p.m. to dark when I quit, fearing moss might be growing on my north side.

Along about 4 p.m. I went by a young fellow sitting on a stand who admired my stylish crouch but noted that the way I was twitching my butt around I could get it shot off for a white tail. I crouched and twitched along, not having the heart to tell the impertinent young whippersnapper that Herself had committed the cardinal sin of washing my Stanfields' Red Labels and the crouch and the twitch were both caused by the fact they had shrunk enough to cut me in half.

Signs were everywhere, just as they invariably are when I do my trail-sitting. Still, as the old-timers say, you can't fry tracks. Last year at least I saw a few does, but this year not even that although, as always, I am surrounded by deer. In a little hollow at the crown of the ridge, the brush had been torn to shreds. A couple of spots had been pawed up down to the turf, and then something had been done to them that left the spots steaming, but which can not be mentioned in a family newspaper. They say bucks do this when the rut is on, but if one does not believe in bucks, what is one to say of the rut?

The day ended like all my deer hunting days: I have seen nothing but encouraging signs. Still, I was warm, have had some fresh air and sunshine, and had not bored myself sitting on a frozen stump freezing to death. It is worth pondering what will happen on the day of disillusionment when my cherished beliefs are shattered and a figment of my imagination appears before me and proves to be a real buck.

For five years running, a couple of friends of mine happily packed up to go elk hunting. Each time they returned, one of them moaned the invariable refrain, "There is no elk." The sixth year they spotted elk on a hillside as they were on their way to their campsite. Both had bulls and were back in town after being gone less than a day, without even having to set up camp. Reliable authorities report to me that neither gentleman has gone elk hunting since.

A Shot Refused

When I finished my duties in my Rocky Mountain House office about a week ago, I just had time to encase my business suit in overalls, don the blaze orange and spend the last 45 minutes of daylight watching a game trail near my Stump Ranch. The first customer to come by was a spike bull moose who peered near-sightedly at me, decided he could not smell me, and spent five minutes munching away in a small swamp while I congratulated myself that there was no one present with a moose tag.

I am a poor sitter and must ease my *gluteus maximus* at frequent intervals, so I strolled downwind to the other point of the bluff where the wind was all wrong. A deer, probably a white-tail, was stomping Rice Crispies down there, but soon stopped when he got the evening downhill drift of me. I did not even bother to sit down but turned to return to the upwind stand.

"Just another of those fat mule deer does in the clearing across the river," I told myself. I looked again. "Scammell! That is no doe and you know it!" But I rationalized, "Surely that's a diamond willow behind its head, not antlers."

I inspected with binoculars as the critter gave me a profile, a head-on, a look-over-the-shoulder pose, a little of this, a little of that. Antlers! At least four points to each side! Head-on, wider than the rump; sideways, at least twice as high as the ears: what the book says is a trophy. Perhaps not a record, but the finest mule deer buck I have ever seen, even in Montana, Idaho, and Wyoming.

I estimated the range at 300 yards. The downhill angle, 30 degrees. I have been hunting thick bush all fall with one of Ruger's rare Model 77's in .358 Winchester. Tonight, for some mysterious reason, I have chosen my only 400-yard rifle, a 6.5 x 55 Husqvarna with a hot load for a 125-grain Nosler bullet.

In front of me is a sturdy tree with a crotch at just the right height, and I snug my left hand and the forearm of the rifle into it. So steady and sure it is that I am already apologizing to the buck's departing spirit. Maybe that is why I look at my watch. It seems to me that in Faulkner's great hunting story "The Bear" the hunter gets rid of his watch first thing.

But there really are only 15 minutes of light left. I do not need a watch to tell me that. If only I were not so familiar with the country! I know I can get Old Jeep on the other side of the river to within only half a mile of that deer, from which it is a dizzying drag uphill over rough sand hills to the vehicle.

The river is at its deepest just here and for hundreds of yards each way. It bears a thin glaze of ice. Scenario: soaking wet I dress out that deer, huff and puff its huge carcass back to the bank, enter the water again all heated up, and wade back with the floating deer in the pitch dark, go find Jeep and churn it into position, pull out winch cable and extra cable. Estimate: 10 days in intensive care and two weeks resting at home.

For two days I kicked myself until the following Saturday when I got my waders full crossing the same water. Then I knew I had made the right decision. That day a companion 200 yards away said that my intake of breath, as the waters poured over the gunwales, sucked the bullets from all the cartridges in his rifle and stripped the foliage from every tree from there to the correction line.

So I lowered the rifle. That old buck was a ham. He stood and posed a little longer, then decided he was scared to death, blew once, turned, and tore off up the ridge blatting like a hound as he went.

Some believe that when Manitou smiles so broadly, it is the worst of bad luck to spurn the offering, to refuse the shot.

13. Homo Sap: the Wildest Creature

Weedless Revenge

Devoted readers will recall that I related in this column in 1968 or 1969 how my fanatical brother-in-law yarded in a three-pound brown trout from under my nose. We were working our way up opposite sides of a good run of water when I got winded and wallowed out to the bank to ruin my wind with a cigarette. While I was thus engaged, brother-in-law mooched his Mepps spinner into a rocky little pocket at my side, grunted in satisfaction, and announced, "I think I'll need help with this one."

At least that's what he thought until I netted the fish three times and the brute jumped out twice, being secured on the third netting only when I clasped the open side of the net to my bosom, so choked was I by the language, while brother-in-law heaved on the line and pulled me, net, and fish half a mile from the stream into a convenient pasture.

Many times since then have I fished with brother-in-law without taking revenge, although I came close the day I did not go along on a trip and he mired to the roof the half-ton hotrod he was then driving and walked to civilization 10 miles the wrong way instead of three miles the right way. It would have been much, much sweeter had not my dear old dad plodded every step of the way with him, in hip boots. We brothers-in-law have both changed over the years in two respects: we are both off the weed, and we have both converted 90 per cent to fly fishing.

He smoked a pipe and quit a couple of years ago. No more need the masters of small craft quail at that fearsome peril to navigation, my fanatical brother-in-law, immersed to his pectorals, glassy glaze in his eyes, forging ever upstream and belching black clouds of smoke. Last November I forsook the weed. No more do west country streams bear the brownstained water, thought to be natural, but really the result of me fishing upstream and being careless about where I deposited my quid of Beechnut. No more is pastoral serenity rent by the odd dull explosion as my cheroot ignites the fumes of my paraffin and naptha fly floatant.

Quitting tobacco actually was easy, as I knew it would be, until fishing season, when complications set in, as I knew they would. Little did I guess that our quitting tobacco and the complications that brings to angling, would fashion my revenge on my brother-in-law. He has been busy with calves and crop and has not been fishing this spring. You can't really pray for rain and good fishing too, so he did not complain when all last Friday we flang flies fruitlessly.

Saturday the clouds thinned and a fair hatch of *Acroneuria* stoneflies came on. I took a couple of 14-inch browns, then came one of those rises to my fly that leaves a froth of bubbles, not just one, and reveals a trout to be measured in pounds, not inches. The procedure was to rest the fish, which I had not touched, and let brother-in-law have at him for his first fish of the year. Generally one pipefull or one cigar would do it, but for a non-smoker, changing the fly, anointing it, and then changing the leader tippet takes not half as much time. We tried the fish again too soon, and he was not buying.

Then brother-in-law was fishing the pool above me when I heard a sharp crack and some sharper language. For this early in the season, his touch was a trifle heavy. He had struck too hard, he said, snapped a six-pound leader and left the fly in a heavy fish. Ordinarily this is a next-day proposition, but a smoking man would still sit down, finish a cigar, and then try the fish again, knowing full well that a brown trout with a fly stuck in its mouth is not going to feed again that day.

Perhaps angling literature and tradition are either all wet or are

178

formulated by anglers hooked on the weed. Not five minutes after the crack, I stepped into the tail of the pool and put the fly up beside the rock where brother-in-law said the big fish had taken. The fly floated past me on the second cast, and there came a gush and a twang that caused brother-in-law to turn around as the big fish hooked himself with the violence of his rush.

After about 20 minutes, brother-in-law faultlessly netted my 21½-inch brown. We held the fish in the water so I could release him after removing my fly. It turned out that I had to remove two flies first, as brother-in-law's was stuck in the lip right beside my own. I know because I tied them both myself.

"Thought that fish sounded mad, like he wanted revenge," said brother-in-law, as he picked up his fly and moved back up to the next pool.

Boy, Dog and Old Angler

For many years I have adhered to one principle on the kids and angling subject: take a boy fishing and push the little b_____ in. A couple of weeks ago, just before his third birthday, son John participated with me in catching a fairly nice rainbow trout.

Scant days later, in fact just the day after the celebration of the third birthday, the squirt announced that he was going fishing with me. Previously he had been outvoted by mother and me, but this time Herself, plagued by little sister's colic, voted with John, and before I really knew what had happened I was embarked on that occasion dozy new fathers dream of, my first fishing trip with my son.

What had started out as a half-decent day was in shambles anyway, so I also packed up Quince, my Brittany, who is becalmed between seasons as it were and who has never been fishing. Actually I tried to take Quince fishing once, but as I was opening the farmyard gate, Quince went hunting and in three seconds found, pointed, and plucked the prized black hen of the lady of the ranch. So this time we went further down the road, and after a delicious lunch of peanut butter sandwiches, salt and vinegar chips, and chocolate milk, the troops headed through the hay to a river.

A guide friend of mine once found that on those days he wasn't guiding a sly old devil, s.o.d. was in visiting the guide's wife. So the next time he was guiding s.o.d., he carried him across a roaring channel of the Madison River, placed him on a island, said "We'll see you around, Romeo," and went fishing. Good idea, I thought. So I carried John across a channel to the lowest of a series of islands to a repeating barrage of "Don't drop me" and "Watch out for the hole". Quince is a frustrated Labrador retriever. He swam.

As long as there is a supply of rocks to throw and a logjam to tear apart for sticks to throw, John is happy. There was an abundance of both on all these islands, so I went fishing. The #8 Le Tort hopper is about as large as a Hungarian partridge and smells of deer, which Quince loves more than huns. So the bonehead stood on the edge of the island, etched against the summer sky, and pointed the fly on its first two floats. On the third float a 15-inch brown rolled and took the fly, and Quince went berserk. He knocked John down before the sprout could get to the net to perform his promised duty. Anguished human roars joined excited barks.

The brown was a jumper, and I reefed in the line and let it fall at my feet. Quince ran back and forth through the line like a shuttle, producing a reasonable facsimile of a gill net. The fish came out, and I set him in the grass, set John on his feet, and made a stab at untangling Quince. It became obvious that the only way to untangle Quince was in the water, so I caught him by the scruff and the butt and fired him right into the middle of the river. The floating line floated free for the most part, and as I reeled the pup in, I noticed the squirt was silent. I thought I caught the first fleeting look of respect in those big brown eyes. Of course the kid, the dog, and I have been through this sort of thing before.

So I moved camp up to the next island. As luck would have it, I had not seen this stream in such excellent shape all year. The fish thought so too, and I was getting take after take on the stonefly nymph I had switched to after having seen what that first fish had been eating.

Fishing a nymph upstream requires concentration, which it was getting up to a microsecond before each strike. At that point I would turn to the splash behind me, only to find it was just Quince trying to retrieve another boulder or sawlog heaved in by this delicate child who is sometimes too weak to climb into his bunk at bedtime. Every time I turned back, I was too late. Still, fishing is fishing. I went on till we had cleared every island in that stretch of the river, and John announced the fishing was no good because there were no more rocks and sticks and we should go home. Boy and dog slept all the way in, just as they had slept all the way out. When we arrived home, they immediately ran off to deal with a supply of rocks and logs they know about.

I fell into a quivering heap and contemplated a liquidation sale of a fortune in fishing equipment. Whether or not the boy is too young to be an angler, I know an angler who is too old to be a young father.

My Fanatical In-Law

Hot sun, a little breeze, a stretch of rapids on a big river. The time of year when the big browns, addled by instinct, quit the remote holes in the river to seek their lady loves. A fine day for catching big brown trout.

There was an outdoors columnist, his brother-in-law—hereinafter referred to as FIL for "fanatical in-law"—and one faithful fishing companion, hereinafter referred to as AB for "angling buddy". It is doubtful if a more determined array of brown trout antagonists has ever been assembled. The river, however, did not appear to be noticeably agitated by fearful trembling of the big browns.

The other two chose spinning tackle, and I, a man of deep conviction, took a fly rod. By noon I had provoked an assault on the fly by an ambitious six-inch whitefish and, just before lunch, as I was remembering where I had left my fish knife, the one with the bottle-opener, I missed a tremendous rise from a big fish.

I had been pleased to spot FIL doing labourious battle with a fish that proved to be a pound and a half brook trout, lured in a manner so in defiance of all angling convention that I will not describe it. AB turned up for lunch with two small browns, a decent brookie, and a story of having lost two browns of a least three pounds each. FIL and I nodded sympathetically in the manner of brother anglers.

Inner man satisfied and principle forsaken, I joined the other two with a spinning rod and headed downriver. In the best brotherly-in-law tradition, FIL and I started fishing a long rapid side by side, me in chest waders lumbering up the middle and fishing the right bank, he in hip waders fishing the left. At the top of the rapid, I floundered ashore to catch my wind and have a smoke to ruin it. As we were moving up to the next pool, FIL says, "That looks like a good place", and lobs his spinner into a little pocket over on my side of the river. "I think I'm going to need help", is what he said next.

We see nothing in the rough water until a big brown, the brown of browns in its gold, cream, and red colors, heaves himself into the air. This homebody brown undoes himself, always keeping his head upstream, always trying to get back to that little pocket. Freedom is the other way, down the long, brush-lined rapid, and he forsakes it.

Twice I cram all of that fish into the net, and twice he heaves himself back into the water, the second time while being borne three feet above the water to shore. Still he stays on, and FIL says nothing to me, although he does know the words. Finally, the exasperated fish turns and drives himself deep into the mesh and sticks. After leading me about half a mile from the water, FIL dared a peek at his fish, a 19-inch brown of nearly three pounds. I touched the taut line, the fish gave the tiniest twitch in the net, and the line gave way right at the hook.

Then came the pool where I missed the good rise in the morning, and FIL gracefully retired to a fallen log. Oozing finesse from every pore, I draped the spinner over a bush on the opposite bank. With unspeakable control, I reefed it out of the bush and plopped it and yards of slack into the water about five feet upstream from where the fish had risen that morning. I reeled like a dervish to take up slack before the spinner fouled the bottom, and the line came taut and started to run out simultaneously.

In his haste to return the favours I had done him earlier, FIL nearly throttled me getting the net from around my neck. At one point the fish mistook FIL for a friendly tree and dashed between his legs. A graceful leap and one-foot pirouette over the line by FIL in a foot of water averted that crisis. This fish, too, bagged himself by trying to torpedo through the net. Another brown, this one a silvery color with a few red spots, better than 16 inches and nearly two pounds.

AB soon hove on the scene back at the car and the usual guarded conversational jockeying for position took place before fish were displayed and congratulations exchanged. AB produced a brown of about 18 inches and two and a half pounds in an all-silver phase, no red, only black spots, looking like a landlocked salmon.

AB was mysteriously silent concerning the demise of his fish, although he listened to FIL and me with relish. I suspect a story lurks in AB. No doubt the same skill and cunning went into the capture and landing of AB's fish as was required for those of FIL and me. The brown is a wary creature, but some days nothing is wrong enough.

Wes on Ice Fishing

Two, three years ago I was dead certain I was burnt out on ice fishing for good. I ain't saying nothing about wenching and shovelling in to the lake.

I've saw worse, just like any genteel old fly-angler who ever was damn fool enough to go to the Stoney in June knows. Haw haw. But they had these great sheets of 5-ply on two-by-two frames, and if yarding 'em down to the place through snow up to a geeraff's crutch wasn't work, then I ain't never done none. And you can shut your dirty mouth.

They was a barn-roller of a shinhook howling slightly more than somewhat, and the most of us with them sheets made more time than we cared to when we got to the bare ice. But "Say lavee," as the Prime Minister said the other day, just before he give up the ghost. Anyhow, we all more or less arrived at the place, and the dudes I was with hooked all them sheets together into a kind of instant biffy. Then we all got in there in the dark and disconnected our shoulders gouging holes through two foot of ice with a huge brace and a bit contrapted by some Swede, I think.

Things got not half bad for a while. Somebody opened a couple cans of these here tasty little shrimps for bait. Lo and behold! Somebody else cracks a crock of Ernie's Ambrosia.

At first it was right entertaining in that six-holer, seeing right to the bottom at all them great lunky brookies ignoring all them shrimps. Then one of the dudes gets exgasperated and jigs a two pounder up through the hole on one of them Len Thompson lake trout grappling hooks. That fish went around that biffy like the button on a backhouse door and slapped all present in the face before someone put it out of its misery.

Then someone annouces we've et all the shrimps, drunk all the sauce, and someone's started one wall of the biffy on fire. Time we put her out. It's time to take the whole mess back down and snake her back up the hill to the jeep.

Ice fishing. What I mean to say is that was the first time I ever tried her. I wasn't going no more and that was for damshur.

Haw! Sap springs eternal as the feller says, and we had another shinhook this winter which started her running again. Feller I was with heard one lake was hot which I'd heard was cold, so I persuaded him to go to one I'd heard was a shur thing.

Nice day, but we almost put her in the roobarb a time or two getting out there. And suffice it to say that we disconnect our vertebrates drilling hither and yonder for water and crushed ice

And there must've been fish down there, because one citizen sits in a snow bank beside a hole and a dwindling bottle of Rosay Porchclimber wine and ever once in a while sticks his arm down the hole and comes up with a fish. Trouble is he was no help howsoever about the secret of what they was takin, because he'd cram shrimps and a gob of salmon eggs garnished with a ripe olive on his hook ever time and chuck the whole schmorgasboard down the hole any old how. Could be even the odd libation of old Rosay he was sloshing in the hole to keep her from freezing over had something to do with ossyfying them fish. I ain't saying. He never offered me some.

Then they was the dude sitting in the mist of a bunch of holes, fishing 'em all with one line connected from hole to hole. It was bad enought the other dudes walking into them lines, but the fit really hit the man when a yokel in one of these new-fangled motorized stone-boats fouled the dude's lines at about 40 per. Talk about birds nests and backlashes! But even the anticks of them lunaticks that ice fishes ain't really enough to keep a cultured angler amused long. So we agree it's cold, damp, all fishing and no catching, and pack her in.

Next day the government man over to the fish and game place tells me the lake we went to which had use to be hot had got cool on the weekend we was there and the lake we was going to but didn't had hotted up something fierce. Anyhow, you know.

And that's ice fishing. Once is enough; twict is a insult to the brains God give man. I have plumb took the pledge, at least until next shinhook, and in these parts that could be forever. And when one comes along a man ain't responsible for his acts anyhow.

Here's hoping.

Your friend,
West Country Wes.

Down with Sweet Little Old Ladies

A gentleman angler in the west country last weekend might well have muttered a motion that they should declare open season on sweet little old ladies. If the meeting will come to order, an outdoors writer would like to second that motion.

Actually my father reported the ominous beginnings of this story.

184

My father came upon aforesaid sweet little old lady and the gentleman with her, fishing a deep corner pool of one of our darkest brown trout meccas.

"How's fishing?" the Guv asked.

"Wonderful," chirped the sweet little old lady.

"Lousy," grumped the old gentleman.

Later I spied on them, noted her handsome, serviceable ensemble of red strap overalls and that whether or not she knew her onions she did know her brown trout. Oh yes, she had applied sufficient ballast to her worm to make every cast sound like a depth charge seeking marauding submarines. But after she got it in the water, she knew how to swim the worm under the cutbanks. The gentleman cursed his tangled line, slapped horseflies, and built better excuses for his own lack of success.

I was flush with success, having made the right decision the day before when the rain quit. Never had I fished this stream with anything but flies, but the water was too high to wade, murky, an unpromising 45° F, and no fish were rising. So up with the old spinning rod, out with the gold Mepps #0 and #6 Five of Diamonds, and out to explore an old stream by a new method.

I caught fish, and I learned things by catching them in places I never bothered to fish before, shallow backwaters and riffles and flats beside deep runs. The hook got there sometimes simply because I can reach further with a spinning rod than with a fly rod, but most often because I have not been using a spinning rod much this year.

Once there was a genuine *tour de force*. I was seated on the bank of a huge round pool looking for my bottle opener when a huge cave in the bank across the fast water in a backwater about 75 feet from me took my eye. First cast and the Five of Diamonds clanked against a rock at the back of the cave, and then the waters rose up. The fish swam upstream in the fast water abreast of me, and gave me visions of those huge old lunkers one reads about but never catches. It was only 13 inches long, but in this stream that is a lunker, or so I thought then.

The next day I decided to be a sport and fish with flies. The day was bright and sunny: the waters had gone down some and cleared to the extent you could see the bottom in 4 feet, 6½ inches of water. I know, because that is the distance from the soles to the tops of my chest waders, and I shipped 94 gallons of water, now warmed to 50° F, from those 4 foot, 6¾ inch deep holes.

After three hours of nothing, I witnessed one of those magic moments in fly fishing. For 10 minutes I stood in the tail of a pool gnashing my teeth and watching in vain for rises. Then a fish above me started to rise under the outside bank, another above him, and so on as the pool came alive. The first one came twice to my own deer hair hopper, and refused it. The second time he slapped it playfully with his tail and chortled gleefully. Revenge was called for.

Out came one of the McGinty's I had tied as a hedge against short supply in August, and that hopper-disdaining trout came and got elbowed aside by a larger fish who was soon in the bag. Others followed, including a 14-incher which I was sure then was the largest brown in the stream. Conceit, it seems, is catching fish on your own McGinty.

Just before the cocktail hour, I got half my come-uppances. Basso profundo "slp-slups" were coming from a profound old brown who ignored my 50 throws of 10 different flies, although he continued to graze noisily on whatsits within three inches of my frauds.

The rest of my come-uppance waited back at camp. My dear old mom admired my fish and announced: "One of the ladies caught a pound and a half trout. I saw it. There she goes now." There went my sweet little old lady off fishing again, her sensible red straps profaned now by a great floppy fuchsia sunhat. To add insult to my injury and comfort to her hopes of yarding in even bigger insults, she also carried a folding lawn chair.

I would consent to an amendment to the main motion: when they open the season on sweet little old ladies, there should be no size limit and no closed streams.

Wes on Blaze Orunge

I take pen in hand on account of where you said in your colyum a whiles back that them as was convinced being saw whilst big game hunting was the way to be safe would invest in a suit of these here blaze orunge duds, now that the govermint has made blaze orunge or scarlet legal, whichever you druther.

Seems to me that there was some sort of incineration like they's something wrong with blaze orunge or with the govermint for having made her legal. Anyhow, you didn't expand her from the sublime to the ridicklous like usual, so I ain't certain you was aware of the whole truth about blaze orunge. If you was, she never come acrost.

It ain't your fault. You just don't know from nothing about big

186

game hunting cause you ain't one, a big game hunter. They is even them got gall enough to say you ain't man enough to hunt big game, but that is a outright prefabrication. The fack is you ain't boss in your house and you can't shoot worth a damn and I tell 'em so, too!

You was half right in that colyum. They is indeed something wrong with blaze orunge, but they is method in the govermint's madness for having brought her in. They is plain a lot of heifer-dust (you should parn me) spread about. Like hunters getting shot in the bush being accidents, and hunters not shooting at what they can't see, and such like.

I've only wore scarlet wunct and blaze orunge never. That wunct I sees a dude likewise in scarlet up the end of a draw. I gets nervous after a while and whistles a few bars of Hogwaller Hoedown when I gets close.

"Haw! Now you whistle," this dude snorts, "I've had the drop on you for half an hour."

"Whyn't you shoot?" I asks.

"Wouldn't have been sporting," he sez. "You wasn't doing no shooting."

I ain't wore bright colors in the bush since. The plain unadulterous fack is that the way to keep the old liver from being ventilated by other dudes in the bush is to be neither saw, herd, nor smelt by said dudes. Some of them ain't bad shots, you give them a full magazine, and I druther take a chance on them not even shooting at what they can't see, than strutting around in blaze orunge inviting them to see if their scopes is screwd on tight enough so's they can shoot a nice tight group in your brisket.

You don't catch them game ossifers in no bright duds whilst pussyfooting about the bush, and that's because they got the inside dope on why the govermint brought in blaze orunge in the first place. A whiles back the govermint noticed welfare, public health, etcettery, was causing a big increase in numbers of summer golfers and teevee watchers to be found in the bush in the fall, and that these dudes was killing each other and generally making the bush an obnoctious place for the rest of us. So they decided to use the principles of game management to reduce the herds of these dudes, and the principle used is that of natral selection. You know, how the pheasants that fly gets shot, so pretty soon only them as runs on the ground is left.

Anyhow, they way they figured it was any dude that would dawn that blaze orunge has about the same mental equiptment as them as shoots fellow animals attired likewise. Now if you dress all them dudes that has the habit of shooting other dudes so they presents a standout target, sooner or later they'll kill themselves off, and the bush will be safe for us other dudes that do not shoot dumb animals, only big game.

The only quibble I got is that they should make blaze orunge compulsory if the full benefits of the dude-management program is to be got, instead of still allowing scarlet. That scarlet is plumb hard to see in some light, and some of them dudes may miss a few good shots and slow the whole plan down.

But rest sured they will come a day that they is only one blaze-orunge dude left, and I shall have no compunkshun however about getting the drop on him and dooming his kind to extermity. And if I should not live so long, I know you'll do the same for me. Here's hoping.

Your friend,
West Country Wes

Never Too Old

This column was to have been a diatribe against plans of Calgary Power to dam the North Saskatchewan River at the Big Horn site. Bert Pruden would have enjoyed that. The last time I talked to Bert, on the telephone about three weeks ago, he told me he'd like to see "them" given "what for" about the foolish things that are done with our natural resources in this country.

But Bert Pruden died suddenly last Sunday at the age of 76 and, as I think back over the four years or so that I knew him, I would rather write a short memorial to a gentleman who really appreciated some of the things we Canadians are too inclined to take for granted regarding fish and game. Two very significant things about Bert are that his love of the outdoors, of hunting and fishing, did not wane as his years increased, and that at the age of around 72 he packed up with his wife and the two of them left their native England for Canada.

It seems to me that Bert never ceased to look in awe at the rights hunters and fishermen enjoy in Alberta. In England, Bert often told me, he enjoyed the dark mysteries of angling for coarse fish with strange sounding names—bream, tench, gudgeon, etc.—but trout and salmon were reserved for other people. Occasionally he enjoyed the rare treat of an invitation by a fishing owner or lessee to fish for pike. Hunting of any quality came even more rarely. Here he found, to his constant wonderment, that all fish and game were there for the hunting and fishing by anyone with the modest price of the licence.

When Bert first came to Canada, age was somewhat against him, and he restricted his fishing to the stocked lakes and potholes of the area. He became a familiar figure, spruce and natty in the best tradition of British sportsmen, sitting on his tackle basket and staring at his float as he fished, not for carp or dace but for stocked rainbow trout. The exacting coarse-fishing methods of Great Britain were devastating, and Bert became as successful a pothole and lake trout fisherman as I know.

One day a couple of years ago a friend and I took Bert fishing with us to the boondocks, to a muskeg creek with a beaver dam, right beside the road. Bert found a firm hummock for his basket and throne beside that beaver dam, and proceeded to dazzle native brown trout with his methods. A large black bear followed me up the side of the creek opposite Bert, and when the animal came into the open we tried to draw Bert's attention to it so he would stand up and see it. Nothing doing. Eyes and ears too, apparently, were intent on that float. Afterwards, when we told Bert about the bear, his eyes took on a suspicious glint as if he wasn't having any of the greenhorn snipe hunt stuff. "I should like to have seen that," was Bert's only comment.

Advancing age and declining health put hunting all but out of the question, but Bert was always ready to go. After the Grey Cup telecast a couple of years ago, the same friend and I decided to go on a short hunting run and, without giving him prior warning, to go and see if Bert would like to come. There he was, ready, willing and able, guns out, boots polished and laced, and in a new addition, a screaming red hunting cap. What is more, Mrs. Pruden confided, he had been ready for a couple of days.

On occasion Bert would express mild regret that he had not come to Canada when he was younger. His real annoyance was reserved for the advancing age and declining health that was interfering with his enjoyment of the fish and game of the country, now that he had come.

In the call I had from Bert three weeks ago, it was plain that while the desire to be out and at it was as strong as it ever was, illness was prevailing to keep him in. He spoke with relish of a trip he had taken to the new stocked pond built by the Eckville Fish and Game Association which Bert, an expert, pronounced a marvellous place full of lovely fish.

Bert's passing leaves me with regrets, among which are that my own convalescence following his phone call prevented me going to see him and that I never got around to taking a picture of Bert on that tackle basket. But I will never forget how he has proved for me that a man's love of the outdoors, of hunting and fishing, endures in spite of years, and that a man should indulge this love whenever and as long as he is able.

Fishing Biologists

I slept not a wink the night before the first time I ever went fishing with a fishery biologist. As I tossed and turned, I conjured up visions of all the things I would learn from this young savant who had a master's degree, yet, in the subject I, a mere amateur, hold most dear: fish. Anyone knew, I assured myself, that fishery biologists are not even interested in fishing but go along to be polite and then spend their time making marvellous scientific discoveries.

Ward Falkner was the biologist, then teaching biology at the junior college. All the streams were muddy the next day, so we wound up pitching spinners at Mitchell Lake. Nothing happened for some time, then Ward got a look in his eye that I have seen before on fishermen. He added a huge bell sinker about 18 inches ahead of the spinner and a tiny chunk of worm to the spinner.

I was about to explain in a kindly manner that weight and bait destroyed the action of the spinner. "Got one," Ward announced. He inserted a thumb in the brookie's mouth, expertly broke its neck, and threw it behind him. I went and performed an autopsy and found the brookies to be crammed with a curious little insect which abounds in Mitchell Lake.

"What are these, Ward?" I asked, holding a handful of stomach contents under his nose. "Yech!" he replied. "Bugs." If he was going to say more, he got interrupted by another fish. After he landed it he offered me a sinker and a worm. I accepted.

We spent some time companionably yarding in brookies. I cleared my throat and asked one of the controversial questions in fishing circles: "Can the rainbow-cutthroat hybrid reproduce?"

"Who knows?" Ward said, as he set the hook in another brookie.

I remember remarking bitterly that biologists don't seem to know anything and Ward replying to the effect that he knew everything about the Q-ion or something in the hemoglobin molecule of whitefish blood, because that's what he did his thesis on.

That evening my wife wiped away my tears and reminded me

gently how much I hated anyone asking me any questions about my work when I was fishing. "But everyone says fish biologists don't fish," was all I could sniffle by way of reply. Now Ward is gone to his reward, taking his Ph.D. at the University of Manitoba in some even more esoteric aspect of fish blood. I just hope they don't try to hold his oral exam while Ward is trying to fish.

So I was prepared for Carl Hunt. Carl is one of the Alberta Fish and Wildlife Divison fishery biologists stationed in Red Deer, and there is no doubt he loves to fish. But I was not prepared for the Carl Hunt jinx. I am a famous guide: people who go with me catch superlatives; I catch cold. Carl was interested in catching fish, so away we went.

How many trips was it? Anyway, Carl caught nothing. He didn't do anything wrong; he just caught nothing. Not that I was doing all that well, but I remember feeling so guilty once last season that I was trying to decide where I would hide a two-pound brown I had on when, sure enough, Carl showed up and helped me land him. After we had had still another bad day, we would have a beer. Carl's wife would sniff the air and doubt we had been fishing. His kids would look at me like I was a criminal.

It got so bad I even forgot Carl was a biologist. Oh, I did slip once and asked him to identify that intriguing looking water weed that waves in the currents of Shunda Creek. "Radishes," he snarled, or something to that effect.

Finally, a little more than a month ago, we broke the jinx. Nothing huge, no fantastic quantities, but on one of our trips Carl did catch a nice batch of brown trout on the McGinty. He was so pleased he forgot that as a government biologist he loves the people and is devoted to the great democratic principle of more fish per man-hour for the masses and had a few choice comments about a member of the masses who went clomping up the bank with his massive wife and mass of children and put down a nice rising brown he was fishing over.

Carl has not, however, told me the real name of that weed.

Pioneer Outdoors Columnist

PINCHER CREEK—The lives of men change and end as fast as the weather. Eighteen inches of snow overnight back in these hills modified my expectations of finishing my holiday fishing the drought-shrunk streams around here in sunny September weather. My father-in-law decided to plough his way to town, so rather than wait in bed for a chinook, I accompanied him.

In town I bought my first *Calgary Herald* in two weeks and, as luck would have it, that was the issue, and the only page I looked at in the store carried the story: Allen H. Bill, 71, outdoors columnist for *The Calgary Herald*, had died in Colonel Belcher Hospital the day before.

Allen Bill's last column was done in hospital, and was a curious blend of nostalgia, sadness, and rage at what money was inducing men to do to some of his favorite streams.

I was a new friend of his and he an old friend of mine, for Allen Bill's columns had given me much pleasure—as they had to thousands of Albertans—long before I ever met him. At one point on the silent ride home, I saw three mourning doves spaced along the top wire of a barbed wire fence, bleakly contemplating nature, their soft graceful bodies etched as sharply against the acres of snow as the cruel barbs that separated them.

Some time following his retirement as managing editor of *The Calgary Herald*, Allen Bill combined journalism with his love of the outdoors in the form of a weekly outdoors column in *The Herald*. Through this new career he became known throughout North America as an informed and ardent outdoorsman and conservationist.

When I first started this column nearly five years ago, I wrote Mr. Bill for advice and help. I got it and it was good. From that time on he became a special kind of friend to me: he gave good advice only when I asked for it, and he offered praise and encouragement when he felt like it.

But Allen Bill would have been the first to snort at me if I tried to convey the impression that his disposition was always sweet. We were lunching at the Alberta Fish and Game convention in Edmonton last spring when an individual Allen had torn up in one of his columns approached to tell Allen he hadn't much liked the column. "Well, what'll it be, bare knuckles or boots?" Allen asked, and the indignant reader retreated from the remarkably fit septuagenarian.

I got my hide etched by Allen's tongue a couple of years ago when we were fishing together on Stauffer Creek. Somehow he confused my already confused directions about where we would meet, got lost, and was nearly engulfed in some of that muskeg. He was a mess and an exhausted wreck but had enough left to let me hear it about directing a man his age into a place like that. Until that point I never would have guessed his age. On the way home we both forgot everything in a good laugh over where he had misplaced his teeth, particularly when he found them under the car seat. The next day we

192

went fishing again.

Allen Bill had been a guest in my home, and a courtly one indeed, so my wife was upset when I returned with my news.

Not the least of the reasons I go fishing is to be alone, so I went to my favorite creek and found it draped by snow-bowed trees on this most unpromising of all unpromising fishing days. Intoxicated with the cool waters added to the tepid soup of August, the fish were mad for me, but I decided I had enough death for one day and was releasing the rosy rainbows one after the other.

I fish this creek so often I feel I have a right to name the holes, and eventually I came to Heartbreak Hole, which generally contains the finest fish in the creek. The name is for the number of times I have hooked said fish without ever having landed one. They always wreck me in the roots along the right bank looking upstream. No such nonsense this time. Six came out on very few casts more than that, including a 14- and a 15-incher, large fish for this water. Unaccountably, all were hooked so deeply that they had to be killed.

I turned my back on the scene of so many defeats and headed home before I hooked too deeply the 20-incher I had seen a week before leading a flotilla of lesser fish on a tour of Heartbreak Hole. Did I just imagine I heard the voice of Allen Bill snort, "You're just quitting because your hands are too cold to go on"?

I know he would have enjoyed the day, and probably he would not have quit.

Grousing with Baby Huey

Faithful readers will recall that Baby Huey is a fine broth of a lad who, only a couple of years ago, at Pneumonia Point, was trying to get his duck-shooting eyes back after umpteen years of ruining them poring over learned tomes at the university. Two years later now, the broth is a little thicker, a beard attests to all that learning, and a fine web has grown between his toes.

So Huey decided he would take up ruffed grouse hunting, just to pass the time of day, mind you, while waiting for the evening flight back to his latest and greatest swamp, to which he had invited us for an evening shoot. When we pulled up beside our favorite grouse cover, Huey surveyed all that beautiful jungle, and his voice went up just slightly when he asked, "We're not going in there?" Oh yes we were, split up into two groups of two hunters and one dog each, the better to avoid dogfights and manslaughter charges.

A grouse, more awake than either of us, was pottering around just where we leave the trail into the jungle, and we easily missed the four shots available between us. Then Quince pointed at a morass of twisted willow surrounding a tiny pothole. I waded in and flushed the bird which went out over the slough where a grouse hunter's companion should have been for a clear shot. Baby Huey was out of harm's way, cursing his route over the high ground.

Next I heard muffled oaths and looked over to see a mass of arms and legs pedalling for altitude. Instead of kicking blowdowns apart in the time-honoured manner of brush-worn grouse hunters, Huey had gone butt over barrel into one and was trying to become a part of it.

Then we topped a ridge and there, just below us, was partridge heaven, a nightmare of gnarled willow, and it was a-twitter with ruffed grouse! Huey was deployed in a nice big clearing on the north edge, and I waded into that willow. Grouse exploded, and I got lucky with two that tried to go out the south side. Quince picked up the first one, then spotted the second, dropped the first, and then stood studying like a donkey torn between two haystacks. Not wishing to confuse the pup on his first double, I picked up the second and let him retrieve the first.

Then the pup pointed a grouse on a low branch, and I stepped in ahead of him. For once it worked, and the bird flew straight for the clearing and Baby Huey. Bang. Bang. "Goodness, gracious, they fly fast!" Top ruffed grouse speed: 35 miles per hour, 9 slower than Huey's beloved mallards.

Undaunted, the pup pointed another, a little higher in another bush, and this one, too, flew straight for Huey. Bang, and again, Bang. "Heavens to Betsy!" and a whole string of great white hunter expressions. But why go on? The lad was at least getting shots away, which was more than I did the entire first season I hunted ruffed grouse.

So we topped another rise, and I called a halt for a bite and to clean the two birds I had. Baby Huey, blowing like a walrus, lay down beside Quince, and they had a panting contest. Touching woodland scene that, on a beautiful, nippy fall day, and me with my camera still in dry dock after my Bow River kayak cruise.

After he got his breath back, Huey philosophized in his usual breathless manner on how those Brittany spaniels made him tired just to watch them, going 40 before they even touched ground, on how a man had to be just a little crazy to follow whirling dervish dogs through cover thick enough to give a snake the bends, chasing after a bird that goes boom! and is behind a bush before you can have a heart attack or a nervous breakdown. I allowed as how I couldn't agree more, and let's get at it.

We struck out umpteen times on wild birds on what I thought was the way back to the car. In frustration, finally I potted one off the limb to which it had flown just as the pup was pointing. I know, I know. I am trying to kick the habit, but a man also has a duty to improve the breed of ruffed grouse by eliminating the odd specimen that displays the regressive gene that makes it roost.

It was the way back, and the only time this year I have hit it first time. The other party—composed of a dog even more grouse-demented than its master, a professional dog trainer who can also shoot, that master who maintains a dose of the D.T.'s in the fall because he claims it sharpens his reflexes, and a small boy who knew where the grouse all hide—had seven grouse.

Huey's diagnosis of dementia was confirmed when we hunted grouse for another couple of hours after lunch and then allowed the panting and babbling lad to lead us to that duck swamp. Sanity to Baby Huey is striding a mile through rushes to the withers and mud to the haunches to put out decoys, and then reverse the whole procedure in pitch dark, handicapped with a load of ducks.

But here our Huey is in his element. Three times he pulled big mallards twisting and turning from such a height that I had time to trim and smoke half a cheroot before they landed with a gush right in his hip pocket. Down they come, and there, framed against the setting sun, is Baby Huey, nonchalantly blowing the smoke from his barrels, the Marshall Dillon of the marshlands. And me without a camera.

Flyslinger's Slow Draw

A ringer of a fly-slinger came to town recently and slew central Albertans, *Homo sapiens* and *Salmo trutta* alike, with his slow draw. Lloyd Shea of the Edmonton Trout Club and current chairman of the Alberta Fish and Game Association Fish Committee, interrupted a central Alberta fishing vacation recently to slip into my office and swap a few lies.

Lloyd is one of that hardy crew of angling experts that considers the North Raven River, or Stauffer Creek as it is often called, to be one of the more rewarding and challenging of Alberta's many fine trout streams. He's embarrassed to admit it, Lloyd says, but he uses a horrendous mess of a fly on the North Raven that is really only a hank of black chenille wound around a #8 heavy wire hook. Yes, yes, I say, sounds very much like my own Despickable pattern, beloved of some of central Alberta's finest and sneakiest brown trout fishermen.

"Fish it only upstream, even on Stauffer," says Lloyd.

"Yes, yes, don't we all," says myself.

"Then I draw it back to me with the rod tip just slightly faster than the current would take it," Lloyd adds.

"What?" I scream. "Not purposely drag a fly, even a wet fly!"

"Sure," says this suave grandfather, whose youth was obviously misspent on trout streams while the rest of us were wasting our time shooting eight ball and snooker. "Move that fly back. As Vincent Marinaro is going to say in his forthcoming book, once you make a trout, especially a big one, chase the fly, nothing on earth will stop him from taking the fly."

"This I got to see," thought I.

"Even tried it a couple years ago in New Zealand," Lloyd said, "and it worked."

So a trip was arranged right then and there for a couple of days hence in the vicinity of Rocky Mountain House on a stream the name of which I shall reveal in print only when the Alberta government decides to designate it a trophy fishing stream governed by regulations designed to protect, not exploit its trophy fish. The late afternoon when we arrived at the stream was not particularly promising, being characterized by the unsettled "wind in the east, fishing is least" weather we seemed to have been having in Alberta thoughout August.

Lloyd Shea does not even have to waste time rigging up a fly rod, as he keeps two or three of them ready-rigged in a special case in the trunk of his car, as befits a visiting fly-slinger. I pointed out the place to start and then caught the first deer trail heading upstream to where I would start. The fish were on the prod in a restrained sort of way, as though they had been feeding steadily all afternoon and were just savouring dessert. For dessert they seemed to like my Le Tort hoppers, and after about an hour I had taken and released one brook trout and three browns in the 12- to 14-inch class, and one magnificent gold, cream, and red brown that would push four pounds.

I should make sure, I thought, that the guest was likewise enjoying himself, so I caught the first deer trail downstream to the stretch where I left Lloyd. But he was not there. Just as I got back to where I started, here he came around the bend on which we had passed each other. Lloyd had taken two or three small trout and had seen one really good one. As we forged upstream, chatting, a tail like a canoe paddle insinuated itself into the air under the bank at the tail of the pool just ahead. The tail flirted monstrously and beckoned us on. Lloyd had not seen it, so I pointed out the general vicinity and went into the streamside brush to dine and watch the process.

The first cast snaked out long, up and under the bank. Then came the slow draw and a gush and a wallow like someone had thrown a small boy into the stream. "Organic fertilizer!" or one word to like effect, Lloyd cursed, "I missed him!" The water under the bank still moved. I imagined question marks etched on the surface as the big fish moved its head from side to side, looking for the missing fly.

"Did you touch him?"

"I don't think so," Lloyd replied.

"Then put it up there again."

Up it went, perfectly again, and lightning flashed from the water to the overhanging tree limbs in as fine a trout leap as I have ever seen.

Lloyd has had his fun when he hooks a fish and does not believe in enjoying the fight to the extent that he kills the creature. Quickly the fish was unhooked and placed in quiet water to recover and swim away, a brown trout of as close to five pounds as makes no difference, only a slightly embarrased victim of the slow draw.

14. Unnatural End

Rod to Gun

Fall is the insidious season for the way it stalks us foolish humans with our absurd hopes that Indian summer will never end and winter will never come. Last weekend an angler went south to fish a stream he has fished perhaps 10 times a season for the last seven years. Seldom, however, had he ever fished the little stream after Labour Day.

This past summer the fishing had been particularly good in the stream, and memories of Labour Day's limit dry-fly catch of rainbow trout averaging 12 inches drove the angler south. He believed that summer had not ended, could not end, and he hoped for two months more of the fishing he had been enjoying.

The bad signs were there as he walked up the valley to the first pool. The mountains to the west had recently received dustings of new snow. The stream was a starved trickle, lower than he had ever seen it. It was so clear that were it not for its burble one would not be certain from a distance that any water was there at all. A pocket thermometer gave a water temperature reading of 48° F, about seven degrees cooler than a month earlier.

Rather than fill the angler with any misgivings, these signs challenged him. The water temperature, particularly, satisfied him with his earlier decision to use a tiny spinner rather than flies. Even the fallen leaves that the spinner hooked on nearly every cast could not drive away the optimism that is the companion of every angler. Nor did the bare branches from which the leaves had fallen, etched against the slate clouds, bring even the slightest suspicion that anything was amiss. The angler did not pause to consider that the deer tracks punctuating the usual mink sign were a little early, or at least that the deer that made them had fled the hills early.

The fish were not co-operative. In fact it seemed that there were few trout left in the little stream. Occasionally a trout would be frightened by the spinner's splash, and a large ghostly form would scoot past the fisherman on its way downstream. But these fish would not pause at the lip of the pool and then scoot back upstream as they do in the summer when the pool was home. Now the frightened fish would plunge over the lip, making a bow wave in the shallow riffle at the head of the next pool downstream. They seemed bent on beating something to the mouth of the little creek where it flows into the big river.

As the angler walked along the grassy bank there were no grasshoppers taking evasive action as they had by the hundreds only four weekends before, and nowhere on the stream could be seen the peculiar quick flips that dotted the water so often during the summer as the trout gorged on the hoppers. A new insect was in evidence. Everywhere along the stream crickets were singing a belated September song. Thinking himself very wise in his desperation for fish, the angler switched to a spinner with a black blade. Promptly, in a rocky little pool, he took an 11-inch cutthroat with the head to tail rosy sheen of late-season good health.

The angler sought the shelter from the stubborn north wind provided by the wall of a small canyon through which the stream flowed. There he sat, puffing a cigar, admiring the fish, and for some strange reason, not really anxious to be on up the stream.

A sound he knew well startled him. From the bushes in the canyon wall above him came the flick-flick of wing against branch and a ruffed grouse cock sailed silently over his head and upstream and landed in a wooded flat on the inside of the next bend. Twice more, at about two-minute intervals, the same sound came, and two other grouse followed the first, the last of which was followed by the angler shouldering an imaginary shotgun.

Musing that the grouse were going upstream and the trout were going down, the angler began to be sure that the single cutthroat was a good way to end a season. Moving away from the creek, the angler took a shortcut back to his starting point through low grassy foothills spotted with clumps of rosebushes, saskatoons, and willows. Halfway back, 18 forms exploded from the grass and 18 sharptailed grouse whicker-whickered their way east. It came to the angler suddenly that the next weekend would be Thanksgiving and with it the probability of the traditional "chicken" shoot with valued hunting companions.

It is not in a flash that the old season passes and the new comes upon us, but in the minds of men it seems that way. Especially to the angler did it seem that way, for that night, wet, heavy and sudden— or so it seemed—came the first snowfall of the year.

Fall Fishing

Fishing in the fall in central Alberta has a strange, mysterious quality that attracts and repels at the same time. The angler gets the impression that something he does not understand is going on, and far too often bores himself to death trying to find out what it is.

Master anglers Cec Head and Mike Burrington were reported ready to take the gas pipe, or at least turn to worms and marshmallows, after lashing to a froth and to little avail the surface of various allegedly teeming waters last weekend. Fall reverses the misery of spring: the water is becoming colder, the hatches of aquatic insects diminish to nothing, and the fishing promises only to get worse and worse instead of better and better, as it does in the spring.

There are always alleged bright spots, and it was to one such that I took Jake Reimer on Labour Day when he decided to take his annual fishing trip. In the same location exactly one year ago I had achieved my finest catch of last season. This year of queer years we got only fresh air and sunshine, so we went exploring elsewhere, notwith-standing Jake's pious protests that fish have nothing to do with going fishing.

Out of the corner of an eye I hazarded a glance at the river we were passing and couldn't believe it. The Clearwater—clear at last! The umpteenth rule is if the Clearwater has its clear day for the year on a holiday, go fishing in it.

Although I had not frequented them for a couple of years, I remembered that sidechannels in various of the braided portions of the Clearwater had provided me with some excellent fall fishing. So we went to the nearest such place and, for a couple of hours, found the fishing to be every bit as bad as at the place we had left. Oh, the crisp fall air and the leaves just starting to turn were like a tonic and all that nonsense that is part of the magic of the torture that is fall fishing.

Jake had been using hardware, and I had even seen him doing a lumbering *pas de deux* on the gravel bars as he snaffled the odd grasshopper. I had gone through all the same options in the hundreds of flies I own and was now down to the secret weapons, those confections I purchase purely on impulse. As it happened, a fly called a Bumble Wulff was on the leader as I came around a bend and saw what has to be the finest pool in the west country, the sculpted handiwork of the high water of June and July.

One of the only satisfactions of the day had been how beautifully that Bumble Wulff floated and how visible it was on those crystal waters, so I cast it up the throat of this masterpiece of a pool. Then the true magic of fall fishing set in for me. All the way from the bottom, six feet down, came the largest brown trout I have hooked this year, and I hooked him so soundly it was hard to believe I had been fishing fruitlessly for five hours. Just as I was getting set for an epic battle, the fly came back to me and the fish was gone.

Consolation came quickly in the next pool upstream where, unaccountably, two fish were busily rising as though it were not fall and there was actually something to rise for. These fish liked the Bumble Wulff well, engulfed it, and were both deeply hooked, two male browns in the breathtaking colors of the fall Clearwater browns.

Then the other magic of fall fishing returned, and we saw neither skin nor scale of another fish for the rest of the day.

Late Season Form

Every angler occasionally has one of those days when he is sure his rod hand should be registered as a deadly weapon. This is the kind of day when every cast lights like a butterfly and stings like a bee, and when the fish can do no right and the angler no wrong. On such a day such an angler is the greatest, and convinces himself that angling is an affair of skill, not luck.

I fished my favorite south Alberta stream last weekend, and everything was perfect: water the right height, color, and temperature, sun shining but not too bright, a bit of a west wind but not too strong. Not a bit of luck in all this, of course, just living right.

Except for the small initial problem of having #8, #10, and #12 Joe's hoppers refused until I got down to the #14's, which were immediately lapped up, there was no difficulty with the fish. They took the flies with calm deliberation, turned, and swam for home until hooked. When the odd hooked fish swam under a flat rock or into a submerged bush, it availed him absolutely nothing. He stayed hooked until the rock was kicked over or the leader untangled from the bush.

The fish did not hold the hot hand that day. In fact, in the clear water one rainbow was seen taking the hopper three times in succession; getting stung each time, and simply dropping downstream a little to look for that disappearing, delicious, but prickly grasshopper. It was, of course, only the skilful presentation of the fly that caused a wild trout to act with such reckless abandon.

So well did things go that morning, that I had the courage to go over to the Castle River for round two with the rabid rainbows there who had cleaned me so thoroughly in round one last year about this time. Six of these chunky, rock-hard maniacs did I K.O., as they found to their utter rage that a light #8 fly cannot be thrown like spoons and spinners. There was no luck in the fact that this was the one day out of 365 when the wind was not howling down the Castle River gorge so that flies, rather than scrap metal, could be cast in the first place.

The next morning I was back on the little stream of the first morning, and things were not quite so good. A "whar's the barn?" wind was howling straight downstream, fit to lynch a man with his own fly line. When I did come to a pool where there was some shelter from the wind, the sun would emerge so brightly from behind a cloud that neither fly nor strikes could be seen in the dazzle on the water.

But the conditions are no excuse, for the fish still flung themselves violently on the fly and impaled themselves. The true skill was displayed in the manifold methods of losing these fish. The first two fish were struck hard enough to pull the hook out but not hard enough to break the leader. Then an exacting adjustment was made which enabled me not to strike at all or with a discreet delay, so that umpteen fish were played for two seconds, then simply opened their mouths and faded into the depths, unencumbered by any fly.

One fish headed for the brush, and I whipped the rod smartly sideways to head him off. The rod smacked into a tree with enough force to snap the leader, but not so much that the rod was damaged. A touch like this comes not from luck, but from many misspent hours of toil on the streams.

Anyone who fly fishes knows about getting the fly line tangled around the boots. Three fish struck while I was in this position, and skill alone kept two of them from getting hooked. The third hooked himself, and only dazzling footwork allowed the leader to be snapped again, instead of myself slipping, sliding, and maybe even being pulled over onto my stupid behind. I got so confident that, as each fish struck, I knew I was going to lose him. Yet no tribute was paid to skill. I do recall roaring into the wind frequent remarks about giving up any fool occupation that was all luck, all of which was rotten.

The final straw came when I hung the fly on a branch, pulled hard enough to break the leader, and the fly fell into the water, floating prettily along a cutbank toward me at the tail of the pool. "What luck," I think, "I can recover the fly without disturbing the pool." When the fly approaches the spot over which I have just put 15 casts hoping for a big fish, there is the almighty suck and gush of a big fish, and my 70-cent Joe's hopper disappears and does not reappear. I wind up and head for home where I know I can be the fourth for bridge, which is a true test of skill.

The two days may even have been show business. They certainly were fishing, which is why I, like a million other anglers, will be rushing the new season two days after Christmas.

The Unnatural End

In a year of weather like this, the hunting season does not end naturally. If a man is not cajoled by bitter weather into feeling like quitting, then his pace just becomes more frantic as the arbitrary, unnatural end of the season approaches.

Even something like the fresh skiff of snow two weeks ago is regarded as an opportunity. It sent me out into fields near home looking for the pheasants that would stand at the end of any fresh tracks I might find. As pheasant habitat goes, the best found in Alberta is marginal, and that around Red Deer is by no means the best. But even around here there are pockets of ideal cover inhabited year after year by a few pheasants.

Snow is the stool pigeon and more to these secret pockets; around here the cover is so thick you need some fresh snow to show you exactly where in that tangled pocket the pheasants are to be found. So that fresh skiff of snow drew me to a known pocket to look for fresh tracks. Somehow Mac and his dog went off in another direction when I announced that I and my dog were going to inspect a clump of brush where we generally find birds.

Halfway around and things seemed still. No huffing and puffing and cracking brush from the dog. I peered in and young Quince was standing there taking great sniffs. As I watched, his stub tail started to rotate. Then his whole rear end started to gyrate. So in I went, and as I reached the dog I heard the cuk! cuk! cuk! of a cock pheasant taking off six feet in front of me. The bush was so thick I saw nothing. A man on the other side would have had a clear shot.

A wide hedgerow on the other side of the quarter bordered barley stubble, and pheasnt tracks were everywhere going in and coming out. Almost immediately Quince bumped a rooster, and again I only heard his going out the other side. Then another, protesting mightily, clambered above the brush and flew down the hedgerow, again out of my range but well within the range of that hypothetical hunter on the other side.

At various intervals two more roosters went out the other side, away from the dog, and especially the gunner. Then the pup pinned one down, and the great gaudy cock jumped up in a tree and cursed the dog, the bird not for a moment realizing how ridiculous it looked as it fought against gravity to balance on its own tail. When it flew, it too was well out of range over the far side of the bush.

By the time we reached the end of the bush, I was so agitated that when the pup sent out a rooster straight away from my feet and up over the bush, I missed with both barrels. What I needed was a gunner, and there he was, back at the car, sound asleep.

A few days later I was back with another gunner to have another go at those pheasants before the season ended. In a sunny corner of the first bluff, a rooster took off and crumpled just as I was about to touch off the first barrel. Another bird flew and my gunner got that one too. Quince retrieved the second first, a stone dead bird, but the first, running over a disced field, was long gone, when we got to where he should have been. Quince got hot umpteen times in the hour we hunted and trailed that bird, but the wounded cock had too great a start and got lost.

205

That day ended with a picture. The two of us hunting down a willow border of some slough grass, me and the dog in knee-high crested wheatgrass on the high side. Point! I walk up to the dog and nothing happens. I order him on, and he stomps two feet to the side and points again. I stir around in that grass. Still nothing. Then as I stand cursing training books that do not tell you what to do in a situation like this, a cock pheasant wipes my nose on his rise straight up over the willow. High and higher he climbs, his color softened by the sun setting in the clear sky of the chinook arch. At his apex, we each fire one shot and miss, the bird levels and cruises straight away, and we each salute his performance with clean misses of our second barrels, then dissolve into laughter. As good a way as any to end the season, I think.

But this season will not end naturally, and a day later, the arbitrary final day, Mac and I manage to get out to the same place for a couple of hours. Despite its being like a day in June, we find birds in a small tule patch, the only one in this pheasant pocket. Mac is his old self again and collects two birds with three shots. We hunt the rest of the cover and see only a couple of roosters who are far too clever for us or our dogs.

Back at the tule patch just before dark, we give it one last go and after great snuffing, pointing, and pouncing, Plum comes up with a wounded rooster, undoubtedly the lost one of my gunner's from two days before.

Recovering a lost bird and confirming a double for a friend: now that is the way to end a season.